Fourth Edition

Practice Exercises in News Writing

George A. Hough 3rd
The University of Georgia

HOUGHTON MIFFLIN COMPANY   BOSTON
Dallas   Geneva, Illinois   Princeton, New Jersey   Palo Alto

Acknowledgments

Page 186: Excerpts from Southern Newspaper Publishers Association Bulletin, July 14, 1983, by Robert J. Wussler. Copyright © 1983. Used by permission.

Page 186: "Alive and Well," by Barber B. Conable Jr., from The New York Times, November 14, 1984. Copyright © 1984. Used by permission.

Page 187: Excerpt from an editorial in The Enterprise, Falmouth, Mass., October 6, 1985, by Bernard Lown, MD. Copyright © 1985. Used by permission.

Pages 187–188: "Secrecy Vs. Security," by Sissela Bok, from The New York Times, February 23, 1983. Copyright © 1983 by The New York Times Company. Reprinted by permission of The New York Times and the author.

Pages 189–190: Excerpt from a speech on May 16, 1984, by President Miguel de la Madrid. Copyright © 1984. Used by permission.

Page 190: Excerpt from "A Challenge to Protect the Integrity of Dr. Martin Luther King Jr.'s Legacy," by The Reverend Jesse L. Jackson. Copyright © 1986. Originally appeared in The New York Times, January 13, 1986. Used by permission.

Pages 191–192: Excerpt from a letter by Representative Don Edwards in The New York Times, October 30, 1985. Copyright © 1985. Used by permission.

(Acknowledgments continued on page 338)

Library of Congress Catalog Card Number: 87-80261

ISBN: 0-395-35938-4

ABCDEFGHIJ-A-9543210-898

Contents

Preface

This fourth edition of "Practice Exercises in News Writing" has been completely reorganized and revised. Much new material has been added, and earlier exercises have been revised. It is still, however, a very basic workbook intended for a first course in news writing or reporting.

"Practice Exercises" asks students to assume that they are reporters and news writers for a mid-size daily newspaper, The Morning Record, in a mid-size city called Carolton, in which a mid-size college, Northwest College, is located. In this setting, the student has the opportunity of writing very real news stories, working with a believable cast of characters — from the Record's city editor to college faculty and students to public officials and residents of Carolton. In their work as reporters, students will write local news stories presented variously as notes, telephone conversations or assignments to cover speeches. They will learn to localize wire stories and to rewrite other stories to update or improve them. A city directory and a college directory and maps of Carolton and vicinity will enable them to check names and addresses and the location of streets, public buildings and places.

Organization

"Practice Exercises" is divided into 12 sections. Each section introduces one or more news writing skills, starting with the preparation of news copy, then news leads, the inverted-pyramid story and so on. At the beginning of each section, students are given specific references to chapters and pages in "News Writing" where they will find background and discussion of the relevant writing skills.

New to This Edition

Two new sections have been added: "Broadcast News" and "Public Relations." The broadcast news section is supported by a new chapter in "News Writing," which describes the similarities and differences between

v

writing for newspapers and for broadcast. "Practice Exercises" asks students to fill in for a news writer at the radio station owned by The Morning Record Co. During their stint in the station's newsroom, students will write for news broadcasts that are carried the first five minutes of each hour and for longer news programs at noon and at 6 p.m. Thirty-nine broadcast news assignments are included in this section.

The "Public Relations" section assigns students to The Morning Record's promotion department, which handles public relations and promotions for the Record, publishes a monthly employee magazine, develops community programs and co-sponsors an annual Press Institute with Northwest College. Students will find they need all their news writing skills in this public relations setting.

The speech texts in "Speeches," Section 8, are almost all new. They are topical and relevant discussions of issues and public affairs that not only provide students practice in writing but can be used to stimulate discussion in the classroom.

Police beat stories — fires, accidents, fatalities — have been gathered together in "Some Hard News Stories," Section 6. Obituaries and a number of stories requiring the interpretation of numerical data are also included in this section.

An additional bit of reality has been added with a section titled "Second-Day Stories," Section 7, that provides practice in writing follow-up or second-day stories that require adequate background on earlier events.

New exercises have been added at the end of each section to provide practice in punctuation skills, usage, grammar and style. A number of exercises provide practice in revising weak or badly written leads.

A reverse directory has been added to the Directories, Appendix 2.

Appendix 4, "Job Hunting," is new. This section includes a sample resume, a sample letter and suggestions about seeking summer jobs or internships — tips that my students have found extremely helpful.

Reporting Skills

While "Practice Exercises" is primarily a primer in news writing skills, it also introduces a number of important reporting skills. First of all, every exercise in "Practice Exercises" is based on a real event and a news story published in a daily or weekly newspaper. Students can learn about news values through classroom discussion of each story and its relevance to real newspaper readers and to real newspapers.

Exercises can also teach the student the need for careful handling of facts, for verification of names, addresses and other details, and for care in spelling difficult words and in making clear the meaning of technical terms. The exercises also suggest the value of direct quotation and demonstrate the kind of facts a reporter needs to gather in order to write a story that will satisfy a reader. A number of writing exercises raise questions about libel, privacy and good taste.

Many of the exercises require the student to seek additional information: the name of a college from The World Almanac or biographical information from Who's Who, for example. A number of exercises will require students to visit the library and verify information in an unabridged dictionary or a reference on quotations. All good reporters know how to use a library.

Language and Spelling

Each section in "Practice Exercises" includes a spelling list consisting of words that present various spelling difficulties and a usage list of words whose meanings are commonly misunderstood.

Language drills are included at the end of each section, and suggested spelling quizzes are included in the "Instructor's Manual."

A Complete Package

In this new edition, "Practice Exercises" is closely coordinated with the fourth edition of my text, "News Writing, " although it may easily be used alone. Both "Practice Exercises" and "News Writing" have been revised and reorganized around a number of basic news writing skills or competencies. A list of these competencies, accompanied by carefully worded instructional objectives, is included in the "Instructor's Manual" that accompanies "Practice Exercises."

The "Instructor's Manual" also includes a model story or key for every exercise or drill. Notes on ways to expand on or follow up a story or to tie it to material in the text are included with many of the models.

Acknowledgments

I developed the first version of this workbook some 25 years ago. Since then it has been shaped and improved in a number of ways. I owe a great deal to the thousands of students who wrote and rewrote the exercises in the introductory news writing course at Michigan State University, where I taught for 22 years, and to the many students who have used this workbook at The University of Georgia. Their reactions to the exercises have suggested many changes, refinements and improvements. Much has been contributed, too, by the graduate teaching assistants who have worked with me in my news writing courses.

I also owe a great deal to colleagues who have reviewed this and earlier editions of "Practice Exercises." I am especially grateful to the reviewers of this edition: Larry Bohlender, Northern Arizona University; Ellie Chapman, University of Missouri, St. Louis; James Fisher, University of Idaho; George L. Garrigues, University of Bridgeport, who has been a helpful critic since the first edition was published; Luther Keith, Detroit News; Stephen Lacy, Michigan State University; Lois D. Matthews, Western Michigan University; and Shirley B. Quate, Indiana University at Indianapolis.

G.A.H. 3rd

How to Use
This Book

This workbook of news writing exercises supplements the fourth edition of my text, "News Writing."

The text and workbook are closely coordinated. At the beginning of each section in "Practice Exercises" you will find notes on the writing skills to be practiced and the chapters and pages in the text where these are explained.

The Exercises

The practice exercises are presented in consistent fashion throughout the workbook. They include, first, instructions that explain the assignment and, second, the information — the facts — you will need in writing a story. In some instances, additional notes or suggestions follow the facts provided for the story.

The facts you are given to work with are raw, unedited material — the type of material news writers have to deal with every day. Whatever the form of the facts — a press release, notes given you by another reporter, a wire service story, a memo from an editor or your own notes — they may contain inconsistencies, for example, ambiguities in reference that will require you to verify names, addresses or identities in the directories in the appendix to the workbook or from some outside source.

In addition, the raw information is presented in most exercises in a deliberately disorganized manner — much as it is in real life — so that you will be forced to think through the story and to make an independent decision about the lead and the structure. Many exercises contain more facts than you need to write the story. Some may include irrelevant material. You will have to learn what to include and what to leave out.

There will be inconsistencies in style in most exercises. You will be expected to learn style and follow the rules in the "Basic Guide to News Style" in the text.

Before attempting to write, read the assignment carefully and ask yourself: "What is the point of the story? What am I being asked to do?" In most news writing assignments there is one obvious requirement, for example, to demonstrate the ability to write a summary lead or to make use of direct quotation.

There are no tricks in the exercises, but you are working with raw material. You will have to give the facts shape, form and emphasis. In every assignment you will find the everyday traps that every news writer must avoid: style errors, incomplete names, incorrect or missing addresses, ambiguities, irrelevancies, too much or too little material to work with, even errors in fact.

The Setting

This workbook asks you to assume that you have a new job. You are a reporter and news writer on a medium-sized daily newspaper in a medium-sized city. You may very well get your first job on such a newspaper. The city and the newspaper are not real, but they have counterparts in real life.

The Morning Record is a fairly representative daily newspaper. It is published seven days a week for distribution in the early morning. The first edition deadline is 5:50 p.m., and the final edition goes to press at 10:45 p.m. The Record is delivered by carrier to homes in Carolton and is delivered on motor routes outside the city. Circulation is now 45,623 in the city zone and retail trade zone. This is a market penetration of about 62 percent. This means that the Record is delivered daily to 62 percent of the households in its circulation area — excellent these days.

The paper is respected in the community and among faculty and students at the college. It gives thorough coverage to college affairs and to the college's athletic programs.

The Record has a superior editorial staff. The executive editor is Marilyn Carter. She has been at the Record for 15 years, first as assistant city editor, then city editor, managing editor and now executive editor. She is a highly competent reporter, writer and editor, and holds the Record staff to exacting standards.

The Record's city editor — the editor you work for — is Linda Miller. She is a former United Press International reporter who worked most recently for UPI in the state capital bureau. She is a graduate of Northwest College where she had a double major — journalism and political science. She is 35 years old and a little hard to work for — impatient of delay and intolerant of anyone who turns in a story containing errors. She dislikes bad leads, misspelled words and sloppy writing. She is, however, infinitely patient and helpful with beginners who try. She is fiercely loyal to the Record and to the best standards of journalism. You can learn a lot from an editor like this.

The Record has a small staff — 22 reporters and editors, about half of them women. There are two black reporters and one Hispanic reporter. You will work general assignment much of the time, but may be asked to work rewrite occasionally. Most of the staff work days, but you may be asked to work nights once in a while. On the day shift you will start at 7 a.m. and work until 4 p.m. Most of those on the night shift work from 2 p.m. to 11 p.m.

The Record is not listed in the Editor & Publisher International Year Book, but if it were, you would learn these additional facts about it:

The Morning Record
Carolton, Washington County

Population City Zone and Trade
  Area: 307,511
Households City Zone and Trade
  Area: 73,270
Circulation: 45,623 ABC
Advertising: (flat line rate) 48 cents
**National Advertising Representa-
  tives:** Shannon & Cullen, Inc.
Independent: AP; Est. 1920; offset
No editions published Christmas,
  New Year's Day, July 4, Labor
  Day, Thanksgiving Day.
Special editions: Progress
  (January); Welcome Week
  (September)
ROP Color — Full color. Minimum
  1,000 lines.

Publisher	Fred Courtwright III
Executive Editor	Marilyn Carter
Managing Editor	William H. Irving
City Editor	Linda Miller
Assistant City Editor	Kellie Ellenburg
Editorial Page Editor	Eric Latham
Sunday Editor	Frank Cuomo
Sports Editor	Mark McCallum
Controller	Ralph Boggs
Production Mgr.	Donald E. Peters
Advertising Mgr.	Henry B. Quirk
Circulation Mgr.	Arthur E. Madeiros
Promotion Mgr.	Deborah Williams

Carolton is a hypothetical city in a hypothetical state somewhere east of the West Coast and somewhere north of the Gulf of Mexico. Carolton could be your hometown or the city in which you are attending college. Its residents are much like the people you know at home and much like those in your college or university city.

The things that happen in this city and on the college campus here are, I hope, familiar, for they are the ordinary and everyday events that occur everywhere.

In short, in suggesting that you act as a reporter for The Morning Record in the hypothetical city of Carolton, I expect that you will find yourself in familiar surroundings.

To add to the sense of reality, maps of the city and its neighborhood and of the campus have been created and will be found in the back of the workbook. And people, buildings, clubs or organizations named in the practice exercises will be found in the directories in the back of this workbook.

Real-Life Assignments

Every news story assignment in this workbook is based on something that actually happened and on a story published in a newspaper. The workbook contains a real and lifelike series of assignments that simulate the kind of news writing experience you would get during a summer's work on a newspaper almost anywhere. Approach your work — your job as a reporter on The Morning Record — with this in mind.

The Goal

The text, "News Writing," and this workbook were written primarily for the student who intends to make a career of newspaper journalism. Many of you who will use the text and workbook will, however, be looking toward other careers — in public relations, advertising, magazine work, broadcast journalism or other journalistic fields. If you are one of those students, keep this in mind: the purpose of this workbook is to help you learn to write better. All those who work in journalism and mass communications are expected to write well. No matter what your career plans, the mastery of news writing skills will be instrumental, first, in finding an internship or summer job somewhere in journalism, second, in securing and doing well on your first job, and, finally, in moving up the professional ladder.

1 News Copy

Spelling

accessible, conquer, fiend, knowledgeable, adviser,* nemesis, repetitious, surveillance, colossal, mischievous, likable, exaggerate, employee*

Usage

affect/effect, allude/refer, allusion/illusion, anecdote/antidote, among/between, rights/rites, fewer/less

Newsroom Vocabulary

copy paper, newsprint, copy pencil, copy-editing marks, proofreader's marks, slug, more, end mark, thirty, front end system, state of the art, ASNE

News Copy

The following topic is discussed in detail in George A. Hough 3rd, "News Writing," fourth edition:

News Copy
Chapter 3, "News Copy," pages 39 through 55.

Spelling

The spelling words on the section pages in this workbook present various difficulties. Many are trick words. Learn to spell them now, and you will save yourself a lot of difficulty later on.

An asterisk after a spelling word, for example, the word *adviser* on page 1, indicates that spelling follows wire service style. That is, the spelling given is the preferred spelling, preferred by the wire services and preferred also by The Morning Record, the newspaper you are writing for.

See "News Writing," "A Basic Guide to News Style," Section 7, pages 482 to 487.

Usage

The usage list on the section pages in this workbook is a list of words and phrases whose meanings and use cause trouble for writers and editors. As a news writer, a person who works with words, you must use words precisely and accurately. Learn the meanings and uses of the words and phrases in the usage lists.

Newsroom Vocabulary

The newsroom vocabulary on the section pages in this workbook includes words necessary and useful to the news writer. Most will be readily learned by reading "News Writing" and by discussion and practice work in the classroom. They are all defined in the glossary in "News Writing."

Preparation of News Copy

1. In general

   a. All news copy is to be typewritten on 8½-by-11-inch copy paper.

   b. Double space all copy unless, as is the case with some typewriters, spacing is not adequate, in which case triple space.

   c. Set margins on typewriter so as to leave a one-inch or a one-and-one-quarter-inch margin at left and a one-inch margin at right.

   d. Set the tab so as to indent six or eight spaces for paragraphs.

2. Identifying copy

   a. On the first page of your copy, roughly an inch from the top of the page and at the left-hand margin, type your name.

   b. About two inches below your name, also at the left margin, type in a slug line. The slug line is a one- or two-word identification for your story.

   c. Drop down another two inches and begin typing your story. When you fold your copy paper the short way, copy side out, there should be one or two lines of copy above the fold.

   d. When your copy is more than one page in length, on the second and all succeeding pages, type in your name, slug line of the story and a page number. Type this on one line, starting at the left margin, about an inch from the top of the page. For example:

   > smith -- auto crash -- 2-2-2

   Drop down about an inch, no more, and begin typing your story.

3. Clean copy

   a. Strive for clean copy, that is, copy that is typed neatly and clearly with a minimum of additions or changes in pencil. "Dirty copy" is unprofessional.

   b. Never strike over a letter. Strike out the word and retype.

   c. When you strike out, use the capital X on the typewriter — nothing else. No other letter or symbol will cover unwanted material as well. Later, when you edit your copy, run a couple of lines through the X'd-out matter.

   d. When you have an error of even one letter in a word, or a transposition, it is frequently best to strike out and retype the entire word rather than to attempt to make an understandable correction later in pencil.

continued on page 4

3

    e. Do not divide words at the end of a line. That is, do not hyphenate words at the end of a line. Do not divide a hyphenated word at the end of a line.

4. Writing the story

    a. Each page of your copy must be complete. End paragraphs at the bottom of each page. Start a new paragraph at the top of each succeeding page. Never break paragraphs. Keep each page separate, complete and fully identified.

    b. The first paragraph of your story should start just above the center line of the page on the first page and about four spaces below your name, slug line and page number on all other pages.

    c. At the bottom of each page, if there is more copy to follow on another page, type in the word *more*.

    d. When you reach the last paragraph of your story, follow it with an end mark:

`end`	(the word end)
`##`	(end symbol, from typewriter keyboard)
`wtd`	(the writer's initials)
`30`	(traditional newspaper symbol for end)

5. Editing your copy

    a. Edit your copy with a newspaper copy pencil. This is a soft lead pencil suitable for writing on soft copy paper. Keep your copy pencil sharp. Never edit with a pen.

    b. Make no unnecessary marks on copy.

    c. Do not confuse copyreader's marks with proofreader's marks. Use only copyreader's marks on your copy. Make all corrections or changes in the copy, not in the margins.

    d. Do not use the proofreader's delete mark on copy.

    e. If your copy isn't right — re-do it. Penciled apologies for lapses or incorrectly prepared copy are not acceptable.

6. Typographical effects

    a. Type all your copy with normal margins and normal spacing between lines. Special typographical effects such as indenting, boldfacing and so on are matters of typography and are decided by the copy desk, not by the news writer.

continued on next page

b. Type all copy upper- and lowercase. Only in rare instances, when you wish to emphasize a single word, should you type it in capital letters.

c. Never underline in news copy.

7. Meeting deadlines

a. Edit copy carefully and neatly before turning it in. The writer is responsible for making all corrections in fact, spelling, typing and so on.

b. Put pages in order and turn in each assignment complete and folded the short way, copy side out, so that your name and slug line are visible on the first page.

c. You may turn in copy ahead of a deadline, but never after one. Get your copy in on time.

8. Revising copy

a. If your copy is not publishable, that is, cannot be brought up to publishable quality with minor changes made with a copy pencil, you may be asked to rewrite.

b. Copy that needs rewriting should be revised and returned to your instructor or editor promptly. If you are given another deadline, honor it.

9. Typing tricks

a. Always use the letter X to strike out unwanted matter.

b. Use the lowercase letter l in place of the Arabic figure 1 unless you have a figure 1 on your typewriter.

c. Distinguish between a hyphen and a dash in typing. A hyphen will be found on the typewriter keyboard, a dash will not.

1. The hyphen is a linking punctuation mark commonly used in compound words, thus:

   `ready-made`

   `self-employed`

2. The dash is a separating punctuation mark, made by striking the hyphen key twice. Make your dash obvious by leaving one space on either side of the dash. The dash is commonly used in place of a semicolon or in place of paired commas:

   `He was an able person -- a very able`
   `person -- but highly unreliable.`

   `He was an able person -- still, he was`
   `sometimes unreliable.`

Editing Marks

Paragraph this

Capitalize carolton

Make this Lowercase

Abbreviate (street)

Spell out (st.)

Transpose words two

Delete extra ~~extra~~ words

Join words, thus: week end

Separate two words, thus

Insert a single word or phrase

Insert a period

Insert a comma in text

Insert opening quote marks

Insert closing quote marks

Make (twelve) an Arabic figure

Spell out (9,) thus, nine

Insert a semicolon in text

Insert a hyphen in H bomb

Insert a dash

Insert an apostrophe in boys

Insert a colon in the text

Leave copy ~~as it is~~ (stet)

There is more of this (more)

End of copy #

Insert a mising letter, thus

Take out a letter or figure

Delete the quote marks

Copy-Editing Models

The models on pages 7 and 8 will guide you in editing your copy. They follow instructions in Chapter 3 in "News Writing" and the instructions for preparation of news copy in this section of "Practice Exercises." A model of the first page of news copy appears on page 7. A model for the second page of a different story is shown on page 8.

damage suit

Local twenty of the institutional and Public Works
Employees Union has filed a $2.5 million damage suit against
the city of Carrolton for violating work rules for union
employees at the city jail.

The suit was filed in United States district court
here yesterday. Monday.

The suit alleges that the city has radically
changed working hours for employees at the jail. Other
contract violations, the suit charges, include failing to
hold meetings with the union once a month, failing to
establish a safety committee at the jail and failing to
discuss quarterly employee evaluations with employees.

Jose Garcia, business agent for the union said
Monday yesterday that the suit was filed only after the city had
refused to discuss problems at the jail with the union.

more

The Federal Deposit Insurance Corp. is the agency ~~XXXXX~~ that insures bank deposits up to $100,000 for some 15,000 ~~XXXXXXXXXXXXXXXXX~~ member commercial and savings ~~XXXXXX~~ banks.

In this state, two banks, both owned by Capital City Bankcorp, were declared ~~XXXXXXXXXXXXXXXXXXXXXXXXXXXXXXXXXXX~~ insolvent last week. ~~XXXXXXXXXXXXXXX~~ The Westminster Savings Bank, with assets of $29.1 million, and the Polk County ~~XXXXXXXXXXXXXXXXXXXXXXXXXXXXXXXXXXXXXXXXXXXXXXXXX~~ ~~XXXXXXXXXXXXXXXXXXXXXXXXXXXXXXXXXXXXXXXXXXXXXXXXX~~ National Bank, with assets of $37.2 million, were closed on Monday and reopened on Tuesday as branches of BankOne Corp. of Capital City.

The closing of these two banks by the state increased the year's total of bank failures to 115. Last year 120 banks failed, a post-depression ~~XXXXXXXXXXXXXX~~ record.

The closings, according to Harold Williams of the FDIC, are a reflection of ~~XXXXX~~ growing ~~XXXXXX~~ problems in some sectors of the economy, particularly agriculture, energy and real estate.

"We're not out of the woods yet," Williams said. "We look for more bank problems."

FDIC officials have predicted that as many as 150 banks could fail or need government ~~XXXXXXXXX~~ assistance before ~~XXXXX~~ the end of the year.

##

8

EXERCISE 1-1

This is an exercise to show you how to prepare news copy in a professional manner.

Retype the story that follows these instructions. Follow the directions given in "Preparation of News Copy" on the preceding pages. Do not change or revise the story in any way. Just retype.

The finished copy will give you your own model for news copy.

Edward Lewis, a Carolton High School senior, has been honored at the 16th National Junior Science and Humanities Conference at Brown University for producing the nation's best high school paper in mathematics and applied physics.

He is one of five U.S. high school students who will attend the International Youth Science Fortnight in London, England, next summer.

Last spring Lewis and two other Carolton High School seniors, Ellis West and Mark White, were chosen to present papers at the Third Annual Chicago Region Junior Engineering, Science and Humanities Symposium at the Illinois Technological Institute.

Lewis' paper was one of 42 presented at the national conference.

##

Slug your copy *conference*.

Don't forget the end mark.

Type as carefully as you can. Strive for clean copy. If you do make a few errors in typing, correct them with the editing marks shown on page 6.

EXERCISE 1-2

This is an exercise to show you the proper way to prepare the second and succeeding pages of news copy.

Retype the paragraphs below. Follow the instructions in sections 2d and 4b of "Preparation of News Copy" on the preceding pages.

Do not change or revise the copy in any way. Merely retype as if these paragraphs were a continuation of the symposium story you typed in Exercise 1-1.

The finished copy will give you your own model for the second and succeeding pages of news copy.

Lewis built his own microcomputer system in order to complete his project, which was titled "An Error-Minimizing Solution to the Three-Body Problem."

Robert Brown, a professor of physics at Northwest College, directed the regional competition and accompanied the winners to Providence.

Lewis is the son of Mr. and Mrs. Elwyn Lewis of 345 W. Ohio Ave.

##

What is the slug line for this page of your copy?

Don't forget the end mark.

Type as carefully as you can. Strive for clean copy. If you do make a few errors in typing, correct them with the editing marks shown on page 6.

EXERCISE 1-3

Using the standard copy-editing marks, make the changes asked for in the examples that follow.

1. Indicate a paragraph at beginning of second sentence:

   The quick brown fox jumped over the lazy dog. The quick

   brown fox jumped over the lazy dog.

2. Capitalize the word *midwest:*

   The midwest is a large and prosperous industrial region.

3. Do not capitalize the word *Democratic:*

   Both speakers extolled the Democratic system.

4. Abbreviate the word *August:*

   They asked for a roll call vote on August 1 because . . .

5. Write out the word *August:*

   They want to meet before Aug. in order to . . .

6. Transpose the words *only won:*

   He only won the first relay before leaving the field.

7. Delete the second occurrence of the word *time:*

   No man may tether time time nor tide.

8. Close up the space in *an other* so that it reads *another:*

   He gave an other man his seat in the train.

9. Change the Arabic figures to words:

   He left 2 books, a bicycle, 4 empty bottles and 3 boxes.

Student's Name _____

11

EXERCISE 1-4

Using the standard copy-editing marks, make the changes asked for in the examples that follow.

1. Separate the words *another* and *man:*

   He gave anotherman his seat in the train.

2. Insert the word *the* after *all:*

   Where have all flowers gone?

3. Insert a period after the words *waste time:*

   Don't waste time Time is what life is made of.

4. Insert a comma after the word *party:*

   He owed a lot to his party his state and his country.

5. Insert quote marks around the phrase *special interests:*

   He said his opponent was a tool of special interests.

6. Delete the quote marks around the word *maverick:*

   He called his opponent a "maverick."

7. Insert the missing letter in the word *illustrated:*

   The tattooed man was ilustrated all over.

8. Delete the extra letter in *inoculated:*

   He was innoculated for diphtheria.

9. Indicate that the Arabic figure *9* should be written out:

   Spell out numbers one through 9 in news copy.

Student's Name _____

EXERCISE 1-5

Using the standard copy-editing marks, make the changes asked for in the examples that follow.

1. Insert a colon after the word *said:*

   The speaker said "My fellow Americans, now is the time . . ."

2. Indicate that the word *ten* should be an Arabic figure:

   Use Arabic figures for numbers ten, 11, 12 and so on.

3. Insert a semicolon in this list after the word *president:*

   Jane Doe, president John Q. Public, vice president; and Martha

   Washington, treasurer.

4. Insert a hyphen in *civic minded:*

   Some words, like civic minded, require a hyphen.

5. Insert a dash after the words *right way:*

   There's a right way and the Navy way.

6. Insert an apostrophe in the word *shes:*

   Shes very ambitious, but the others are not.

7. Indicate that the words *and women* are to remain in the copy:

   Now is the time for all good men ~~and women~~ to come to the . . .

8. Put a *more* mark at the end of the copy:

   A strong performance by General Motors also increased

   investor confidence. The market closed at the highest level

   since last August.

Student's Name _____

EXERCISE 1-6

Using the standard copy-editing marks, make the changes asked for in the examples that follow.

1. Delete the unnecessary letter in the word *occurred:*

   The accident occurrred at Broad and Main streets.

2. Insert the missing word or figure:

   The Declaration of Independence was signed on July, 1776, in

   Philadelphia.

3. Put an *end* mark at the end of the copy:

   It works out to $2.08 a share of common stock, compared

   with 41 cents a share in the first quarter of the year.

4. Delete the unnecessary comma after the word *shortstop:*

   He played first base, shortstop, and center field equally well.

5. Insert space between the words incorrectly run together.

   Hesaid the treaty negotiations were a completedisaster.

6. Insert a hyphen in *A bombs* and *H bombs:*

   The committee expressed concern about A bombs and H bombs.

7. Correct the improper spacing:

   He acted un interested but actually was verymuch concerned.

8. Correct capitalization:

   They lived in Albany, N.y., and then moved to a new Suburb

   outside Baltimore, Md., where they remained for 20 Years.

Student's Name _____

Instructions for Exercise 1-7

Mark all paragraphs.

line 01   Put quote marks around words *New Games*.
line 02   Delete word *local*.
line 03   Insert apostrophe in *citys*.
line 04   Insert missing letter in word *recreation*.
line 05   Delete words *recent event* and insert words *first tournament*.
line 06   Use your copy pencil to draw a couple of lines through X'd-out matter.
line 07   More deleted matter.
          Insert a hyphen in the word *nonstructured*.
line 08   *Special* is one word. Close up space.
          Make word *six* an Arabic figure.
line 09   Delete quote marks around words *balloon bash*.
line 10   Insert missing letter in word *creative*.
          Delete comma after *day*.
line 12   Capitalize word *traditional*.
line 14   Insert a space between words *pottery* and *and*.
line 15   Lowercase *A.M.*
          Delete *12*.
line 17   Abbreviate *August*.
line 19   Deleted matter again.
line 20   More deleted matter.
line 21   Insert a period after the word *fee*.
Place an end mark at the end of the copy.

Instructions for Exercise 1-8

Mark all paragraphs.

line 01   Make *fire fighters* one word.
line 02   Words *circuit court* should be capitalized.
line 04   Spell out *depts*.
line 05   Capitalize *civil service*.
line 06   Insert word *of* after *21*.
line 08   Capitalize the word *college*.
line 09   *Carolton* is spelled with one *r*. Delete the extra letter.
line 10   Use your copy pencil to draw a couple of lines through the X'd-out matter.
          Abbreviate *Nevada*.
line 12   Make *Electrical Engineering* lowercase.
line 13   Delete periods in *F.B.I.*
line 14   Abbreviate *Oklahoma*.
line 15   Make *Police Chief* lowercase.
          Spell out *west* in *W. Palm Beach*.
line 16   Make *Key Punch* lowercase.
          Capitalize *co.* in *General Telephone co.*
line 18   Make *Court's* lowercase.
line 19   Make *Legal Adviser* lowercase.
line 21   Make *City* lowercase.
          Spell out *4*.
line 22   Make *thirty* an Arabic figure.
Place an end mark at the end of the copy.

19

Instructions for Exercise 1-9

Mark all paragraphs.

line 01   Abbreviate *Company*.
line 03   *United States* should be abbreviated: *U.S.*
line 04   Delete *yesterday* and insert day of week.
line 05   Spell out word *Dept.*
line 07   Spell out *Ft.*
line 08   Abbreviate *November*.
line 09   Spell out *Sept.*
line 10   Delete extra letter *r* in *Carrolton*.
line 11   Indicate with appropriate editing mark that *SBA* should be spelled out.
line 14   Indicate with appropriate editing mark that *assoc.* should be spelled out.
line 15   Insert comma after *Carolton*.
            Delete opening quote marks before word *to*.
line 17   Insert word *people* after *disadvantaged*.
            Delete closing quote marks.
line 18   Insert closing quote marks after *set-aside*.
line 19   Spell out *3*.
            Make it read *Parks said*.
line 20   Insert comma in *2000*.
            Make it read *$100 million*.
line 22   *Eighty* should be an Arabic figure.

Place an end mark at end of copy.

Instructions for Exercise 1-10

Mark all paragraphs.

line 01   Insert a comma in *1000*.
line 02   Insert a dash after word *gasses*.
line 05   Capitalize word *county*.
            Delete word *more*.
            Change words *two thousand* to Arabic figures.
line 06   Delete *last night* and insert day of week.
line 07   Make Arabic figure a word.
line 09   Insert period after *inhalation*.
            Deleted matter again.
line 11   Change cap *P* in *Paraquat* to lowercase.
line 12   *Sodium* is misspelled. Change the *o* to *u*.
line 13   *West* should not be capitalized.
line 15   Insert opening quote marks before word *It*.
line 17   Title *fire chief* on lines 17 and 18 should be uppercase.
line 20   *Manufacturing* and *co.* should be uppercase.
line 21   Deleted matter again.
line 22   A word is misspelled here.
            Deleted matter again.
line 23   Insert a period after word *storeroom*.

Place an end mark at the end of the copy.

EXERCISE 1-7

This is an exercise in using standard copy-editing marks. Make the changes in the copy that are asked for in the instructions on page 19. Do *not* make any other changes. Follow instructions carefully. Refer to the examples of copy-editing marks on page 6.

01   New Games, a modern recreation concept recently

02   tested by 400 Carolton residents at a local tournament,

03   will be a regular feature of the citys vacation

04   recreaton program.

05   Susan Cristo, who coordinated the recent event, will

06   also direct a program XXXXXXXXXXXX that stresses

07   XXXXX active involvement in nonstructured games.

08   Other spec ial events planned for children aged six

09   through 13 will be the great "balloon bash," a

10   nature-oriented scavenger hunt, a cretive dramatics day,

11   and a physical fitness award day.

12   traditional camping activities and other events,

13   including camping, painting, ice skating, tennis, arts

14   and crafts, tumbling, potteryand baking, will be the

15   major focus. Morning classes from 9 A.M. to 12 noon and

16   afternoon sessions from 1 to 4 p.m. will be offered

17   through August 20.

18   Extended supervision before and after regular hours

19   will be available for XXXXXXX children of working

20   parents. Prepared lunches will be available at XXXXXXXX

21   a nominal fee

Student's Name _____

EXERCISE 1-8

This is an exercise in using standard copy-editing marks. Make the changes in the copy that are asked for in the instructions on page 19. Do *not* make any other changes. Follow instructions carefully. Refer to the examples of copy-editing marks on page 6.

01   The first of the new fire fighters the city of

02   Carolton must hire as a result of a circuit court

03   decision will begin work next week. The court has

04   ordered all city depts. to hire from a statewide

05   civil service list.

06   William A. Hughes, 21, Lynn, Mass., and Stephen P.

07   Choate, 24, of New Orleans, have been hired. Choate is a

08   part-time student at Northwest college.

09   Hughes is a newcomer to Carrolton. He has been

10   working in XXXXXX Reno, Nevada, and finds the move to

11   this area not an easy transition.

12   Choate majored in math and Electrical Engineering at

13   Purdue. His father is an F.B.I. agent in Tulsa,

14   Oklahoma, and his mother is a lawyer. A brother is

15   Police Chief in W. Palm Beach, Fla. His wife, Nancy, is

16   a Key Punch operator with the General Telephone co. in

17   Carolton.

18   The city had expected to appeal the Court's decision,

19   but last week Marion Orr, the city's Legal Adviser, and

20   members of City Council decided against appeal. Mrs. Orr

21   said the City will hire 4 more firefighters within the

22   next thirty days.

Student's Name _____

EXERCISE 1-9

This is an exercise in using standard copy-editing marks. Make the changes in the copy that are asked for in the instructions on page 20. Do *not* make any other changes. Follow the instructions carefully. Refer to the examples of copy-editing marks on page 6.

01   The Carolton Construction Company has been awarded the

02   largest building contract ever granted a minority firm in

03   United States school construction history.

04   The contract for $1.5 million, announced yesterday by

05   the Dept. of Education and the Small Business

06   Administration, will finance an addition to a school at

07   Ft. Dunbar.

08   The building project will begin November 1. Completion

09   is set for Sept. of next year.

10   The contract to the Carrolton firm was granted through

11   a special SBA program that allows government agencies to

12   negotiate contracts with firms owned by minority people

13   or other disadvantaged business owners.

14   Marshall Parks, assoc. administrator of the SBA office

15   in Carolton said the program is intended "to use

16   government procurement to get minorities and other

17   disadvantaged into the economic mainstream."

18   The program, known as the 8-A "set-aside effort, was

19   created 3 years ago, said Parks. Since then, more than

20   2000 contracts valued at almost $100,000,000 have been

21   signed.

22   Contracts have gone to eighty minority firms in this

23   state.

Student's Name _____

EXERCISE 1-10

This is an exercise in using standard copy-editing marks. Make the changes in the copy that are asked for in the instructions on page 20. Do *not* make any other changes. Follow the instructions carefully. Refer to the examples of copy-editing marks on page 6.

01   More than 1000 people -- evacuated Sunday when a

02   chemical fire released deadly gasses have returned to

03   their homes.

04   A second chemical fire, this one in rural Washington

05   county, forced more two thousand people from their homes.

06   Officials in Carolton said last night that 72 people,

07   including 5 firefighters, were treated for chemical

08   burns.

09   Many others were treated for smoke inhalation XXXXXXX

10   Police in Carolton said one chemical agent released by

11   the fire was Paraquat, a defoliant, and another was the

12   bleaching agent sodiom hydrosulfide.

13   Police cruised up and down streets on the West side of

14   Carolton, using bullhorns to warn residents of the fumes.

15   It smelled like sewer fumes coming through the door,"

16   one Carolton resident said.

17   Residents said Carolton firefighters, especially fire

18   chief John Wiggins, did their job well.

19   The first fire started in a warehouse owned by the

20   Shook manufacturing co., in the Carolton industrial

21   XXXXXXX park. The second fire was caused by an explosion

22   that occured when XXXXXXXXXXXX a spark from an acetylene

23   torch ignited waste paper in a paint factory storeroom

Student's Name _____

2 News Leads

Spelling

vernacular, satellite, resistible, supersede, temblor, reconnaissance, privilege, nitpicking, liaison, hemorrhage, existence, ballistics

Usage

consul/council/counsel, censor/censure, apposite/opposite, appraise/apprise, character/reputation, accept/except

Newsroom Vocabulary

copy, story, lead, five Ws, summary lead, blind lead, byline, deadline, style, stylebook, news hole, ANPA, First Amendment, FYI

News Leads

The following topic is discussed in detail in George A. Hough 3rd, "News Writing," fourth edition:

News Leads
Chapter 4, "Writing the Lead," pages 58 through 64, for a discussion of summary leads.

Chapter 4, "Writing the Lead," pages 65 through 67, for a discussion of blind leads.

Chapter 4, "Writing the Lead," page 68, Figure 4.3, for a model of a summary lead and a blind lead.

"A Basic Guide to News Style," pages 459 through 490.

EXERCISE 2-1

A good lead requires precise use of language. Once you have determined the subject of a lead, you must find a verb that is directly related to the subject, a verb that creates the right picture in the mind of the reader.

In the spaces below, supply appropriate verbs for the nouns on the left. Item 1 is an example of verbs appropriate to a story about a fire.

1.   fire   destroys   damages   injures

2.   robbery   _____   _____

3.   holdup   _____   _____

4.   theft   _____

5.   accident   _____   _____   _____

6.   appointment   _____

7.   promotion   _____

8.   grant   _____   _____

9.   speaker   _____   _____

10. taxes   _____   _____   _____

11. sentence   _____   (as to prison, to jail)

12. fine   _____   (a legal penalty)

13. reception   _____

14. inauguration   _____   _____   _____

15. conference   _____

16. temperatures   _____   _____

17. author   _____

18. chairman   _____   _____

19. voters   _____   _____

20. warrant   _____

Student's Name _____

EXERCISE 2-2

Write a one-sentence summary lead based on these facts:

Fact 1   A local man has a new job.

Fact 2   He has accepted a job beginning the first of the month with Graham Associates, a public relations firm.

Fact 3   He has been city editor of the Record since 1979.

Fact 4   He is a 1970 graduate of the School of Journalism at Northwest college.

Fact 5   His name is Fred W. Nelson.

Fact 6   Nelson spent last year in Washington on an American Political Science Association fellowship.

EXERCISE 2-3

Write a one-sentence summary lead based on these facts:

Fact 1   Women's golf team from Northwest college is taking part in an invitational tournament at Guadalajara, Mexico.

Fact 2   The college's team score yesterday was 304. The team finished in 4th place.

Fact 3   Maryanne Sims, a senior at the college, had lowest score for the college team. She shot a 72.

Fact 4   Yesterday Florida finished first, Oklahoma second, Southern Methodist third and Northwest 4th.

EXERCISE 2-4

Write a one-sentence summary lead based on these facts:

Fact 1   The Franklin library is expanding its programs.

Fact 2   One new program is called "Book Buddies."

Fact 3   In this program, adults read children's books to patients in the pediatrics wards at local hospitals.

Fact 4   The library is also trying to find volunteers who speak Spanish to help with other library programs.

Fact 5   The library wants to add Spanish-language stories to the English-language stories now available on tape and needs volunteers to record the stories.

33

EXERCISE 2-5

Write a one-sentence summary lead based on these facts:

Fact 1 Northwest college is planning to build a new residence hall.

Fact 2 The college has raised $4 million toward the projected cost of eight million dollars and earlier this year asked the federal government for additional funds.

Fact 3 Yesterday, at a meeting of the college's board of trustees, you learned that the federal government has given the college the money it needs.

Fact 4 The federal grant is for $4 million.

Fact 5 Construction will start early next year.

Fact 6 Architect for the college is the Carolton firm of McKim, Oglethorpe and Dodge.

Fact 7 The new residence hall will be built near the Chartwell residence hall.

Fact 8 The building will accommodate 400 students.

EXERCISE 2-6

Write a one-sentence summary lead based on these facts:

Fact 1 Carolton applied for and has been awarded a state youth employment grant.

Fact 2 Grant comes from the state Human Resources Commission.

Fact 3 Purpose of the grant: to provide part-time summer jobs for low income students ages 16 to 21.

Fact 4 The $45,000 grant will permit hiring between 60 and 70 students.

Fact 5 They will work 25 hours a week for ten weeks at the minimum wage.

Fact 6 Work will consist of general cleanup and maintenance around city hall and other public buildings.

Fact 7 Applications for summer work and selection of those who will be employed will be handled by the Carolton public schools.

Question: Will your readers know what the minimum wage is?

EXERCISE 2-7

Write a one-sentence summary lead based on these facts:

Fact 1   The state vocational rehabilitation services office in Carolton has been looking for a new director.

Fact 2   A new director was named yesterday.

Fact 3   Her name is Janice Sanders.

Fact 4   She has been assistant director of the Massachusetts vocational rehab services office in Taunton, Massachusetts, for the past three years.

Fact 5   Her salary will be $50,508 a year.

Fact 6   She replaces Herbert Krug, who resigned last month.

Fact 7   The vocational rehab office here serves residents of Washington County and three adjacent counties.

EXERCISE 2-8

Write a one-sentence summary lead based on these facts:

Fact 1   The city clerk has been given the ok to buy a new computer.

Fact 2   The clerk's office uses a computer for budgeting and accounting for all city departments.

Fact 3   The city's present computer, purchased in 1981, is no longer able to handle all the city's work.

Fact 4   Purchase of a new computer was approved by city council last night at its regular weekly meeting.

Fact 5   The new computer will cost $65,000.

Fact 6   Donna Williams, the city clerk, told the council that she will ask for bids for the new computer as soon as possible.

EXERCISE 2-9

Write a one-sentence summary lead based on these facts:

Fact 1   The Presbyterian Home is building an addition to its infirmary located on East State road.

Fact 2   Facility will have twenty two beds and will cost $1,250,000.

Fact 3   Construction will start Monday after a ground-breaking ceremony tomorrow at 4 in the afternoon.

35

EXERCISE 2-10

Write a one-sentence summary lead based on these facts:

Fact 1   The Carolton Area Chamber of Commerce held its annual banquet last night.

Fact 2   The chamber's new president was installed at the banquet.

Fact 3   Term of office for the chamber president is two years.

Fact 4   The new president is Nancy Johnson.

Fact 5   She is owner of Carolton Hardware Co.

Fact 6   She is a director of the Farmers and Merchants bank and is a trustee of Carolton General hospital.

Fact 7   Other officers were also installed last night.

Fact 8   The new vice president is Walter Hillman.

Fact 9   The new secretary is Bruce B. Hikok.

Fact 10   The new treasurer is Charles Banks.

EXERCISE 2-11

Write a one-sentence summary lead based on these facts:

Fact 1   The power company has started a new and unusual service.

Fact 2   Service has been developed with the assistance of the Washington county association for the blind.

Fact 3   This service will be available at no cost beginning next month.

Fact 4   About 400 of the power company's 1,300,000 customers are blind.

Fact 5   Gas and electric bills for area residents who are blind will be sent out in braille.

Fact 6   These customers will get regular bills, followed a few days later by bills in braille.

Fact 7   Association for Blind will get billing information from the power company and put it into the association's computer, which will transcribe the data into braille.

EXERCISE 2-12

Write a one-sentence summary lead based on these facts:

Fact 1   Local hospitals have completed their reports for the past fiscal year. The fiscal year ends June 30.

Fact 2   At Carolton General 200 births for fiscal year; 188 in the previous year.

Fact 3   At Holy Cross, 608 births for fiscal year; 654 in the previous year.

Fact 4   At St. Luke's, 475 births for fiscal year; 501 in the previous year.

Fact 5   Over past several years, births at local hospitals have averaged about thirteen hundred.

Fact 6   Receiving hospital — the city hospital — does not have a maternity ward.

Fact 7   These figures come from reports filed by the hospitals with the Washington County Health Department.

EXERCISE 2-13

Write a one-sentence summary lead based on these facts:

Fact 1   New programs for elderly residents of Carolton will be available soon.

Fact 2   Program will include recreational activities, social events and craft sessions.

Fact 3   Residents sixty years of age and older are invited to take part.

Fact 4   Program will be at the Carolton-Washington Adult center at 412 East Main. This is a new city facility.

Fact 5   The center will open for the first time on Monday.

Fact 6   Plans call for the center to be open weekdays from 9 in the morning until 5 in the afternoon.

Fact 7   The center will be operated by the Washington county department of public health.

Fact 8   Funding for the center is coming from a state grant and from funds provided by the city and county.

EXERCISE 2-14

Write a one-sentence summary lead based on these facts:

Fact 1   Temperatures yesterday at the airport: high 91, low 68.

Fact 2   Rainfall: none.

Fact 3   Yesterday's high temperature set a record. Previous record for this date was set here in 1941 when temperature reached 89.

Fact 4   Yesterday was 17th consecutive day with a temperature over 80.

Fact 5   Yesterday was 22nd consecutive day without precipitation. This part of state is extremely dry. Average rainfall to date is 26 inches. Up to yesterday, total for year is 18 inches.

Fact 6   Weather service gives you this forecast: No change expected in next four or five days. Continued hot and dry.

EXERCISE 2-15

Write a one-sentence summary lead based on these facts:

Fact 1   Children starting kindergarten in Carolton schools will need a birth certificate and a certificate of immunization.

Fact 2   School district staff will be at elementary schools tomorrow and Monday from 8 in the morning until five so parents can register their children.

EXERCISE 2-16

Write a one-sentence summary lead based on these facts:

Fact 1   The Women's Studies Center on the Northwest College campus had a reception this noon.

Fact 2   Guest of honor was Carol Ellis, director of Women's Opportunities for the American Association of Community and Junior Colleges.

Fact 3   She is a 1982 graduate of Northwest college.

Fact 4   She is in Carolton to visit Northwest College and to study its women's program.

Fact 5   About 200 faculty, students and Carolton residents attended the reception.

Fact 6   The reception was held in the student union building on campus.

EXERCISE 2-17

Write a one-sentence summary lead based on these facts:

Fact 1   The Eric Griswold Prizes for this year were announced yesterday.

Fact 2   Two Northwest College faculty members won the awards.

Fact 3   Each will be presented a gold medal and $1000 in cash.

Fact 4   Prizes are for quote original research contributing to the welfare of humanity unquote.

Fact 5   The prizes are given by the Griswold Foundation. Nominations for the prizes are submitted by colleges and universities in this and other countries.

Fact 6   Winners are Professors Julia Trosko and Charles Tsui.

Fact 7   They have been experimenting with new varieties of plants that have potential as sources of food in semi-arid areas of the world.

Fact 8   The prizes will be presented Saturday at a faculty convocation in the LaFollette auditorium.

EXERCISE 2-18

Write a one-sentence summary lead based on these facts:

Fact 1   Washington County Public Relations Club held its annual "Awards Celebration" last night.

Fact 2   Program was held at the Commerce Club.

Fact 3   The club made two major awards.

Fact 4   One award was given to Alfred Carew. He is superintendent of the Carolton public schools.

Fact 5   He was given the club's "distinguished public relations award."

Fact 6   A second award went to W. H. Handy III, vice president for community relations of the First National Bank.

Fact 7   Carew's award is for "improving the image of the Carolton school system."

Fact 8   The award was given to Handy for his continuing contributions to the club.

EXERCISE 2-19

Verbs have been called the muscle of good writing. These sentences need a little more muscle. Review Exercise 2-1. Then rewrite and use a strong, vigorous verb. For example:

Weak   The stabbing of a 31-year-old man occurred Friday morning in front of the First National Bank.

Better   A 31-year-old Carolton man was stabbed Friday morning in front of the First National Bank.

1.   Three teen-agers charged in connection with the random shooting of vehicles that left one man wounded have been arrested and turned over to County Family Court.

2.   The state Highway Patrol is investigating two accidents that resulted in injuries Friday.

3.   A Carolton man has been arrested in connection with the March 12 burglary of the County Line Liquor Store.

4.   Washington County police received calls from people reporting nearly a dozen burglaries.

5.   A traffic accident on Highway 30 yesterday Friday left a 27-year-old Carolton man in serious condition.

6.   A winter storm that battered the midstate area yesterday left hundreds of motorists stranded on highways and in emergency shelters.

7.   A Carolton man and two juveniles have been arrested in connection with two school burglaries here last month.

Student's Name _____

41

EXERCISE 2-20

Verbs have been called the muscle of good writing. These sentences need a little more muscle. Review Exercise 2-1. Then rewrite and use a strong, vigorous verb. For example:

Weak   A collision between a car and a Carolton police unit resulted in the death of a Florida man last night.

Better   A Florida man was killed last night when his car collided with a Carolton police car.

1. Carolton police yesterday investigated a two-car wreck on California Avenue in which both drivers were injured.

2. A police shoot-out in the City Hall parking lot yesterday left two men injured and in police custody.

3. The Washington County Sheriff's Department has asked for an armed robbery warrant against a Carolton teenager.

4. Carolton police reported yesterday that a thief entered an automobile belonging to James Wang of 504 E. Utah Ave. while the vehicle was parked at Wang's home and stole a stereo.

5. A 13-year-old Carolton boy ran into the path of a car near the high school and remained hospitalized yesterday.

6. Judge John Rowland gave suspended sentences and $300 fines to the four men convicted of trespassing.

7. The Athenian Grille on East Main Street was the victim of vandals last night.

Student's Name _____

EXERCISE 2-21

It's time to get acquainted with the stylebook.

Fill in the blanks in this news story, using the key at the bottom of the page. The key tells you what words or numbers go in the blanks, and the numbers in parentheses refer you to the appropriate sections of the "Basic Guide to News Style" in "News Writing."

01   A Canadian poet will lecture on her work _____

02   on the Northwest _____ campus.

03   Carol Greenwood, author of _____ volumes of poetry,

04   will speak on _____.

05   The lecture will be in the LaFollette Auditorium at

06   _____. Tickets are _____.

07   Miss Greenwood's only novel_ "Singing Women_" is an

08   ____ utopian story set in the future in what was once

09   the _____.

10   The lecture is one in a series scheduled during

11   _____ and November by the department of English.

12   The next lecture will be on _____.

line 01   tomorrow night (see 6.3)
     02   college (see 2.1)
     03   twenty (see 3.1)
     04   The Poet's Voice (see 4.7)
     06   eight o'clock at night (see 3.6, 6.1 and 6.4)
          four dollars (see 3.7 and 3.12)
     07   paired commas (see "News Writing," pages 397 through 399)
     08   anti (see 4.4)
     09   U.S. or United States? (see 1.13)
     11   October (see 1.12)
     12   November first (see 1.12 and 3.13)

Student's Name _____

EXERCISE 2-22

Fill in the blanks in this news story, using the key at the bottom of the page. The key tells you what words or numbers go in the blanks, and the numbers in parentheses refer you to the appropriate sections of the "Basic Guide to News Style" in "News Writing."

01 _____ of the Carolton Community Mental

02 Health _____ have a new _____ contract.

03   Wage provisions of the contract will be renegotiated

04 after _____ year.

05   Board members approved the contract _____.

06 ____ Mary McLeod, _____, said

07 the contract will be signed _____.

08   The _____ professional, _____ clerical and six

09 other workers at the clinic are represented by

10 _____.

11   The union's previous contract expired _____.

line 01   Employes or employees? (see Section 1 spelling list in this workbook)
    02   clinic (see 2.1)
       two year (see 3.1 and 4.4)
    04   one (see 3.1)
    05   last night (see 1.14 and 6.3)
    06   Miss McLeod is a medical doctor (see 5.6 and 5.7).
       director of the clinic (see 5.12, 5.13 and paired commas)
    07   next Monday — day or date? (see 6.5)
    08   one hundred and ten; nine (see 3.1)
    10   AFSCME, the American Federation of State, County and Municipal
       Employees (see 1.1, 1.2 and 1.3)
    11   the 30th of last month (see 1.12, 6.5 and 6.7)

Student's Name _____

3 Writing the Story

Spelling

judgment, flaccid, aerial, sheriff, tariff, bailiff, plaintiff, restaurateur, temperament, rendezvous, prejudice, accidentally

Usage

continual/continuous, eminent/imminent, empathy/apathy, expatiate/expiate, parameter/perimeter, media/medium, noon/midnight

Newsroom Vocabulary

editorial, editorial matter, assignment, inverted pyramid, brief, paragraph, body, development, attribution, identification, lowercase, uppercase, down style, up style

Writing the Story

These topics are discussed in detail in George A. Hough 3rd, "News Writing," fourth edition:

Inverted Pyramid/Single-Incident Stories
Chapter 6, "Writing the Story," pages 89 through 92.

Identification
Chapter 6, "Writing the Story," pages 97 through 102.

Attribution
Chapter 6, "Writing the Story," pages 93 through 97.

Time Elements
Chapter 6, "Writing the Story," pages 102 through 108.

Paired Commas
Chapter 19, "Newspaper Grammar and Punctuation," pages 397 through 399.

Style
"A Basic Guide to News Style," pages 459 through 490.

Errors in News Copy

Errors in news stories are serious matters. At the very least, they annoy readers who know better, undermine confidence in the reliability of the newspaper and may even provide grounds for a libel suit against the newspaper.

You must make every effort in writing news stories to avoid errors in fact or interpretation. The byword of the professional journalist is "accuracy always."

The news writing exercises in every section of "Practice Exercises" may include errors deliberately placed there to test your journalistic reliability — the care with which you check and verify facts that you use as the basis for a story.

First, the exercises probably will not follow news style as it is set forth in the "Basic Guide to News Style" in the appendix of "News Writing." You will have to know the style rules and follow them.

Second, you will find discrepancies in names and addresses in the exercises. You will be expected to check every name and every address against the model directories in the appendix. The directory is correct. The exercise may omit a middle initial, misspell a name or give an incorrect address.

When you have completed a news story assignment, read your copy over carefully. Check your story against the assignment and verify the accuracy of names and addresses. Check your copy against the style guide.

When — and only when — you are sure that all names, addresses and facts in your story are correct, write "all names verified" at the top of your copy.

You will be penalized for errors in news story assignments. First, you will have to revise and correct your story. Your instructor will lower your grade. And, finally, you will be asked to write a correction.

Most newspapers publish correction notices as soon as errors are discovered. These are sometimes published under standing heads like "For the Record" or "Getting It Straight." Sometimes they are simply labeled "Correction." Slug your correction stories *correction*.

Your correction story, following in general form the model in Figure 20.3 in Chapter 20, will begin:

> A story in (day)'s Morning Record incorrectly
> reported that . . .

Then set the record straight by explaining what the facts were.

If something was left out of the story that should have been included, your correction story might begin:

> A story in (day)'s Morning Record omitted the
> (name of) (fact that) (date of) . . .

Develop the habit of careful workmanship. Check, check and check again. Don't let errors creep into your copy.

EXERCISE 3-1

This morning your city editor handed you a press release from Northwest College. "Here," she said, "write something on this."

The press release said that the National Institute of Education has decided to provide funds for a research project to study how ninth graders solve algebra problems.

The Institute has allocated $37,300 for this study.

The study will be conducted by Dr. Sigrid Wagner. Dr. Wagner is on the faculty of the School of Education at Northwest College. She is an assistant professor.

Her grant is one of three being made by the Institute. The grants continue the Institute's funding for studies of learning disabilities.

Dr. Wagner's grant is the only NIE grant awarded in this state.

Dr. Wagner is nationally known for her research in early childhood education.

EXERCISE 3-2

While you were on campus this morning, you stopped in at the college bookstore. During a conversation with the manager, he asked you if you had the story on Charlie Applegate. He told you that Applegate had been elected president of the booksellers association. He gave you these facts:

The Mid-State Booksellers Association held its annual meeting in New Orleans Thursday and Friday of last week. Mr. Applegate has been active in the association for the past 10 years. This past year he was vice president.

The association has about 2000 members in 50 states. At this year's meeting Applegate was elected president. He will serve until the next annual meeting.

Applegate, the manager reminds you, is owner of the bookstore on New York avenue.

The association holds an annual trade show and meeting. It also watches legislation that may affect book publishers and booksellers.

About 1000 bookstore owners and managers were at the convention.

Applegate is on the city council and is chairman of the county Democratic committee.

EXERCISE 3-3

You are working the early shift today. When you came in at 6:45 a.m., the assistant city editor asked you to do a story on last night's storm. You made a few phone calls and picked up enough information for a story.

From the weather service office at the airport:

When the storm struck, temperature dropped from 70 to 55 degrees in less than an hour. Rainfall in 24 hours ending at midnight was 1.1 inches. Weather service at airport clocked wind at times at 45 miles an hour.

From the power company:

There were several outages during the evening. Lightning struck a transformer on Old Meetinghouse Road, and about 1500 homes and businesses on the east side of Territorial road were without power for from one to three hours. Power company crews worked until four this morning repairing the transformer and wires knocked down by falling limbs. Worst hit was West Wisconsin Avenue, where several big trees fell across power lines.

From police:

Traffic was a problem for a while on West Wisconsin Avenue. Cars had to be diverted for a couple of hours until trees were removed and power lines repaired. The problem was in the 300 block. There were no serious auto accidents. Just a few fenderbenders.

From the fire department:

One call, to 503 East Vermont, about 11:30, house fire. Damage about $7,500. Lightning struck the house.

From department of public works:

City crews worked from 11 last night till after 4 this morning clearing fallen limbs and assisting power company crews.

From a reader who calls as you are getting ready to write:

East of Old Meetinghouse road where he lives there was a lot of wind. Some trees down, fallen tree limbs. He lost some shingles off his roof.

FYI: The storm blew up too late last night for the night staff to get a story into the final edition of today's paper.

EXERCISE 3-4

Because of the holiday next week, many businesses and offices will be closed or have irregular hours. You have been asked to write a story explaining the situation.

Your notes for the story:

Closed: all banks, city hall and city offices, county offices, all courts
Closed: schools — city and parochial
Closed: post office (lobby open)
Closed: federal building and all federal offices
Mail deliveries: no
Trash pickup: no (pickup next day)
Delta Mall: stores closed/restaurants open
Food stores: 10–6 only
Library: Franklin closed/college library 9–5

EXERCISE 3-5

On a visit to the Northwest College campus this morning, you picked up an announcement about an undergraduate book contest sponsored by the library. Write a story for tomorrow's paper.

The Bloomfield Library is sponsoring an undergraduate book contest.

The contest is intended to identify and reward students who have displayed particular aptitude in assembling and organizing their personal libraries.

Collections of any type will be considered for the awards. Personal libraries may be subject-centered, deal with an individual author or be more general.

Students must submit lists of their books, including author, title and date of publication. Book lists should be annotated.

There is no upper limit on the number of books. Numbers are secondary to discriminating selection. To be eligible for an award, student libraries should consist of at least 35 titles.

The collections will be judged by a nominating committee consisting of Dr. Granville Holmes, journalism; Robert Shaw, Department of Natural Science; and Don Harmon, romance languages.

Annotated lists of books may be taken to the main office of the library. Deadline is the 15th of next month. Winners will be announced at the end of the month.

Only full-time undergraduate students who are enrolled during the present term are eligible to apply.

EXERCISE 3-6

The public relations office at the college called this story in this morning. Write it for tomorrow's paper.

An award to Joan Lawrence — presented Saturday at Iowa City, Iowa. She is a senior at Northwest College majoring in speech. Her home is in Austin, Tex. She is a member of the Northwest College forensics team.

The award was made by the Central States Forensics Assoc.

Joan was in Iowa City with the forensics team for a meet at the University of Iowa. The meet was sponsored by the Central States Forensics Assoc.

Joan won first place in expository speaking.

Teams from 76 colleges and universities took part in the meet on Friday and Saturday. Northwest sent a team of six. The Northwest team placed 34th in the meet.

EXERCISE 3-7

You got a phone call this morning from Al Souza, head of the Chamber of Commerce's committee on industrial development. He told you:

Chamber will hold a press conference tomorrow noon. Plans to announce that a high-tech industry has decided to locate a new plant in the city's industrial park on the northwest side.

Won't announce name of firm until tomorrow. Firm will move into an existing building. May build later. Expects to start production early next year.

Firm will employ about 200 people. About a dozen executives will move here before production starts.

Firm makes optical products, including night scopes used in aiming firearms at night. It is a supplier for the U.S. defense department.

Press conference will be held at the civic center.

The firm has plants in several states. Decided to expand and start new production line here because of available buildings, labor supply and favorable climate.

Souza says the firm's decision a direct result of an aggressive campaign by the chamber to bring new industry to Carolton.

He says several other manufacturing companies are also looking at sites here.

EXERCISE 3-8

Joyce McLaren, director of public relations for the Tri-State Education Association, called just now with a story. Write it for tomorrow's paper:

The Tri-State education association has had an acting director for the past six months. He is Bernard E. Palmer. Palmer was principal of Carolton Central High until he retired last June. Yesterday the association hired a permanent director.

The new director has been executive director of City Charities in Paoli, Pennsylvania. He will start his new job here July 1st.

His name is Anthony L. Rhodes. He is 42, a native of Lancaster, Pennsylvania, and a graduate of Teachers College at Columbia university.

His wife's name is Amy, and they have two children, Frank, eight, and Sarah, five.

The Tri-State education association has about 2500 members in four states. Its headquarters is in Carolton at 255 Washington Road.

You ask, but Miss McLaren will not tell you what Rhodes' salary will be.

EXERCISE 3-9

Your editor handed you a press release from the state highway department and asked you to check it and write a story for tomorrow's paper.

You learn from the press release:

The interstate will be closed from a point five miles east of Carolton to the state line beginning this morning. The highway department is beginning construction of a three-span bridge over the Yellow river and repaving about a mile of the highway on either side of the bridge.

You call the public information officer for the state highway department in Capital City and learn:

The interstate will be closed about six months.

You call the county highway department and learn:

To detour around the construction work, eastbound traffic will have to leave the interstate at Battle road, go south on Battle road 6 miles to Highway 20, then east on 20 to the junction of 20 and the interstate at Greenfield.

FYI: Greenfield is in Green County about eleven miles southeast of Carolton. Green County adjoins Washington County on the east.

EXERCISE 3-10

While you were in the office this morning, a subscriber called with a story she would like to have in the Record. She told you:

Her daughter, Cheryl Ann, is a 1984 graduate of the high school here. She enlisted in the Air Force a couple of months ago. Now she has finished her basic training at Lackland Air Force Base. She is an airman.

After her leave, she is going to Rickenbacker Air Force Base, where she will be attached to the 310th Combat Support Group. She's home now on a 10-day leave.

Lackland is in Texas. Rickenbacker is in Ohio. Mother is Mrs. Virginia Main.

EXERCISE 3-11

Write a news story based on the information given to you today by the publicity chairman of the Women's Club. Verify all names. Write a blind lead.

The Carolton Professional Women's Club offers scholarships each year to teachers in the Carolton and Washington county school system.

The names of the teachers who are being given scholarships this year were announced yesterday at a meeting of the club.

Scholarships are $500.

Susan Christo teaches at O'Higgins junior high. Alice Short teaches at Central high.

The scholarships may be used toward a graduate degree, enrichment courses or continuing education courses.

EXERCISE 3-12

You were in the college library this morning to return a book and saw that the annual book sale sponsored by the Friends of the Library was being held in the lobby.

You didn't have time to browse through the books for sale, but you did get a few notes on which to base a story for tomorrow's paper. Your notes:

5,000 books on sale — sale started today, runs through Saturday. Prices range from 50 cents up — books have been collected by the Friends — some new, some used — some are books discarded by the college library. Proceeds from the sale will go toward purchase of tapes for the library's special collection for the blind.

EXERCISE 3-13

Your city editor has handed you a press release that came in the mail this morning and asked you to write a story based on it. You read it and learn:

The University of Austin has awarded a number of fellowships for the study of foreign languages. Among the recipients is a graduate of the local high school.

Linda Anne Vogel is a graduate student at Ohio Wesleyan University. She is studying Romance languages.

The fellowship will enable her to spend next summer traveling and studying in Portugal.

Her parents' names are in the press release, so you call her mother, Mrs. Helen Vogel, and verify the facts in the release. She tells you that Linda graduated from high school here in 1983. She got her BA at Wesleyan in June 1987.

Write a story for tomorrow's paper. Some of your readers may not know where Ohio Wesleyan is, so include that in your story.

EXERCISE 3-14

You got a call from Bill Morrissey in the college public relations office today. He had a story he thought you might want to run in the Record. He told you:

A local woman who is pretty well known in the city and has been very active in supporting the college's art museum has been added to the board of Citizens for the Arts.

Citizens for the Arts is an organization for people who want to support the arts in the state, stimulate public awareness and appreciation of the arts and promote increased state funding for the arts.

She is Anne Dickens. She is a member of the board of Friends of the Museum. She is also a member of the Turner committee, which is helping the museum prepare for and promote the coming exhibition of paintings by J. W. M. Turner. The Turner exhibit opens the first of the month.

She is also on the board of the Washington County Heritage Foundation.

Mrs. Dickens is a free-lance writer. At one time she was a reporter on the Record.

Some of your readers may not recognize the name J.W.M. Turner. Please identify him in your story.

EXERCISE 3-15

While you were having coffee this morning in the Hotel Lenox coffee shop, you chatted with Ralph Turner, secretary of the Franklin library board. Turner told you that the board has finally found a head librarian.

You recall that Mrs. Helen Kirby is retiring the first of the month and that the library board has been conducting a search for someone to replace her.

Turner told you that the board has picked Richard Tassinari for the job. He is a 1980 graduate of the school of library science at the University of Michigan. Since then he has been a branch librarian in Ann Arbor.

He will start work here at the end of next month.

Write a story for tomorrow's paper. The library board hasn't announced Tassinari's appointment officially, so attribute the story to Turner.

EXERCISE 3-16

Marlene Brackett, public information officer for the city schools, brought in a story she thinks is newsworthy. You can write it for tomorrow's paper. She told you:

A senior from Central high is one of several area students who are in Chicago this week for the National 4-H Congress. The congress began yesterday and will end Saturday. She is the daughter of Eugene and Evelyn Lyons.

Suzanne Lyons is editor of "The Blue and Gold," the student newspaper at Central, a member of the debate team and Future Business Leaders of America.

At the Congress, she will give the speech that won her first place in public speaking at the state 4-H competition last summer. Title of her talk is "Leadership."

She is 18 and has been in 4-H work for the past six years.

EXERCISE 3-17

A local woman, Mrs. James McGregor, called you this morning to tell you that both her sons have made the dean's list at college. Write a story for tomorrow's paper.

Michael on fall semester list at Babson College. He is 1987 graduate of Central high. Majoring in computer science.

James Jr. on fall semester list at University of Wisconsin at Madison. He is a journalism major. He is a 1986 Central high graduate.

EXERCISE 3-18

The Record's police reporter called in with a tip on a railroad wreck. Here's what you learned from her and from other sources:

From the police reporter:

At about 7 this morning a freight train went off the tracks about 5 miles west of the city. One man was injured. She doesn't have the man's name, but she knows that he was taken to Carolton General.

From the hospital:

Name of injured man is Frank Korth. Age 37. Works for the railroad. He has abrasions and contusions about the body, and his left leg is broken below the knee. His condition is "good." He is being held for observation.

From Ray Vanderpol, district superintendent for the Territory and Western railroad:

Korth was one of several Carolton men on the crew of the wrecked train.

Freight train consisting of engine and 18 freight cars was en route here from Chicago with a mixed cargo. Nothing hazardous in the cargo. Engine and seven cars went off the track. He estimates damage to the railroad equipment at more than $250,000. No estimate of damage to cargo.

Accident caused by a faulty switch. Railroad crews are at work clearing the track and getting the overturned cars back on the track. Line should be open for rail traffic by tonight.

From Morning Record reference library:

There have been two other accidents this year on the railroad's lines in the Carolton district, one six months ago, one last week. In both instances several freight cars were derailed.

In writing your lead, you must decide which are more important, people or property.

EXERCISE 3-19

You got a call this morning from a real estate dealer who gave you these facts. Write a story for tomorrow's paper.

Local real estate agent — elected to board of national real estate association — nation's largest trade association — Lorraine M. Worthington — she's with Higginbotham Sons — will be director of National Association of Realtors.

EXERCISE 3-20

While you were on campus this morning, you stopped in at the Air Force ROTC office and picked up a story about the honors banquet held last night. You learned:

Banquet was in the Gold Room at the student union.

Awards were presented to 27 cadets for scholarship, leadership and military service.

Two of the cadets honored are from Carolton. They are Nancy Riley and James Wang.

The awards:

Daughters of Founders and Patriots award for leadership and discipline: James Wang.

Air Force ROTC leadership and service ribbon: Nancy Riley. Allied Dynamics award for sophomore cadet with most exemplary attitude: James Wang.

Background:

Wang is a sophomore majoring in computer science. Member Arnold Air Society. Father on college faculty.

Riley: a business ad major, member Delta Mu Delta business honorary, member Alpha Phi sorority.

Cadet Riley lives in married student housing with her husband, an Air Force sergeant, who is on leave to complete his undergraduate education at Northwest College.

EXERCISE 3-21

The Record reporter who covers the campus called in with this story. Write it for tomorrow's paper.

Robert Rodale was on campus yesterday. He was here to give the Luther Burbank lecture, an annual lecture sponsored by the college. His title was The World Food Crisis.

He was presented the college's Founder's Medal for quote distinguished contributions to agriculture unquote.

Rodale is chairman of the board of Rodale Press, Emmaus, Pennsylvania, and editor of "Organic Gardening."

The lecture was in LaFollette auditorium. About 300 faculty and students attended. He was introduced by William Donnelly, head of the school of agriculture.

61

EXERCISE 3-22

Earl May called you this morning with a story. May is director of the Washington County Extended Care Facility. He told you:

The federal government has agreed to loan the facility nine million dollars to build an apartment complex for elderly people with low or moderate incomes.

The loan is coming from the Department of Housing and Urban Development.

The facility has 16 acres of land on Washington road, adjacent to the existing facility building just east of Old Meetinghouse road. May says the facility has plans for a three-story complex consisting of studio and one-bedroom apartments. There will be 160 units in the complex.

Construction will start early next year.

HUD has also agreed to provide two million dollars annually to subsidize rents for occupants of the complex.

You ask May about zoning. He tells you that the land is outside the city and suggests you check with the county. You call Henry Dickens, the county manager, and he tells you:

The land the center plans to build on is in a single-family residential area. Zoning will have to be changed to multifamily residential. That will require approval by the county plan commission and the board of county commissioners. Dickens expects no problem getting approval.

A check of clips in the Record's reference library refreshes your memory about the facility. It is operated by the county and is managed by a board appointed by the county commissioners.

EXERCISE 3-23

While you were on campus this morning, you picked up this story:

Beverly Gibbs — professor — business administration — and assistant dean of the school of business —

Governor named her to state banking commission yesterday. Commission has four members. She will fill a vacancy on the commission. The apppointment is for three years.

She is a Democrat. Home address: 605 West Florida.

You ask the college public relations office for a biographical sketch, but there isn't much to add. She is 42, has been on the faculty for 10 years and has written a book on bank regulation. She teaches, among other things, a course on money and banking.

EXERCISE 3-24

Write a news story for tomorrow's paper based on these facts, gleaned from a press release from the Marine Corps Development and Education Command at Quantico, Va.

The Corps maintains a basic school for newly commissioned officers. They spend 26 weeks at the school, after which they are assigned to a duty station.

Among recent graduates of the basic school is George D. Main of Carolton.

He has been assigned to Fleet Marine Force as a rifle platoon commander — he will be stationed at Norfolk, Virginia.

Main is a graduate of high school here — and a graduate of the U.S. Naval Academy — earned a Bachelor of Science degree at the academy.

You want a little more information, so you call Main's mother. You find out from her that he completed the course at Quantico last month and has been home on leave since then. His leave is up next week. Mrs. Main tells you it was just a coincidence, but his sister, who is in the air force, has also been at home on leave.

EXERCISE 3-25

You were at city hall this morning and in talking with the director of the Community Development Agency learned these facts. Write a story for tomorrow's paper.

Agency met last night. Finally approved purchase of a site for the new city hall building. Approved a site on West Virginia. Roughly an acre, now vacant. Most of it used now for parking. Cost is 375 thousand dollars.

New building will be eight stories. Cost at least fifty million.

City will ask for bids next month.

FYI: There isn't much new here. Most of this information has been in the paper. The fact that the site has been determined and the purchase okayed, however, is new.

EXERCISE 3-26

In news writing, it is necessary to be as clear and as definite as possible. Vague words and general descriptions don't inform the reader adequately. Be specific. For example:

vague   several students   *specific*   six students

1.   local school   Harvey O'Higgins Junior High

2.   middle-aged man   _____

3.   tall high school senior   _____

4.   member of the faculty   _____

5.   a local resident   _____

6.   a college senior   _____

7.   for many years   _____

8.   store owner   _____

9.   state official   _____

10. prominent businessman   _____

11. small foreign car   _____

12. unmarked currency   _____

13. public transit system   _____

14. car crash   _____

15. senior citizen   _____

16. taught school here   _____

17. earned a master's degree   _____

18. a young girl   _____

19. several months ago   _____

20. missing for several days   _____

Student's Name _____

EXERCISE 3-27

These leads are cluttered with details and could be improved by judicious trimming and rearrangement. See what you can do. For example:

Weak   Carolton police are trying to identify a man killed last night after he was hit by a train on the Territory and Western tracks about five miles north of the city.

Better   An unidentified man was struck and killed by a train Monday night about five miles north of Carolton.

1. A federal judge sentenced a Carolton woman charged with embezzling $340,000 from the Washington County Chemical Co. where she was a bookkeeper to three years in prison yesterday.

2. Police arrested two men and a woman in connection with burglaries last month in the Cedar Village and Colonial Village Apartments, Detective Thomas Worth said.

3. A Washington County couple convicted of using counterfeit credit cards to bilk banks out of more than $91,000 were sentenced yesterday by a judge who said they should both spend some time in prison.

4. Arthur Becker made a lot of green over the years watching grass grow. His small grass business has sprouted into one of the largest suppliers of grass seed in the state.

5. A jump in layoffs of adult men sent unemployment climbing in January from 6.5 percent to 7.3 percent, the highest rate in 18 months and a possible sign of an approaching recession.

6. A Carolton woman and her 91-year-old mother yesterday became the victims of a street robbery. Two young men knocked them down and fled with the woman's purse. It held all of $5.

Student's Name _____

EXERCISE 3-28

Edit this news story. Correct errors in style. Use standard editing marks and practices. Do *not* rewrite.

01   A Carolton service station owner was seriously injured

02   yesterday in a two car accident in front of his service

03   station on Territorial Rd.

04   Don E. Waldron, 115 E. Main St., and Mrs. Helen Vogel,

05   504 West Vermont Avenue, were taken to Carolton General

06   hospital.

07   Police said the accident attracted an unruly crowd.

08   Fifteen persons, including 7 juveniles, were arrested

09   for loitering.

10   Both cars were badly damaged. Waldron said it would

11   cost him $2000 to repair his car.

12   Police said Mrs. Vogel's car was heading north on

13   Territorial Road at 5 P.M. Waldron was driving south.

14   Mrs. Vogel, a retired teacher, is a volunteer at a

15   24 hour crisis center at Carolton General Hospital.

Number Correct _____

Student's Name _____

EXERCISE 3-29

Edit this news story. Correct errors in style. Use standard editing marks and practices. Do *not* rewrite. There may be errors in spelling, usage or punctuation.

01   Two Carolton Central High school seniors won awards

02   yesterday at the Washington County Youth Science Fair.

03   They are Harold Baker, 17, son of William and Mary

04   Baker, 84 Oak Street, and Nancy Williams, daughter of

05   Henry and Samantha Williams, 710 East Main St.

06   Baker and Williams will share a $2,000 cash award and

07   are eligible for a freshman scholarship at Northwest

08   college.

09   Central High administrators were pleased with the

10   award won by the two student team.

11   James Hardy, head of the high school physics

12   department called the two seniors knowledgable, bright,

13   and ambitious at an "honors day" program yesterday.

14   The two worked together on a study of the affect of

15   marigolds on nematode infestations in commercial tomato

16   crops.

17   The Science Fair opened Monday at 9 a.m. and will

18   close Saturday at 12 p.m.

Number Correct _____

Student's Name _____

71

4 Quotation

Spelling

hypocrisy, inseparable, misspelled, parishioner, dietitian, relevant/irrelevant, subtle/subtleties, siege, chauffeur, limousine, innuendo, consistent

Usage

flout/flaunt, healthful/healthy, historical/historic, illusive/elusive, persuade/convince, half-mast/half-staff

Newsroom Vocabulary

speech tag, direct quote, indirect quote, newsman, reporter, legman, journalist, working press, press, stick *or* stickful, dateline

Quotation

This topic is treated in detail in George A. Hough 3rd, "News Writing," fourth edition:

Quotation
Chapter 7, "Quotation," pages 111 through 132.

Models

Direct and indirect quotation fall into three categories that for convenience can be referred to as Type 1, Type 2 and Type 3.

Type 1, in which the speech tag comes first and the direct or indirect quote follows:

>Smith said, "I am in this race to win."
>
>Smith said he is in this race to win.

Type 2, in which the order of quote and speech tag is reversed so that the quote comes first and the speech tag follows:

>"I am in this race to win," Smith said.
>
>He is in this race to win, Smith said.

Type 3, in which the speech tag is inserted at some natural break in the quote:

>"It's not likely," Smith said, "that I would do that."
>
>It's not likely, Smith said, that he would do that.

Type 1 quotes are used most often for indirect quotation. Type 2 quotes are preferred for direct quotation. Type 3 quotes provide a useful alternative to Type 1 and Type 2 quotes.

EXERCISE 4-1

Indicate by writing the appropriate number in the space at right whether the sentence is a Type 1, Type 2 or Type 3 quote:

1. "I'm on my way to Dublin Bay," she said. _____

2. They chimed in, "Of course you'll take the train." _____

3. "Pack my box," she ordered, "with a dozen roses." _____

4. "Now is the time to pack your suitcase," he said. _____

5. He ordered: "Pack my box with two dozen roses." _____

6. She told him she would stay two or three weeks. _____

7. "Congress must be more cooperative," he said. _____

8. The country expects more of the Congress, he said. _____

9. The country, he said, expects more of the Congress. _____

10. "Help," she cried, "and please hurry!" _____

11. "Help, help, and please hurry!" she cried. _____

12. The instructor said he wanted the work done at once. _____

13. "Turn this assignment in right now," he ordered. _____

14. She said, "Develop the idea along these lines." _____

15. "This way to the egress," the sign read. _____

16. They cried in unison, "Don't go out that door!" _____

17. "There's a fool born every minute," he said. _____

18. She said, "No, no, a thousand times no!" _____

19. "Keep moving, keep moving," the traffic officer said. _____

20. The speaker said that he had one more question. _____

Number Correct _____

Student's Name _____

EXERCISE 4-2

Revise these Type 1 quotes and convert them to Type 2 quotes. Type your revision directly below each Type 1 quote.

1. He said, "The council has no authority for such an act."

2. Mayor Harold Orleans said: "I can't go along on this one."

3. Councilman Mary Hawks said, "I resent the mayor's attitude."

4. Another councilman said, "That's negative thinking."

5. City Clerk Donna Williams said, "I hate these arguments."

EXERCISE 4-3

Revise these Type 1 quotes and convert them to Type 3 quotes. Type your revision directly below each Type 1 quote.

1. Smith said, "Nevertheless, I think the mayor will win out."

2. He added, "The mayor seems to be on top of the situation."

3. The mayor said, "Just like the council, always bickering."

4. He said, "They can never agree, but they'll never admit it."

5. Councilman Lambert said, "We'll take our stand right here."

Student's Name _____

EXERCISE 4-4

Revise these Type 2 direct quotes and convert them to Type 1 indirect quotes. Type your revision directly below each direct quote.

1. "I won't go along with the council this time," Jones said.

2. "I resent the mayor's attitude," Councilman Lambert said.

3. "The mayor seems to be on top of the situation," Smith said.

4. "I may have to vote against the mayor," Boyle said.

5. "I need the money to pay off a bad check," the man said.

EXERCISE 4-5

Revise these Type 1 indirect quotes and convert them to Type 2 direct quotes. Type your revision directly below each indirect quote.

1. He said his men would just have to search for the money.

2. The sheriff said that nobody knew the trouble he'd seen.

3. The mayor said he'd just have to wait until the next election.

4. The candidate said that he was all right on that question.

5. The city clerk said that it was all a matter of dirty politics.

Student's Name _____

EXERCISE 4-6

Your city editor looked over the story you wrote about the new librarian (Exercise 3-15) and suggested that you call Tassinari and see what he had to say. You did, and this conversation took place:

You: Mr. Tassinari, I understand that you are going to be the new librarian at the Franklin library.

He: Yes, that's right. I just heard from the board. It was decided last night.

You: Very good. Congratulations. You're starting the first of the month?

He: Yes, but I'll be in Carolton before then, of course.

You: Have you any plans for changes in the library?

He: Not at the moment. I think the Franklin is a fine library. I'll have to look things over carefully before I make any changes.

You: What's your special field of interest in library work?

He: Well, I'm especially interested in children's literature. I have done a lot, too, with early reading programs here in Ann Arbor. I want to do everything I can to help children develop a love of reading.

You: Great! That sounds good. Thanks very much. I'll look forward to talking with you again when you get settled at the library.

He: Fine. Thanks. Goodbye.

Now go over your notes and select two one-sentence quotes. Use the first as a Type 1 indirect quote and the second as a Type 2 direct quote. The indirect quote must (1) identify the speaker and (2) tell the reader what he is talking about. The direct quote, which will follow in the next paragraph, will give the speaker's views in his own words. Insert these quotes, the second immediately following the first, into your earlier story. Follow the model on page 131 of "News Writing."

EXERCISE 4-7

Your editor suggested that you could improve your story on the college faculty member's appointment to the banking commission (Exercise 3-23) if you talked with her and got a couple of quotes. You called her, and she told you:

I am very pleased, of course, to have been appointed to the banking commission.

I expect to be a working commissioner, and I hope I can do a good job.

Both these statements are direct quotations. Put the first in the form of a Type 1 indirect quote. Put the second in the form of a Type 2 direct quotation. Insert the two quotes, the second immediately following the first, into your story. Your story on the new librarian will serve as a model.

EXERCISE 4-8

While you were in the office this morning, your city editor asked you to take a call. You found yourself talking with Ray Vanderpol, superintendent of the railroad. You learned enough for a story. Write it for tomorrow's paper.

The railroad has started a program of rebuilding and improving grade crossings here. Several crossings north of the city need work.

First grade crossing to be improved will be the one on Western avenue. This crossing will be closed to traffic for two weeks beginning next Monday.

Quote we're going to rebuild the whole thing unquote.

You thanked Vanderpol for the information and then called the county highway department for further information. You talked with Lamar Wilson, superintendent of roads for the county, and learned:

The county will not be involved in this work. It will be strictly a railroad effort.

Note: Attribute carefully and use the direct quote.

EXERCISE 4-9

At city hall today, the mayor's administrative assistant gave you a story about an award to the city. Write the story for tomorrow's paper.

The National Automobile Safety Association makes 2 national awards each year for traffic safety. One is for large cities — more than 100,000. The other is for cities with less than 100,000 population.

Carolton won this year in the small city category. Seattle won in the large city category.

The awards will be announced today. The award will be presented formally next week by someone from the Carolton Safety Association office.

Carolton won for quote outstanding efforts to prevent pedestrian traffic accidents unquote.

You talk with the mayor and he tells you:

This is great. We're very pleased with the award. We owe it all to the fine work done by the police traffic safety division.

You check with the Accident Prevention Bureau and are told:

Past year (12 months ending 30th of last month) city had only 27 traffic accidents involving pedestrians that involved any injuries. Year previous: 51 injury accidents involving pedestrians.

You know the population of Carolton. What is the population of Seattle? You'll want to put both figures in your story.

EXERCISE 4-10

While you were at the high school this morning, you were told about the Special Olympics program that will be held this weekend. It's worth a story. Write it for tomorrow's paper.

Your notes:

Special Olympics — program for handicapped children — sponsors — public schools and civic organizations — program open to the public — at the high school field

for ages 5 through 13 — includes track events — softball tournament

expect about 250 to participate — Saturday — 9 to 3 — kids have been practicing for weeks

You talk with Kenneth L. Miller, school district phys ed specialist, and he tells you:

We've got a great program. The kids are as excited as any kids would be before a big athletic event. They're great. Every one of them wants to go out there and win.

Review the use of *extended quotation* before you write.

EXERCISE 4-11

Revise these paragraphs to bring the quotations within guidelines suggested in Chapter 7 of "News Writing."

1.   Jacobson said he believes that fundamentalists are "never the mainstay of believers in any religious philosophy ... The vast majority of Christians are entirely comfortable with science, and particularly with biology."

2.   Jones said that in the second incident, Smith "was threatening us when we were outside the house. But when I had enough of it, I took after him. I met him on the stairs. He threatened me (with a knife), and when I took off after him, he took off and ran ... jumped out the window and the officers below took him ..."

3.   If Johnson had run with the president in 1980 or 1984, he "would have won a convincing victory," Smith said. But "we would have lost anyway in 1982," he said.

EXERCISE 4-12

These paragraphs are examples of extended quotation. For a full discussion of extended quotation, see "News Writing," pages 121–123.

Are these examples acceptable or not acceptable according to the guidelines in "News Writing"? Indicate your choice — to accept or not accept — by writing A or NA in the blanks at right.

1.   "As far as I am concerned, there's no such rule. I have to wonder about the motivation for this thing. It's a phony issue," Smith said.   _____

2.   "I just walked away," Jones said. "It was easy to walk away. I had some personal problems at home to take care of."   _____

3.   "As far as I am concerned," he said, "the company's probably doing it. I know our people aren't."   _____

4.   "In order for classes to be on a full schedule, it was necessary to consolidate the smaller classes and eliminate some class offerings," he said. "This, in turn, reduced the number of teachers needed."   _____

5.   "Farmers know how to deal with them, but your average backyard gardener is unprepared. I certainly wouldn't advise homeowners to spray either, because most of them don't know what they are doing," he said.   _____

6.   "We've seen one good hit out there. I think you see by the empty seats that the fans are disgusted," Lesinski said.   _____

7.   "I think it's terrible so far," a fan said. "They might just as well forget it. You're watching second-rate football but paying first-rate prices."   _____

8.   "Frankly," Snyder said, "if the duck season were any better, I'd be hunting instead of sitting here. This game is the worst I've ever seen."   _____

9.   "We've seen one good hit out there. I think you can see by the empty seats that the fans are disgusted," Jones said.   _____

10.   "What happens to the complex doesn't affect our decision," Smith said. "We purchased the land in 1980. It's an excellent location and we plan to build in the future. But we have not decided just when."   _____

Number Correct _____

Student's Name _____

EXERCISE 4-13

This is an exercise in punctuating quotes within quotes. The words "hard to please" in these sentences are direct quotation and should be enclosed in quote marks. Make no other changes.

1. He said that the attorney general is hard to please sometimes.

2. He called the attorney general hard to please.

3. "The attorney general is hard to please," he told reporters.

4. Smith said the governor considered himself hard to please.

5. He told me the attorney general is hard to please.

6. "The governor says he's hard to please," Smith said.

7. "My opponent is being unfair," the attorney general said. "He

    said I am hard to please. I am not hard to please."

8. "I said he is hard to please and I meant it," Smith said.

9. Is the attorney general hard to please or not? people asked.

10. Editorials asked why the attorney general is hard to please.

11. Readers asked, "Is the attorney general hard to please?"

12. The attorney general said the governor is hard to please, too.

Number Correct _____

Student's Name _____

EXERCISE 4-14

This morning at city hall you noticed a change in the art exhibit. This month the artist is a city employee.

Donna Williams, the city clerk, tells you that the artist is Emma Daggett, an illustrator and cartographer who works for the city planning commission. And this is a first for the city hall art gallery — the first time the artist has been a city employee.

Miss Williams tells you quote her art exemplifies the fine work being done by city employees unquote.

You talk with the artist, and she tells you she has worked for the city for three years. She does maps and illustrates city publications. She has an MFA degree from Northwest college.

Her last exhibit was at the art club.

Also from the artist: quote I'm pleased to have the recognition of the city hall exhibit ... at first I was a bit concerned about the reaction to some of my abstracts ... I've had a lot of compliments, though ... people seem to like them unquote.

The Record runs a story every month about the current exhibit at city hall. Attribute carefully and use the quotes.

EXERCISE 4-15

Revise these paragraphs to bring the quotations within guidelines suggested in Chapter 7 of "News Writing."

1.   Frazier also said: "We need to be very aggressive markets (of American agricultural products). We need to be very aggressive salesmen. We have not been."

2.   With Patrick Leahy (D-Vt.) as his Senate counterpart instead of Jesse Helms (R-N.C.), "the Democratic philosophy for agriculture will be given a higher priority," Anderson predicted.

3.   He said that philosophy advocates funding "the necessary tools" to help farmers survive but not "just throwing money at the problem."

4.   For Smith's latest venture, Jones said, "there is reasonably broad appeal. There may even be broad appeal. I think they have between a fairly good and an excellent opportunity."

EXERCISE 4-16

The Record's police reporter was off today, and you filled in on her beat. At Carolton General Hospital you learned that a state health department doctor had been in to look at a Carolton man who has been in the hospital for a week with an illness the hospital had not been able to diagnose immediately. Now the state health people say the man has bubonic plague. The patient is William Cleveland, age 34. His doctor, Dr. Alpha Bates, tells you:

He has been quite ill. He's better now that we know what his illness is and are able to treat it. He'll go home in a day or so.

We think he contracted the plague from an infected rabbit. He was hunting upstate. He cut his finger on a bone while cleaning a rabbit he shot.

You talk to the county health department and are told:

He had two rabbits in his freezer, and we sent these to the lab at Fort Collins for examination. They found evidence of plague immediately.

You call the state health department at Capital City and talk with Dr. Foster Saruda in the communicable disease division. He tells you:

Quote There's no reason to panic . . . There is almost no chance of an epidemic unquote.

He also tells you:

Hunters, though, should wear gloves while cleaning rabbits and not handle them at all if they have any break in the skin that might facilitate the entry of disease-causing organisms.

This is the fourth case of plague in the state since 1975. One man died in 1981. There were two cases last year.

The Fort Collins lab the doctor referred to is the U.S. Centers (correct) for Disease Control. If you're not sure what bubonic plague is, your readers may not know either. Do a little research and include a brief explanation of bubonic plague in your story. Quote and attribute carefully. This is a somewhat technical story.

EXERCISE 4-17

In today's mail you got a press release from the state Department of Transportation that has some local as well as statewide interest. Write a story based on these facts, excerpted from the press release:

(Names of members of new Disadvantaged Business Enterprise Minority Advisory Committee)

Henry Johnson, an attorney from Newton

Theodore Lake, executive director of the Westville Minority Business Development Center, Westville

Horace Wise, vice president of the Trust Company Bank, Centralia

Gerald A. Cook, chairman of the School of Business, Northwest College, Carolton

The press release says that Cook will be chairman of this new committee and quotes T.C. Moore, state DOT commissioner, as saying:

I'm happy to say that we have an outstanding advisory board. I'm delighted that Dr. Cook has agreed to help us. I'm looking forward to working with Dr. Cook and with the committee.

The press release says that the advisory committee will quote advise the department in its administration of the DBE program and assist the department in identifying methods to increase minority participation on highway department projects unquote.

Use a blind lead. Quote Moore. The cities mentioned in the list are cities in your state.

EXERCISE 4-18

Revise these paragraphs to bring the quotations within guidelines suggested in Chapter 7 of "News Writing."

1.   "Here in this house, he (Robert) felt close to his father. His world was here," said a cousin.

2.   "I think a lot of it (his problems) was caused by the breakup of Robert's marriage," said Smith. "He always hoped they could get together again."

EXERCISE 4-19

While you were on campus today, you talked with Dr. Shanks at the Student Health Center. He told you:

The health center has completed a study that was begun last year in an effort to find ways in which the center could do more to educate students about alcohol-related health problems.

Shanks says quote 15 percent of students graduate with an alcohol problem and go on to develop more serious problems in later life unquote.

Many students don't realize the role alcohol has come to play in their lives.

Shanks says 87 percent of Northwest college students use alcohol.

Most students think they don't drink more than anyone else, yet some drink every night of the week.

Students who would like to take a closer look at alcohol and how it fits into their lifestyles can, if they wish, complete a questionnaire prepared by the center. Those who express further interest will be referred to health center staff members who have expertise in dealing with alcohol-related problems.

Shanks says quote we think we can be helpful unquote.

He also says quote what some students consider normal consumption of alcohol is considered overuse in the real world unquote.

Shanks' 15 percent figure is a national figure. Overindulgence in alcohol may not be as serious a problem at Northwest. Nevertheless, there is a growing awareness of the dangers of heavy drinking. There's a story here — with some good quotes.

EXERCISE 4-20

Marlene Brackett called this morning with final figures on the recent fund-raiser for the Special Olympics. Write the story for tomorrow's paper.

The barbecue held last month brought in $3084. The Special Olympics is sponsored by the schools and local civic organizations.

EXERCISE 4-21

Verbs have been called the muscle of good writing. These sentences need a little more muscle. Rewrite them. Try to use a strong and vigorous verb. For example:

Weak   The economy experienced a quick revival.

Better   The economy revived quickly.

1. The governor cited a failed attempt in the legislature last year to create another state holiday.

2. He said that the school had made several accomplishments during his tenure as dean.

3. The Carolton VFW Post held an installation of officers Monday.

4. A two-car accident occurred Tuesday on Highway 30. Both drivers were injured.

5. John Baker pleaded guilty to speeding charges and received a $10 fine.

6. In a holdup Monday night about $100 was taken from the cash register of the History Village Inn by an armed man.

7. An election was held Monday night in Carolton. Mayor Henry Clay Smith was re-elected.

8. Police are making an investigation of the bank robbery.

Student's Name _____

EXERCISE 4-22

These sentences are defective. Delete *there is/are* or *there was/were* and revise the sentences as necessary.

Weak   *There were* 82 cases *reported* during the school year.

Better   Eighty-two cases *were reported* during the school year.

1. There were 83 doors and windows found open.

2. There is already very little brain activity detected.

3. There are still some common interests found in the community.

4. There are several features which appeared in recent issues.

5. There are several magazines published for journalists.

6. There are also feature stories that profile women journalists.

7. There is also some features that do not appear in every issue.

8. There was a holdup Monday night in which $100 was taken.

9. There were some money managers who were quick to cash in.

10. There wasn't a lot of progress being made in the search, a police official said.

Student's Name _____

EXERCISE 4-23

Edit this news story. Correct errors in style. Use standard editing marks and practices. Do *not* rewrite. There may be errors in spelling, grammar, usage or punctuation.

01   A Northwest college faculty member has been awarded

02   the coveted Mark Twain Prize for his history of the

03   Korean War.

04   Albert H. Sawyer, Jr., professor of history will

05   accept the award tomorrow in Charlotte, North Carolina.

06   Sawyer's history, The Forgotten War, was published by

07   the Northwest College Press. More than 4000 copies have

08   already been sold according to Miss Helen Wood, general

09   manager of the press who will accompany Sawyer to

10   Charlotte tomorrow.

11   Sawyer lives with his wife, two sons, and three

12   daughters at 640 East Nevada Ave.

13   Sawyer will be guest of honor at a reception in Old

14   College Hall, Monday, at 4:30 P.M.

15   On Tuesday he will give the keynote address when the

16   Washington County Historical Society meets on campus.

17   The title of his talk is Wandering Through History.

18   Some two hundred historians are expected for the

19   meeting and Mayor Henry Clay Smith has designated next

20   week as "History Week" in Carolton.

21   Smith called Sawyer a likable chap but said that he

22   tends to exagerate things.

Number Correct _____

Student's Name _____

EXERCISE 4-24

Edit this news story. Correct errors in style. Use standard editing marks and practices. Do *not* rewrite. There may be errors in spelling, grammar, usage or punctuation.

01   The first of fifty-seven families whose homes are

02   sinking into a reclaimed swamp has been awarded more than

03    $400,000 in damages in a lawsuit against a local

04   developer.

05   The suit had asked for a million dollars in damages.

06   A jury in municipal court deliberated for more than

07   nine hours yesterday before informing judge Sidney Smith

08   that it had reached a decision.

09   There are 7 other plaintiffs. They seek damages

10   ranging from $4000 to $63,000.

11   Many of the houses in Forest Lawn estates, a 105 lot

12   subdivision were built in the late 1960's.

13   Yesterday's verdict settled the claim of Harry and

14   Mary Johnson, 260 Washington Rd., whose two story home

15   settled and collapsed over a two month period in 1978.

16   Mr. Johnson is an insurance salesman with an office in

17   the Jollity building.

18   He is president of the Forest Lawn Neighborhood Assn.,

19   a member of the Northwest College Alumni club and father

20   of an 8 year old son by his 1st wife.

21   Mrs. Johnson teaches high school English and History.

Number Correct _____

Student's Name _____

5 Developing the Story

Spelling

discernible, compatible, seize/seizure, soluble/dissolve, weird, peninsula, serendipity, irreligious, defendant, veteran, veterinarian

Usage

imply/infer, ingenious/ingenuous, nauseous/nauseated, odious/odorous, damage/damages, loath/loathe, all right

Newsroom Vocabulary

journalism, print media, must, future book, alive, kill, dead, transition, hole, localize, slant, pad

Developing the Story

These topics are treated in detail in George A. Hough 3rd, "News Writing," fourth edition:

Coming Events
Chapter 8, "Developing the Story," pages 135 through 139.

Lists
Chapter 8, "Developing the Story," pages 139 and 140 and Figure 8.2 on page 141.

Localizing
Chapter 8, "Developing the Story," pages 140 through 146.

EXERCISE 5-1

This exercise introduces the news writer's trick of using commas and semicolons to organize lists of names or other items into a concise or readable form. For example:

> John Smith, 127 Wisconsin Ave., treasurer; Jane
> Jones, 11 E. Nevada Ave.;

Assume that you have already written the lead on a story about an election of officers and now need only to list the names. Write a paragraph giving the names and begin it:

> The new officers are

Here are the names of the new officers and their offices. You will find their addresses in the city directory.

president	Marshall Reeves
vice president	Maurice Henderson
secretary	Stewart MacDonald
treasurer	Mrs. George Howe
trustee	Harrison L. Nightingale

Follow the model in Figure 8.2 on page 141 in "News Writing." Don't forget about style for names, courtesy titles and addresses.

EXERCISE 5-2

The school district's public relations officer, Marlene Brackett, has mailed you a press release. You learn:

Central High school seniors have been earning college credits by taking advance college credit exams administered by the College Entrance Examination Board. The credits are for advanced work done in high school courses. The credits can be used at any college. The college determines the amount of credit it will allow.

Advance college credits have been earned by these students:

Dave Brewster	French
Kim Clark	history
John Coolidge	English
Robert Franklin	English
Luis Gomez	history
Eileen Curtis	French
Mary Jones	history
Lorie Twardzynski	mathematics
Debra Green	biology

You don't need addresses or other identification in this story. Make your list as concise as possible. You can combine names of students who have earned credit in the same subject.

103

EXERCISE 5-3

Your city editor has asked you to write a story based on this press release. It came in the mail today from the state Department of Education. If you list the names of the students who do not live in Carolton, omit their street addresses.

CAPITAL CITY — (today's date) — Fourteen state college students are among 550 students nationwide who have been awarded National Science Foundation Graduate Fellowships, the state Board of Education announced today.

The fellowships are awarded for outstanding ability in the sciences, mathematics and engineering. They provide an annual stipend of $6,000 for three years of graduate study, the state board said.

State winners, listed by hometown are:

Dalton: James M. Offer, 337 Third St.; Craig Archer, 417 Lyons Ave.; Rebecca Rountree, 530 Linwood Blvd.

Southfield: Robert Morris, 205 S. Seventh St.

Williamstown: Peter L. Tobias, 551 Foster Road.

East Point: James L. Pye, 1601 Chelsea St.

Livonia: Kenneth J. Brady, 35 Wood St.

Carolton: Helen E. Rivera, 87 S. Meade; Mark H. Stahl, 650 W. Florida; Raymond L. Miskell, 415 E. Maryland.

Washington: John L. Sullivan, 52 Goldcrest Drive.

Mount Pleasant: Michael E. Nathanson, 1011 Deptford Drive.

Eastville: Martha L. Rizzo, 1701 N. Beech St.

Plymouth: Susan Short, 610 W. Lakeshore Drive.

A few phone calls, and you learn that Miss Rivera is a senior at Vassar; Stahl a senior at Fairleigh Dickinson; and Miskell a first-year graduate student at Purdue. Verify spellings for these institutions. Are they colleges or universities? Where are they? Use full names and locations in your story.

EXERCISE 5-4

Your city editor handed you this story, with instructions to rewrite it for tomorrow's paper. "Check the name," she said. "It doesn't sound quite right."

WASHINGTON — The National Advisory Child Health and Human Development Council has invited four distinguished American scholars to join its board.

They are Hobart Ransom, Williams College, Williamstown, Mass.; Eugenia Watson, Vassar College, Poughkeepsie, N.Y.; Jane E. Phelps, University of Minnesota, Minneapolis; and Robert Leavitt, Northwest College, Carolton.

EXERCISE 5-5

You were on the rewrite desk this morning when your city editor handed you the latest copy of a newspaper trade publication. He pointed out a story about the Newspaper Advertising Bureau in which he had circled the name of John L. Wallington. "Write a story about this," he told you. "Wallington is a graduate of Northwest College and worked for the Record while he was a student. A lot of people here know him."

Here's the story:

The Newspaper Advertising Bureau elected officers Monday and added five new members to its board of directors.

New directors are Marguerite Brown, Tacoma News; Ralph Giddings, Houston Telegraph; Robert Mackie, Wausau (Wis.) Observer; Christine Fowler, Rock City (Maine) Blade; and John Secord, Port Royal (Fla.) Sun-Times.

Officers re-elected for one-year terms:

John L. Wallington, publisher, San Jose Morning Post, chairman.

Frank Doolittle, publisher, Virginia Beach (Va.) Times and Record, vice chairman.

Darlene E. Pickett, president and publisher, Lawson (Okla.) Evening Standard, treasurer.

Howard S. Wood, publisher, Fairhaven (Mass.) Daily Camera, secretary.

The Ad Bureau board met in New York in conjunction with the annual meeting of the American Newspaper Publishers Association.

You check with the Northwest College Alumni Office and learn that Wallington was graduated in 1970 with a BA in journalism. Your city editor recalls that he worked for the Record from the fall of 1968 through the spring quarter of 1970 as a general assignment reporter. Rewrite and trim the story. Use a blind lead.

EXERCISE 5-6

While you were on rewrite this morning, the publicity chairman of the Washington County Democratic Women's Organization called in a story about a meeting. She told you:

Meeting at county Democratic headquarters. Open meeting.

Program: panel discussion on proposal to establish a quote women's commission unquote here.

Meeting time: eight o'clock Thursday night.

Panelists: Mrs. Christine Harris (chairman of the county Democratic Committee)
Mrs. H. C. Smith (chairman, Carolton Women's Caucus)
Francis Norton (member state Democratic committee)
Sue Ellen Dendramis (state representative from Carolton)

Women's commission proposal will be on the ballot in next county election.

EXERCISE 5-7

This morning while you were on the rewrite desk, your city editor called over to you: "Hey, take this call, will you? On two." You picked up the phone and found yourself talking to Bill Morrissey at the news bureau on campus.

Morrissey: Say, I thought you'd want to get something in tomorrow's paper on the commencement speaker.

You: Sure. Who is it?

Morrissey: Derek Bok. We were lucky to get him.

You: Tell me about him.

Morrissey: I don't have much. He's president of Harvard. I'll have a bio sketch for you the first of the week.

You: Okay. When's commencement?

Morrissey: It will be on (date). In LaFollette auditorium as usual.

You: What time?

Morrissey: Eight in the evening. Same as last time.

You thank Morrissey and start to write the story. Then you realize you need a little background on Bok. You can check Who's Who in the newspaper library. Ask your instructor to provide day and date for commencement.

EXERCISE 5-8

Your city editor handed you this story and asked you to rewrite it. "Use a blind lead," she said, "and just list the runners-up."

Brian Kane, a senior at Carolton Central High School, Monday won first place in the Northwest College school of engineering's annual design competition.

He will receive a four-year, full-tuition scholarship to Northwest College worth $20,500.

Roberta Wilson, a senior at Lincoln High School, Hastings, won second place in the competition and will receive a four-year, half-tuition scholarship worth $16,000.

Two students tied for third place in the contest and will each receive a $4,000 four-year scholarship. They are Debra King of Meigs High School, Meigs, and John Edwards, Eaton High School, Eaton Rapids.

The students were asked to design a small city bank that wanted to attract new customers and provide both walk-in and drive-in services.

FYI: Hastings, Meigs and Eaton Rapids are cities in your state.

EXERCISE 5-9

While you were on rewrite this morning, your friend George Robinson called you with a story about his service club's monthly meeting. You can write it for tomorrow's paper.

Friend: Will you get this in tomorrow's paper? The Challenge club will be meeting Monday. Jim Wilson will speak.

You: Wilson? What's his full name?

Friend: James L. And the meeting is at the Eagle restaurant as usual. At seven.

You: What's Wilson going to talk about?

Friend: Just a second. Got it right here. Okay. Legislative Trends in Mental Health.

You: He an expert or something?

Friend: Oh, he'll be okay. He's the community health representative of the county mental health department.

You: Okay, he's an expert. What's the correct name of this club of yours?

Friend: Carolton Chapter of the National Challenge Club. By the way, if you want to come, we'd be glad to have you.

You: Well, perhaps, but I may have to work. Do you want your name on this?

Friend: No, that's not necessary. And don't forget the time. Seven.

You: Okay, thanks, got it.

EXERCISE 5-10

Write a news story based on this information:

There will be an interesting lecture next week. A poet from South Africa will speak. His lecture will be in French.

Title of his lecture is: Cultural Rights and the Rights of Man. Lecture will be at 8 o'clock Tuesday at the Maison Francaise, 575 Newton Road.

Speaker is Breyten Breytenbach, the author of The True Confessions of an Albino Terrorist. He spent seven years in prison in South Africa because of his opposition to apartheid.

His lecture is sponsored by the Department of Romance Languages at Northwest College.

EXERCISE 5-11

This press release came in today's mail. Your city editor handed it to you with instructions to rewrite it for tomorrow's paper. "There's a lot of interest in this program in the schools here," she told you.

The press release:

Universal Electric Corporation has announced the winners in its 40th annual science scholarships competition. The winners were chosen from 15 finalists out of 350 entrants from schools throughout the state.

The Universal Science Scholarship Program is designed to encourage the state's most promising high school scientists to pursue careers in scientific disciplines.

Winners of $5,000 scholarships are William Alan Schwartz, 18, son of Mr. and Mrs. Peter B. Schwartz, Lake City; Joel S. Fajane Jr., 17, son of Mr. and Mrs. Joel S. Fajane, Monroe; Scott D. Smith, 18, son of Mrs. Annette W. Smith, Union City; Karen B. Brickhouse, 17, daughter of Mr. and Mrs. Sigmund Brickhouse, Owosso; and Diane Rivera, 18, daughter of Mr. and Mrs. Carlos Rivera, Carolton.

The scholarships were awarded for original research submitted to the panel of Universal judges. The winners are all high school seniors.

Schwartz' entry was a study of the chemical nature of the transport of substances into the cells of bacteria; Fajane studied a number theory introduced by the Pythagoreans, who developed some of the basic principles of mathematics and astronomy; Smith designed and built a computer for use in his school; Brickhouse experimented with a chemical capable of changing the patterns of genetic inheritance in green algae; and Rivera studied the regenerative ability of a type of one-celled organism.

The 10 finalists who did not win scholarships were each awarded a cash prize of $250.

EXERCISE 5-12

As you may know, a city election is scheduled for next month. In preparation, the city clerk is conducting a voter registration drive. The city clerk today gave you a schedule for registration. Write a story for tomorrow's paper.

Dates and places where voters may register:

Franklin library/10th
Central Fire Station/12th
First Baptist church/14th
National Guard armory/17th
Trinity A.M.E. church/19th
Central high/21st

FYI: The election will be on the first Tuesday after the first Monday of the month.

Include street addresses in your story.

EXERCISE 5-13

You are working today on general assignment. This morning you picked up these facts from the public relations office on the Northwest College campus. Write a story for tomorrow's paper.

Conference here Friday and Saturday — at Northwest College conference center — governor will be keynote speaker — will open conference with his address Friday morning at 10 —

For owners of small businesses and of minority businesses — sponsor is the school of business at Northwest college —

Program consists of panels and speeches — names of speakers and participants below —

issues to be examined: employment, incorporation, licensing, taxes, hazardous waste, economic development, and agribusiness

(on the program besides the governor)

> George Murray — state department of trade and industry (director)
>
> Maurice Cleveland — secretary of state (state, not U.S.)
>
> Mark Crimmins — director, state department of revenue
>
> Theodore DuPont — cooperative extension service (director)
>
> John Timmins — state labor department (commissioner)
>
> Marilyn Breed — state department of industry and trade (commissioner)

The handout from the college public relations staff says that small and minority businesses accounted for more than two-thirds of the new jobs created in the state last year.

You check the governor's name in the state government directory: Walker L. Robertson.

EXERCISE 5-14

Your city editor tossed you this story. "Rewrite it," she said. Follow her suggestion. Rewrite to conform to the STOP formula.

"Carnivorous Plants and Their Insect Associates" is the title of a lecture scheduled for Wednesday afternoon by the entomology department.

Dr. Genevieve LaFrance, distinguished professor of entomology and zoology, will speak at 4 in room 125 of the biological sciences building.

109

EXERCISE 5-15

Your city editor handed you this press release. It came in today's mail from the state Board of Education in Capital City. "Fix this up for tomorrow's paper," she said.

CAPITAL CITY — Six colleges and universities in the state have been awarded more than $95,000 by the National Science Foundation to help underwrite research projects that will involve undergraduate students, the State Board of Education announced today.

The participating students, usually juniors and seniors, will be selected on the basis of their work in college-level courses, the state board said.

Following is a list of the institutions receiving the NSF grants, the amount of the grant and the name of the department and science project director:

Wilson College, Oil City, $16,490, Ronald O. Knapp, biology.

Lenox Institute of Technology, Lenox, $7,260, James W. Sleeper, physics, and $15,200, Donald K. Abood, chemistry.

Northwest College, Carolton, $16,500, Charles Huang, physics.

Oakbrook College, Oakbrook, $8,700, Richard L. Tomboulian, biology.

Southern Baptist College, Riverside, $12,000, Lester Huzar, chemistry.

Holy Cross College, Doraville, $19,000, Henry Hunziker, psychology.

You call Professor Huang, and he tells you:

He will select six seniors to work on a project in the college's new cyclotron laboratory. He will be assisted in supervising the project by another faculty member, Julia Feldpausch.

EXERCISE 5-16

There will be another lecture this week in a series sponsored by the Department of English. The lecture will be Tuesday night at 7 in the law auditorium.

The speaker is Dr. Eugene T. Maleska. He is the crossword puzzles editor of The New York Times.

Title of his talk is Fun With Words.

He has an Ed.D. from the Harvard Graduate School of Education.

He has written several books, including Sun and Shadow, a book of poetry, The Junior Crossword Puzzle Book, and The Crossword Book of Quotations. His latest books are A Pleasure in Words and Across and Down.

Write a story for tomorrow's paper.

EXERCISE 5-17

You were on the rewrite desk today, and your editor asked you to write a news story based on these facts:

Lecture this coming week on campus — Wednesday 8 in the evening in the auditorium at the law school.

Title: Nuclear Winter.

Tickets available on campus at the student union and at the Paragon newsstand.

Speaker is Dr. Carl Sagan. He is a professor of astronomy at Cornell university, Ithaca, New York.

Sagan is the author of Cosmos, a book on science that has been a best seller and was the basis for the television series of the same name.

Sagan and other scientists have become concerned about the effect a nuclear war might have on the environment. Soot and dust from a nuclear burst, they believe, might produce a severe, widespread and long-term cooling of the earth's surface.

They have termed this climatic catastrophe a "nuclear winter" and believe that even a brief period of cold and dark would have serious effects on world food supplies.

EXERCISE 5-18

This morning you got a call from the college public relations office. Bill Morrissey gave you these facts on a speech he thinks is of some interest. He told you:

The speech will be in the student union on Friday afternoon. Time: 3:30.

Speaker is guest of the school of environmental design.

Speech is public. Speaker is George Reynolds. He is on faculty of Georgia Tech. He is an associate professor of architecture. Reynolds will talk about building and community design.

Reynolds is an expert on energy-efficient and livable housing. He has been active in developing a living example of an energy-efficient village. He lectures a lot in this country and abroad on energy conservation.

Reynolds is a member of the Club 1000 and the Passive Solar Society of Georgia.

He will be introduced by the dean of the environmental design school.

EXERCISE 5-19

Write a story based on these facts, given to you by the Northwest College news bureau:

Keynote Speaker:	Art Downs.
Topic:	No title, but Downs says he will discuss his column and how he writes it.
Organization:	The Northwest College School of Journalism.
Place:	Memorial Hall.
Day/hour:	Saturday at 10 in the morning.

The occasion is the school's annual "high school newspaper day." Downs is the keynote speaker.

The program will start with Downs' speech and will end after the last workshop at 3 p.m.

The school expects about 500 high school newspaper editors and about 50 of their advisers. Usually about 60 high schools are represented.

Dr. Granville Holmes is director of the program. He tells you:

Newspaper day provides a golden opportunity for young journalists to learn. There will be workshops on such topics as news writing, editing, advertising, sports reporting, ethics, and school press law. Workshops will be taught by members of the journalism faculty.

Dr. Holmes is a bit verbose. Don't quote him directly. Attribute where necessary.

EXERCISE 5-20

You were routinely checking records today at the courthouse and found that tax liens have been filed against several local people by the Internal Revenue Service. The record shows:

Date Filed	Name	Tax	Amount Owed
7	Miller, Robert L.	individual income	$1,043.50
8	Lund, Aaron O.	individual income	2,783.00
9	Barth, Julius	unemployment	7,783.80
10	Teacher, Walker E.	individual income	1,060.00
17	Hawkins, Emma	unemployment	840.73
21	Funderburke, J.L.	individual income	604.28

You will need to identify these people by their addresses. You don't need to include the date the lien was filed.

Write the story for tomorrow's paper.

EXERCISE 5-21

Your city editor handed you this wire story with instructions to fix it up for tomorrow's paper:

CAPITAL CITY — The State Bar Association today released the names of 17 people who passed the bar examination given last month.

They are Mary Martin, Tyler; John Gooch, Monroe; Willis Sims, Haslett; Robert Kemp, Rogers City; Harry L. Richardson, Eastville; Larry Walker, Roseville; Rosa E. Morales, Saginaw; Ernest Beech, New Salem; Lawrence P. O'Donnell, Monroe; Ralph Haroldson, Jackson; Marilyn E. Rauch, Portage; Marcia Williams, Carolton; Harrison Hewins, Stevensville; Ervin Sinclair, Plymouth; Don Myers, Dodgeville; Edna Anderson, Williamstown; Larry Lee Smith, South Haven.

You called Marcia Williams, and she told you that she got her law degree in June at Northwest College. She intends to practice tax law.

EXERCISE 5-22

Your editor handed you this wire story. "Rewrite this for tomorrow's paper," she said.

HILLSDALE — Roger Wells, 28, of Carolton, was killed today when his car went off the road near Hillsdale. Wells was driving home from his job on the night shift at the Hillsdale Iron and Steel Co.

The accident occurred about 4 a.m. on U.S. 210 15 miles east of Carolton.

Lawrence County sheriff's officers said Wells apparently fell asleep at the wheel of his car. The car left the road, traveled 150 feet into a field and turned over.

Wells was dead when he was found by a sheriff's highway patrol officer.

You have no time to get more on this story, but do verify the name before writing. Use a blind lead, please.

EXERCISE 5-23

This morning your city editor handed you this story, a wire story passed along by the news editor. Rewrite it for tomorrow's paper.

LAKE CITY — Dwight McDonald of West Newton was elected president of the state Fraternal Order of Eagles yesterday at the organization's 68th annual convention.

About 300 delegates are attending the convention here.

Other officers elected are Oscar Jones, Cement City, vice president; William Hazelton, Carolton, treasurer; Robert Waldron, Becket, chaplain; and Ronald Shelton, Huron Bay, conductor.

EXERCISE 5-24

The Northwest College news bureau has given you a story about a conference that will be held here Saturday. Write it for tomorrow's paper.

What: Mid-America Regional Conference of the Association for Humanist Psychology.

Speakers: William Tell, author of The Liberated Man.
Jean Bannon, director of the Foundation for Mind Research.
Mary Petruscak, medical anthropologist.
Mike Bozzo, director of the Capital City sports center.

Conference: Theme of the conference: Fulfilling the Dream: Self, Family and Society.

Other: Conference is open to the public. Registration fee will be $5. Conference opens at 10 Saturday morning.

EXERCISE 5-25

Here is a story that came over the state wire this morning. Your editor would like it rewritten for tomorrow's paper.

MONROE — Westphalia, Beaver Falls and Carolton artists won top honors in the State Fair art show, which opened here today.

More than 200 works are entered in three divisions. They will be on display in the Community Arts Building throughout the fair.

Prize winners in the oil painting division were:

Barbara Moore, Westphalia, first; Henry Love, Carolton, second; and Walter E. Shook, Madison, third.

Prize winners in the watercolor division were:

Charles Gifford, Beaver Falls, first; Jane Roberts, Clare, second; and Helen Lutz, Carolton, third.

Prize winners in the prints division were:

Horace N. Gilmore, Carolton, first; Dorothy Bond, Monroe, second; and Laurence Peters, West Allis, third.

EXERCISE 5-26

The secretary of the local chapter of the Embroiderers Guild of America has given you a story about the installation of the organization's new officers. Write the story. Include street addresses.

President: Bette Yaffee
1st vice president: Catherine Tombs
2nd vice president: Jane Bell
Secretary: Harriet Howe
Treasurer: Diana Robbins

The officers were installed Friday at the organization's regular monthly meeting at the City Art Club.

EXERCISE 5-27

While you were on rewrite this morning, your city editor handed you a story that had just come in on the wire. She asked you to rewrite it for tomorrow's paper. You can do it in about three paragraphs.

CAPITAL CITY — (today's date) — The National Labor Relations Board today authorized elections at various state firms to determine what union representation, if any, is desired by employees in their dealings with management.

The firms, locations, number voting in the election, the union or unions seeking representation and the date of the election are as follows:

Willow Run Rubber and Lining Co., Farmington, 33 voting, United Mine Workers, (month) 10th.

Bugent Sand and Gravel Co., Eastville, 20 voting, Teamsters, (month) 12th.

Empire Hotel Co., Dalton, 16 voting, Hotel and Restaurant Employees union, (month) 15th.

Radio West Newton, Inc., West Newton, 16 voting, American Federation of Television and Radio Artists, (month) 18th.

Kelly Construction Co., Carolton, 28 voting, International Brotherhood of Electrical Workers, (month) 20th.

Canteen Service Co., Mount Pleasant, 10 voting, Teamsters, (month), 28th.

You really don't need expert knowledge to rewrite this story. Ask your instructor for the month.

EXERCISE 5-28

Here's another story that needs a list of names. You have learned from the secretary of the Rose Society:

The Rose society's annual show was held Saturday and Sunday in the National Guard armory. It was the 35th annual show. Among the 147 awards presented:

best rose in show	Howard Baker
best hybrid tea	Gerald Ferguson
best arrangement	Mrs. William Miskell

These are Carolton residents, best identified here by their street addresses.

115

EXERCISE 5-29

Your city editor handed you this press release and asked you to follow it up.

CAPITAL CITY — Traffic is moving over all 22 miles of newly widened Interstate 285 in Lake County and Beaufort County, the State Department of Transportation reports.

One lane has been added to both the northbound and southbound routes of the highway from its intersection with U.S. 210 east of Carolton. I-285 is now a six-lane freeway throughout that stretch, and the Department of State Highways expects to start taking bids next month to widen the freeway from White Oak north to the U.S. 10 interchange near Walkerville.

Widening of the freeway began last year, but because of the lack of a detour route and the amount of traffic — up to 55,000 vehicles a day — work was done under moving traffic conditions.

Contractors on the 22-mile, $250 million project were Kelly Construction Co. of Carolton; L.W. Eastman Co. of Bellville; Case and Roach Inc. of Akron, Ohio; and Delta Construction Co. of Cleveland, Ohio.

You call the Kelly Company and ask about completion of the highway work. James Kelly, the firm's general manager, tells you that the I-285 work mentioned in the press release was completed last week, and all the Kelly crews and machinery are moving next week to a new highway construction project near here. Kelly was low bidder on a $5.5 million contract to rebuild the Battle Road bridge over the Indian River. He tells you that there hasn't been anything about this project in the paper since the bids were advertised several months ago.

EXERCISE 5-30

The local American Legion Auxiliary installed officers Tuesday night, and the publicity officer has brought in the list of names. Write a story for tomorrow's paper.

President	Anna Turnbull
1st vice president	Wanda Murphy
2nd vice president	Myra Hall
Secretary	Helen Gillette
Treasurer	Mahalia MacComber
Chaplain	Evelyn Spaulding
Sergeant-at-Arms	Vivian Blake
Executive Board	Mildred Newhouse
	Gladys Powers
	Ella Jackson

EXERCISE 5-31

Edit these sentences to improve punctuation. Use standard editing marks to insert or delete punctuation. Do *not* rewrite.

1. James L. Wilson will address the Challenge Club, at the Eagle Restaurant, Monday, at 7 p.m.

2. Wilson, a community health representative with the state Health department will discuss recent health legislation.

3. Syndicated columnist, Art Downs will be the keynote speaker.

4. The speakers will be: William Tell, author of the new book "The Liberated Man", Marjorie Campbell, a medical student; and Anthony Wilbur, New York Times columnist and author of "David's House".

5. The meeting will be Monday, at 8 p.m., at the County Building.

6. William Cleveland, 34, of 539 S. Grant St. is at Carolton General Hospital. He is in fair condition according to the hospital.

7. Police arrested Jack Tumanis, a Sandusky, Ohio senior, for jaywalking.

8. The cars collided at 2 p.m. on Jan. 11, 1978 in Wichita, Kans., where Smith was living at the time police reported.

9. Commencement will be June 11, in the LaFollette Auditorium at 10 a.m.

Number Correct ＿＿＿＿＿

Student's Name ＿＿＿＿＿＿＿＿＿＿＿＿＿＿＿＿

117

EXERCISE 5-32

Eliminate the *redundancies* in these items. You may *X* them out on the type-writer, draw a line through the unnecessary words or write or type a revision in the space at the right. Some of the items may *not* be redundant.

1. still remains _____

2. at the hour of noon _____

3. spoke on the subject of sin _____

4. an actual fact _____

5. in real life he was _____

6. present incumbent _____

7. made out of iron _____

8. took a walk _____

9. for a period of 10 days _____

10. was engaged in studying _____

11. work has already begun _____

12. strangled to death _____

13. set a new record _____

14. gave birth to a baby boy _____

15. every single day _____

16. at the intersection of _____

17. at 10 p.m. tonight _____

18. during the summer months _____

19. in the event that _____

20. for the purpose of _____

Number Correct _____

Student's Name _____

EXERCISE 5-33

Edit this news story. Correct errors in style. Use standard editing marks and practices. Do *not* rewrite. There may be errors in spelling, usage or punctuation.

01   A Carolton woman was killed last night during an

02   exchange of gunfire between a Carolton police officer and

03   three men suspected of importing drugs into Washington

04   county.

05   Madeline Boomershine, 27, of 386 West Nevada Avenue

06   was killed in the crossfire.

07   Police said Boomershine was crossing the street when

08   detective Sgt. Bert Block exchanged shots with three men

09   in a late-model car with Fla. license plates.

10   She was given last rights by Rev. Sean O'Connor,

11   assistant pastor of St. Thomas Roman Catholic Church.

12   She was dead on arrival at Carolton General hospital.

13   Two of the men fled after the shooting, but the driver

14   of the car, Carl E. Manners, 40, of Sarasota, Florida,

15   was taken into custody.

16   Manners is at Carolton General Hospital with multiple

17   gunshot wounds in the abdomen and chest.

18   Police found a ten pound package of cocaine in the

19   trunk of the Florida car. Estimated street value is

20   $2,000,000, according to police Lieutenant Thomas

21   (Pinky) Maher.

Number Correct _____

Student's Name _____

EXERCISE 5-34

Edit this news story. Correct errors in style. Use standard editing marks and practices. Do *not* rewrite. There may be errors in spelling, grammar, usage or punctuation.

01   Verdicts are expected tomorrow in the lawsuit filed

02   by Carolton families whose homes have been damaged by

03   subsiding land in a former swamp.

04   Walter Nesbitt, attorney for the homeowners is

05   unusually optimistic about the outcome.

06   Nesbit said yesterday that he thinks the jury will

07   award his clients at least 400 thousand dollars.

08   Nesbitt is an experienced trial lawyer. He recently

09   defended a libel suit against "The Morning Record." The

10   Record lost the case, but the jury awarded the plaintiffs,

11   an Albany, New York, couple, only five cents in damages.

12   He is a flamboyant figure who keeps a thermos of

13   coffee in his briefcase and once threw a coke bottle at

14   a bailiff. He is a graduate of the University of

15   Michigan Law School and earned a Master of Arts in public

16   administration at Harvard.

17   He was expelled from college after he rode a unicycle

18   across the platform during a Memorial day program and

19   refused to stand when the band played The Stars and

20   Stripes Forever.

21   His clients have great faith in his judgement, however,

22   and he charges collossal fees.

Number Correct _____

Student's Name _____

6 Some Hard News Stories

Spelling

cigarette,* allegiance, uncontrollable, cemetery, occur/occurred/occurring/occurrence, leisure, implausible, changeable, inoculate, deterrent, strict/strictly, resuscitate

Usage

ordinance/ordnance, perspective/prospective, populous/populace, prostrate/prostitute, alumnus/alumni, alumna/alumnae, vulgar/profane/obscene

Newsroom Vocabulary

breaking news, itemizing lead, obituary, precision journalism, set, overset, morgue, memo, issue, edition, point, pica

Some Hard News Stories

These topics are treated in detail in George A. Hough 3rd, "News Writing," fourth edition:

Chronology
Chapter 9, "Some Hard News Stories," pages 158 through 161; Chapter 5, "News Story Organization," pages 80 through 82; and model stories, Figures 9.1 and 9.2 on pages 158 and 159.

Numbers
Chapter 10, "Numbers in the News," pages 183 through 206.

Obituaries
Chapter 9, "Some Hard News Stories," pages 169 through 180, and model stories, Figures 9.6 and 9.7 on page 172.

Itemizing Leads
Chapter 9, "Some Hard News Stories," page 163.

Libel
Chapter 22, "Legal and Ethical Considerations," pages 441 through 451.

Ethics and Professional Standards
Chapter 22, "Legal and Ethical Considerations," pages 451 through 456.

Attribution
Chapter 6, "Writing the Story," pages 93 through 97.

Hyphens
Chapter 19, "Newspaper Grammar and Punctuation," pages 390 through 394.

EXERCISE 6-1

When you were in your bank this morning, a bank vice president handed you a press release and suggested that it would make a story for the Record business page. He's right. This is news. Write a story. The press release tells you:

The bank is the University City National Bank. The bank's annual meeting of stockholders was held yesterday. Among other matters that came up at the meeting, Mr. Elmer, the bank's president, announced that the board of directors had declared a quarterly dividend on the bank's common stock.

The dividend will be 66 cents a share for the quarter ending this month. Because this is the last quarter of the bank's fiscal year, the 66 cents brings the dividend for the year to $2.64. The quarterly dividend will be paid to stockholders of record the first of this month.

This is the 56th quarter in which the bank has paid a dividend. The bank has assets of more than $150,000,000.

EXERCISE 6-2

Write a story based on these figures just released by the state Department of Revenue. The figures represent state tax revenues for last month and for the same month last year. Insert the current month in the blank in the line beginning *Month of*. To make your story meaningful, you will have to calculate the percentage of change from last year to this year.

State Department of Revenue
Capital City

Revenue Division's report of collections:

Month of _____ this year compared to same month last year.

Revenue Source	This Year	Last Year	Change
Sales and Use	$142,479,549.23	131,942,217.11	_____
Motor Fuel	26,300,584.97	25,759,593.23	_____
Individual Income	190,165,512.46	168,812,306.22	_____
Corporate Income	8,954,394.99	10,464,849.77	_____
Cigar and Cigarette	7,146,779.39	7,706,805.89	_____
Motor Vehicle	1,374,458.93	1,219,445.35	_____
Liquor	2,646,650.24	4,557,948.81	_____
Malt Beverage	5,566,552.62	5,389,824.83	_____
Estate	1,029,796.73	1,050,198.92	_____
Property	2,159,770.12	1,892,358.80	_____
Wine	1,603,701.67	1,307,756.34	_____
Miscellaneous	800,711.59	804,546.21	_____
TOTAL	390,228,462.94	360,907,851.48	_____

EXERCISE 6-3

You were covering the police beat this morning when you were told about the rescue of a child who had fallen into the river. Write the story for tomorrow's paper.

From the report at police headquarters:

Boy saved from drowning this morning. Taken to Carolton General Hospital. Name: Mitchell Stephenson — age seven. Parents: William and Deborah. Address: 125 Indian River Place. Mother said boy had been playing near river.

From Carolton General:

Mitchell is in good condition. He will be held overnight for observation.

From Mercy Ambulance Service:

Ambulance and paramedics went to Indian River Place about 9:40 this morning. Took boy to Carolton General.

From (Mrs.) Kathy Gibbs:

I live next door. I heard Debbie scream and saw her run down to the river. I followed her. When I got there, she had pulled him onto the bank and was trying to bring him to. I'm not sure he was breathing.

From Mrs. Stephenson:

I was so nervous I couldn't do a thing. Kathy tried, too, but we weren't getting anywhere until John came.

From John Gibbs:

I followed my wife. She and Debbie were trying mouth-to-mouth resuscitation, but they weren't doing too well. I was a medic in the army so I took over and got him breathing again.

From Russ Reimenschneider, Mercy Ambulance paramedic:

Mr. Gibbs saved the boy's life. If he hadn't known how to give mouth-to-mouth, the boy wouldn't have made it.

Verify names and addresses. Use direct quotes to help carry the narrative along.

EXERCISE 6-4

You were covering the police beat this morning. From the desk sergeant in the robbery squad office, you picked up the following facts:

Armed robbery — 8 last night — O'Malley's Restaurant and Bar — $250 taken from cash register —

Restaurant owner — Floyd Scissors — age 38 — 104½ North Calhoun — shot — through-and-through wound upper left thigh — taken to Carolton General by police ambulance —

No one else hurt — restaurant busy at time — 50 to 60 people including restaurant help —

From a statement made by Scissors this morning:

Man walked in and ordered dinner — finished his meal — came up to cashier's counter — had a revolver — told Scissors quote if you make any fuss, I'll kill you unquote — said he wanted the money from register — Scissors handed it over — man ran to door — fired one shot in Scissors' direction — hit him in leg — Scissors quote I don't know why he shot me. I didn't do a thing. Just gave him the money unquote —

From desk sergeant:

Description of robber: male — white — 25 to 30 — medium height — blond hair — bushy mustache — had on black leather jacket — wearing red and black running shoes —

You check with the hospital:

Scissors is in good condition. Resting comfortably — a .38-caliber bullet removed from his leg this morning and leg set — bullet had caused compound fracture of the femur.

EXERCISE 6-5

While you were at police headquarters this morning, you picked up this story. Sgt. Harry Oberdorfer, on duty at the desk, told you:

Cheap holdup. Suspect got about twenty bucks. Had a knife and threatened the night man at the gas station at five eleven south Territorial road. Ran off after the robbery. Night man at station is Elwyn Fereira. He wasn't hurt. He called us right away. Headquarters sent a black and white, but they couldn't find the suspect.

This isn't much of a story, but write it anyway. Attribute to *police*. You know, of course, that a *black and white* is police jargon for a patrol car.

EXERCISE 6-6

When you stopped at the Carolton state police post this morning, you were told about a drug bust last night. You talked with state police Lt. Jack Toy, head of the narcotics squad, and he told you:

We're holding these men:

> James Earl March, age 26, St. Louis, Missouri
> John Lambert, age 24, East St. Louis, Illinois
> Harry Rogers, age 30, Kansas City
> Joseph Flag, age 27, Kansas City

Being questioned now. Expect to take them to county court this afternoon for arraignment. Charge will be possession of controlled substance with intent to distribute.

Arrest made by state police trooper Walter Hickok. On highway patrol. Saw car pulling a boat trailer. Trailer had no tail light. Stopped car. Became suspicious, checked car and trailer. Found seven burlap bags of marijuana in boat. Haven't been weighed yet. No estimate of street value.

Arrest was on U.S. 210 east of the city.

Toy told you of another arrest on drug charges:

A Colombian national, Luis Calderon Carbajal, arrested at airport last night. Coming here from Mexico City on Capital Airlines flight. Customs agents found 2.2 pounds of heroin in his luggage. He is being held for questioning. He is at the county jail.

On second reference, refer to the Colombian as Calderon. Avoid police jargon — find another word for *bust*.

You will have to write your story without waiting for details on the arraignment. Your city editor wants to get the story to the Associated Press right away. You can write an insert on the arraignment later.

EXERCISE 6-7

You were on the police beat today. One of your responsibilities on this beat is to cover the fire department. In checking with the fire department, you got a story about a fire in an apartment complex. The facts:

Fire at 347 West Arizona avenue. Rubbish fire in basement storeroom. One pumper and a ladder truck responded. Alarm at 8:45. Equipment returned to central station at 10:05.

Fire Lieutenant Jacob Strauss says building was filled with smoke when firefighters got there. Some residents had left their apartments and were standing outside in the parking lot. Firemen went through the building and got the rest outside.

Building pretty clear of smoke when they left the scene. Occupants were able to go back in.

Strauss tells you it wasn't much of a fire. Maybe $1,500 in damage to storeroom in the basement where fire apparently started. Occupants may have some loss from smoke damage.

Fire marshal Clayton Evans assigned to investigation.

You ask Strauss about the building, and he tells you it is a 24-unit building. Three stories. Occupants are mostly elderly.

EXERCISE 6-8

The relationship between the paired items is expressed in *absolute* terms, that is, in concrete terms. Explain the relationship in *relative* terms. For example:

absolute   The distance from A to B is 20 miles.
          The distance from B to C is 40 miles.
relative   The distance from B to C is twice the distance from A to B.

1. James J. Jeffries (heavyweight)   220 pounds
    Young Corbett (featherweight)   110 pounds

2. Mary Smith (daughter)   age 15
    Harriet Smith (mother)   age 45

3. Carolton tax rate, 1987 $60
    Carolton tax rate, 1967 $30

4. William is 6 feet 4 inches tall.
    His younger sister is 3 feet 2 inches tall.

EXERCISE 6-9

There was a robbery this morning at the First National Bank, and since you were free at the moment, your city editor sent you to cover the story. At the bank you talked with police, bank officers and witnesses:

From Detective Lieutenant John Begg of the robbery squad:

We've got an alarm out for the robbers — three men — two were young — maybe twenty-five — third man was in his 50s — all three medium height — slender — put on ski masks after they entered the bank —

They were driving a 1983 Volkswagen van — dark blue —

From Mrs. Rita Hoffman, vice president of bank:

I was with a customer at my desk. I looked up and saw a man with a mask on pointing a gun at me. He said quote This is a holdup unquote. I thought oh my god, this is it.

I saw three men. They ordered everybody to stand over against the wall — they made me and my customer go with the others. I think the older man was in charge. He held the gun on us.

From Mary Jane Toefel, a bank teller:

I saw them when they came in. One had a can of spray paint and squirted it at the camera. They were putting those masks on as they came across the lobby. Scared? You better believe I was.

From John Ashford, a bank teller:

I saw them in time to trip the silent alarm. One of them jumped over the counter and grabbed the cash from the drawers. The other went into the vault. They had canvas bags to put the money in.

From Kenneth Stieber, 822 E. Nevada, an insurance agent:

I was in the bank to cash a check. It was over pretty fast. They seemed nervous. The guy with the gun, his hands were shaking. He had, I think, a .45 automatic.

We were facing away from them, but I could see a little in a mirror on the wall at my left. The guy with the gun seemed to be in charge. They hadn't been in the bank more than three or four minutes when he yelled at the others to hurry. He said quote let's get out of here unquote and they ran out the door.

From Maurice Henderson:

I was just going into the bank when they were coming out. They grabbed me and took my car keys. I'd parked right in front of the bank. They jumped into the van and took off. I sure hope I get my van back.

continued on next page

You ask Lieutenant Begg for additional details and learn:

The alarm was sounded at 9:17. Uniformed officers in a scout car got to the bank at 9:25. There were about a dozen customers in the bank during the robbery and eight bank employees. Nobody hurt. Several customers frightened and upset. Others just angry. Begg thinks robbers were amateurs.

From Mrs. Hoffman:

Robbers got about $100,000 — all bills — mostly $5, $10 and $20 denominations.

From Begg:

Spray paint did not cover camera lens completely. It may be possible to identify the men — if the camera caught them before they got their masks on.

EXERCISE 6-10

You were on rewrite again this morning when the Riley funeral home called with an obit. Write it for tomorrow's paper.

Deceased is Carolyn (Robb) Dwight. Born Nov. 1, 1920. Died yesterday at St. Luke's hospital.

Born in Winchester, Virginia. Came here in 1946 as a social worker with county welfare department. Worked later for county Council on Aging. Retired in 1985 as director of the agency. Served on the boards of the Family Counseling Center, American Red Cross and Salvation Army.

Graduate of Michigan State University school of social work.

Member All Saints Episcopal church, Washington County Democratic Women, National Organization for Women, Carolton Country Club. She was a veteran of WW II. Served in Europe with the Women's Army Corps.

When she retired she was honored at a dinner given by the Council on Aging. Mayor Smith said of her quote Mrs. Dwight has done a remarkable job in developing the Council (on Aging) — the city owes her a great deal for her work on behalf of the elderly unquote.

Services tomorrow at 10 a.m. at All Saints. Rev. Evers to officiate. Burial in Evergreen cemetery.

Survivors: husband, Robert, assistant general manager of Kelly Construction Co., sons, Robert, Newark, James, Williamsburg, Virginia, a daughter, Marion, Carolton; and a nephew, Harold Robb, Dothan, Alabama.

Funeral home said cause of death was cancer.

EXERCISE 6-11

Carolton assesses real property, land and buildings, at full market value. Value of real property in the city this year:

Residential property	$278,911,500
Commercial property	9,714,500
Industrial property	7,830,070
Total taxable value	$296,456,070

The city council has approved a budget that includes these figures:

Expenditures	$2,994,110.34
Miscellaneous income	$1,274,665.13

How much must be raised by taxation to balance the budget?

_____

If _____ must be raised by levying taxes on a tax base of $296,456,070, what will the tax rate be?

_____

What will the tax on your home be if it is assessed at $75,000?

_____

EXERCISE 6-12

You were on rewrite this morning when the Record's police reporter called in with an accident story. She told you:

One-car accident. Driver either drunk or asleep. Car went off road and hit a tree. Total loss.

Driver taken to Carolton General by Mercy ambulance. He is being held in the police ward.

Accident on Highway 30 about three miles southwest of the city near junction of 30 and County Trunk D.

No witnesses. Deputy Sheriff Larry Tate was on traffic patrol and spotted the car. Found driver near the car.

Tate says driver seemed dazed. Thinks he may have been drinking. Expects to ticket him for DUI.

Driver: Robert Willoughby, age 22. Lives in Carolton. Address 234 River Road. He has lacerations and contusions. May have a concussion.

DUI, of course, means driving under the influence of alcohol. And from your own knowledge of police procedure, you know that the police ward at Carolton General is a locked ward where prisoners are housed.

EXERCISE 6-13

When your editor looked over your weather story (see Exercise 3-3), she asked you to get a little more on the house fire and write it as a separate story.

You have all that the fire department records show (see Exercise 3-3), so you call the Buchanans. Mrs. Buchanan tells you:

My husband and I had just gone to bed. It was raining hard and there was a lot of lightning. Suddenly there was the most awful clap of thunder and everything lit up like daylight. Then we smelled smoke and realized that the house had been struck. Harry went up in the attic and looked around. The attic was full of smoke so we were pretty sure the fire was somewhere up there or in the roof.

I ran to the children's room and got them up. Harry called the fire department from the kitchen. We got the car out and parked it in the street and sat there until the fire trucks came. The fire was in the roof at the back of the house. The firemen weren't here very long. We went back to bed about one. The house still smells a little smoky.

You ask about the extent of the damage and are told:

We've called a contractor to come look at it. I don't think there's much damage, but we'll know when we get an estimate for repairs. Harry checked this morning and our insurance will cover it.

Write your story. Don't be misled by the amount of information you have. Be concise. Are you aware of the difference between *damage* and *damages*?

EXERCISE 6-14

You were on rewrite today when Door Bros. called with an obit. Write it for tomorrow's paper.

Deceased is Mrs. Esther (Keezing) Gold. Died last night at home. Born January 11, 1906, in Germany. Came to this country in 1920. She had lived in Carolton since 1930.

Husband: Morris Gold. They were married in 1923.

Two children, Harold, Carolton, and Dr. Ruth Gold Wells, Chicago. One brother, Charles, Palm Beach, Florida.

There are five grandchildren and one great-grandchild.

Member: Hadassah, National Council of Jewish Women, National Women's Committee of Brandeis University, B'nai Jacob Sisterhood. Was on the board of the Carolton Public Housing authority.

Services tomorrow at Door Bros. at 4 p.m. Burial in Evergreen cemetery.

135

EXERCISE 6-15

While you were on rewrite today, your city editor asked you to get the details on the fatal accident on the river yesterday. You checked with various sources and found:

From the coronor's office:

Name of the dead girl is Kim Clarke. She was brought to the county morgue from St. Luke's hospital. Records show she died at 12:30 this morning. There will be an autopsy.

From the sheriff's office:

Accident happened about 6 yesterday afternoon at the boat dock on the Indian river west of Airport road. Rescue squad from the Carolton fire department was dispatched to the scene. Fire Captain Jack Hope may have more information. Talk to Deputy Medford.

From Captain Hope:

Rescue squad scuba divers found the girl in 20 feet of water near the boat dock. She probably had been underwater for 20 minutes. Rescue squad paramedics worked on her — CPR — then took her to St. Luke's. She was unconscious when they put her in the ambulance.

From Deputy Sheriff Jack Medford:

I was on patrol near the airport. Went right to the scene. Witnesses said the girl was climbing down a metal ladder to get into a canoe. Let out a yell. She just let go of the ladder and fell into the water.

The kids she was with tried to grab her, but she slipped underwater. The divers with the rescue squad got her out. She'd been underwater a while when they found her.

From Dr. H.L. Hirsch:

I was called a little after 6. Paramedics were working on her when I got there. I think she got some kind of electrical shock. Probably from something on the dock.

From Herbert W. Cooper, state department of natural resources officer:

We're investigating. The DNR is responsible for the park. The sheriff's people are also looking into it. If you call me tomorrow, I may have something.

From the dead girl's parents:

Kim a senior at Carolton Central. Age 18. Strong swimmer. They don't know anything at all about the accident. Kim had gone to the park with a group of friends from school.

EXERCISE 6-16

Property tax rates are stated in terms of dollars per thousand, that is, for every thousand dollars of property you own, you will pay so many dollars.

For example, if the tax rate is $6.00 per thousand and you own a home assessed — that is, valued for tax purposes — at $100,000, you will pay a tax of $600.00.

The tax rate in Carolton:

This year	$7.50
Last year	$7.00
Previous year	$6.50

What will your taxes be this year if your home has been assessed at $75,000?

_____

What did you pay last year when your home was assessed at $68,000?

_____

What did you pay two years ago when your home was assessed at $65,000?

_____

EXERCISE 6-17

When you came to work this morning, your city editor handed you this wire story and asked you to check on it and write something for tomorrow's paper. The wire story:

ROGERS CITY — (today's date) — Three people were shaken up but uninjured this morning when their light plane overshot the runway at the Rogers City Airport and overturned in a ditch.

Treated and released at Rogers City Community Hospital were Hugh Morgan, Monroe; John Lodge, Carolton, and George A. Rogers, Carolton.

You call Rogers' office at city hall and learn that he is in Rogers City for a meeting of the state Municipal Officers Association. He is expected back tomorrow. No one in his office has heard about the accident. You call Mrs. Rogers and she tells you:

George called me just now. He's fine. He's got a bump on his head, but nothing serious. He said he's going to the meeting and will be back tomorrow. If the plane can't fly, he said he will take the bus.

FYI: The plane belongs to the city, and you know that Rogers, who was a naval aviator in World War II, frequently flies it.

EXERCISE 6-18

Your city editor has handed you these figures that came in today's mail from the state department of labor. The economy is always a good story, your editor reminded you, and suggested that you write a story for tomorrow's paper.

Last month

County	Labor Force	Employed	Unemployed	Unemployment Rate
Washington	71,051	66,578	4,473	6.3%
Greene	29,127	27,201	1,926	6.6
Franklin	7,104	6,577	527	7.4
Dodge	39,348	36,625	2,723	6.9
Duval	47,858	43,676	4,182	8.7
5-county region	194,488	180,657	13,831	7.1
state	2,874,904	2,706,749	168,155	5.8

Previous Month

County	Labor Force	Employed	Unemployed	Unemployment Rate
Washington	70,948	66,165	4,783	6.7%
Greene	28,797	26,858	1,939	6.7
Franklin	7,032	6,541	491	7.0
Dodge	39,082	36,188	2,894	7.4
Duval	47,993	43,250	4,743	9.9
5-county region	193,852	179,002	14,850	7.6
state	2,864,509	2,685,602	178,907	6.2

You must report changes in the figures for Washington County, for the five-county region in which Washington is located and for the state. You must explain the figures in both absolute and relative terms.

EXERCISE 6-19

You were on the police beat this morning and after making the rounds at police headquarters, you stopped in at the public safety office on campus. From detective Lt. Sean O'Kelly you learned:

Police have arrested six students. They've admitted they cut down the big fir tree on Circle drive on campus night before last. They have been released on $500 bond each. Charge is criminal trespass.

Students: Richard Allen, 20, 540 S. Mead
             Will Henderson, 19, 540 S. Mead
             Daniel Roberts, 21, 540 S. Meade
             Gregory Gould, 18, Hallowell Hall
             Quimby Lawrence, 19, Hallowell Hall
             Harry Matthews, 20, Hallowell Hall

Lieutenant O'Kelly fills you in on the story:

Tree was a 30-foot fir in front of Forestry school building on Circle drive. Valued at $750. Was cut down and taken away night before last. A campus police officer found it yesterday in front of fraternity house, set up and decorated with lights.

You check the Meade Street address and identify it as the Alpha Zeta Omega fraternity house.

You call the student judiciary office and learn from Beatrice Wetherbee, assistant dean for student affairs, that the students have been referred to the student judiciary. She says she understands they are pledges and were sent out to get a Christmas tree.

Write your story. Attribute carefully.

EXERCISE 6-20

You were covering police this morning. After checking at police headquarters, you stopped at the Central Fire Station and learned:

Fire about four this morning at 210 West Main. Smoke damage. Electrical wiring burned out. Damage estimated at $6,500.

Cause given as quote faulty wiring unquote.

One pumper responded.

Remember, early estimates of damage and first thoughts about the cause of a fire may change after fire officials have had time to investigate. You should attribute opinions, even informed opinions. In this story, attribute to *fire officials*.

EXERCISE 6-21

You were on rewrite this morning when the Record's police reporter called this story in. Write it for tomorrow's paper.

Auto accident — on Old Meetinghouse road near bridge. Two cars involved — accident about 2 a.m. Ambulance called at 2:25 a.m.

Car No. 1 — driven by Horace Gilmore — accident report gives his address as 335 W. Oregon. — car had been stopped at side of road — driver was attempting to return to pavement — collided with approaching car.

Car No. 2 — driven by Branson Porter, 506 S. Sherman — heading north on Old Meetinghouse Road.

Sergeant John Talcott (Carolton police accident prevention bureau) is officer in charge of investigation. He says that Porter had been drinking. Blood test taken at hospital. Neither driver has been ticketed.

Gilmore taken to Carolton General. He has multiple fractures of left arm and leg. May have a concussion. Possible internal injuries. Hospital says his condition critical.

Porter also at Carolton General. Abrasions and contusions. Being held for observation.

Virginia Main, 804 N. Sherman, also injured. Fractured left arm. Abrasions and contusions. Possible concussion. Held for observation.

Accident report on file at police headquarters shows Virginia Main was a passenger in car No. 1.

Report gives Gilmore's age as 45; Main, 40; Porter, 52.

No one involved in the accident has been able to give police a statement.

Attribute as appropriate. Police reports are notoriously careless about spelling of names and about addresses. Please verify all names and addresses before you write.

EXERCISE 6-22

You were on the police beat this morning. At the Accident Prevention Bureau, you picked up this story about a fatal accident last night. Write it for tomorrow's paper. Use an itemizing lead.

Accident was at the railroad crossing on Western avenue. An eastbound freight hit a 1987 Dodge Colt. Carried car hundred yards before train stopped.

continued on next page

Four occupants of vehicle taken to St. Luke's hospital. Three were DOA.

Vehicle was going north on Western avenue.

APB officer John Talcott got a statement from the survivor. He said they all had been drinking. He was in front passenger seat. He saw the train. Thinks it was going about 40 miles an hour. Ferreira was driving. He tried to beat the train.

In the car: Ricky Ferreira, 16, 127 Maple
                Lawrence Carew, 17, 221 Sycamore
                Stephen Dawson, 15, 308 South Houston
                Anthony Carter, 16, 212 East Florida

Carter is at St. Luke's. Has abrasions and contusions, sprained left wrist, a concussion. Hospital says his condition is good.

Bodies are at Door funeral home. Talcott says there will be an autopsy.

You check with the railroad and learn:

Crossing signals were working at the time. Train was probably going about 45 miles an hour — normal speed when traveling in a congested area. Engineer of the train, Walter Stroh, is at police headquarters to give his statement.

FYI: *DOA* is police jargon for *dead on arrival*.

EXERCISE 6-23

Riley Bros. Funeral Chapel just called with an obit. Write it for tomorrow's paper.

Deceased is John Souza. Died this morning at Holy Cross hospital. In ill health for some time. Born June 19, 1908, in Funchal, Madeira. Came to this country as a child.

Attended public schools here. Foreman with county highway department forty years. Retired in 1978.

Communicant at St. Thomas church here. Member Holy Name Society. Member Carolton Senior Citizens Club.

Veteran of WW II. Served in army. Awarded bronze star and purple heart medals. Member Carolton VFW post.

Wife, Mary (Costa); sons, Albert, Louis, Donald, Joseph, all of Carolton; a daughter, Linda, Monument Beach, Massachusetts, a sister, Mary, Tampa, Florida.

Funeral mass day after tomorrow at 11 a.m. at St. Thomas. Father Flynn will say the mass. Burial in church cemetery.

EXERCISE 6-24

You were on police today. You heard about the holdup at the Holiday Inn just after it happened and went to the scene. During the morning, you learned the following:

From police officer John Chin:

The injured man was lying on the floor in the middle of the lobby when I got there. He appeared to have a chest wound. There was a lot of blood. I called the ambulance. They took him to Carolton General. I don't know his name. He appeared to be about 40 years old. He was staying at the hotel, I understand.

From Detective Willis Barke:

The desk clerk and his assistant have just given us statements. We have a pretty good description of the suspects, and hopefully we'll find them fast.

From Charles Watson:

I'm the night clerk. I go off duty at 6. It was about 10 to and Frank was just getting ready to take over the desk. I was showing him some new registrations when I heard someone come in. I looked up and there were these two guys with masks on. Ski masks, you know. One of them had a shotgun. The tall one. The other guy had a pistol. That's what he slugged me with. He jumped right over the desk and shoved us back. He hit me with the gun ... I just went out like a light. That's all I remember till the cops were there. I'm going over to the hospital for a check. My head hurts.

From Franklin Swift:

We looked up and saw these two guys. The tall one had a rifle or shotgun. The other one is the one that slugged Charlie. He hit him, then grabbed at the cash drawer. He just pushed me, that's all. He wanted me to open the safe, but I couldn't. We don't have keys. It's locked at night. They were in a hurry. They were running back to the lobby door when this man came in off the street ... a guest ... I don't know his name. They just shot him and ran out the door. I don't think he really saw them. He was heading to the elevators. I called the cops.

You call Carolton General and learn:

Injured man is in serious condition. He has a gunshot wound in the upper left chest. He is still unconscious.

From Gerald Olds, manager, Holiday Inn:

The guest's name is Gerald Blaine. He checked in last night. I think he's an engineer. From what Frank and Charlie told me, I

continued on next page

think he was shot accidentally. He just showed up at the wrong time. I think the robbers reacted before they had a chance to think. This is the first time we have been robbed. I don't think they got more than $150. We never have much money in the cash drawer. The night clerks don't have a key to the safe. I open it in the morning when I come in.

From Detective Lieutenant Pinky Maher:

We have a description of the suspects. First one is about 6 two. Maybe 40 years old. Wearing a plaid shirt and corduroy pants. The other is about 5 six. About 175, we think. Same age, about 40. Had on a tan work shirt and pants. Wearing army combat boots. Both had ski masks on. Both were white.

We don't think they're local. No similar descriptions from recent holdups. Don't know how they got away.

Injured citizen is Gerald Blaine. Papers in his wallet indicate he is 48. Home is Oak Park, Ill. He is with Great Lakes International, Oak Brook, Illinois.

From Mrs. Myrtie Watson, 107 Maple:

You can't talk with Charles. He's in bed. He doesn't feel well. He has a headache and a big lump on his head. The police took him to the hospital, but they let him come home. He says he'll be all right and is going to work tonight. I'm not sure he will. What? No, I'm not. I'm his mother.

You are on deadline for the first edition. Slug your story *holdup/page one.*

EXERCISE 6-25

Jenkins Funeral Home just called with an obit. Your city editor saw that you weren't busy and asked you to take the call. She wants the obit for the first edition of tomorrow's paper. The deadline is fast approaching.

Deceased is Mrs. Mary Theresa Marks. Born in Carolton on December 11, 1926. Died yesterday at home. Had been ill for some time. Husband, Peter; daughters, Mrs. Horace Meade (June), Mary, Patricia and Ellen, all of Carolton; brothers, the Rev. Patrick McGuire, Providence, Rhode Island, John, Harold, Edwin McGuire, all of Carolton.

Her parents were the late Patrick and Kathleen (Grogan) McGuire of Carolton.

Educated in public schools here. Bachelor of Arts from Boston college, master's of medical social work from Catholic university, Washington.

continued on page 144

143

She helped establish the St. Luke's Medical Center here and served as a member of the board of the center for many years.

Member Boston college alumni society; Daughters of Ancient Order of Hibernians; Washington County Democratic Women; board of directors of Washington County historical society; Carolton Professional Women's club.

Communicant at St. Thomas church. Mass of Christian Burial will be celebrated day after tomorrow at St. Thomas at 11. Burial in church cemetery. Father Flynn to celebrate the mass.

Rosary at funeral home tomorrow night at 7.

Family suggests that memorial gifts be made to the Washington County Cancer Society.

EXERCISE 6-26

Tax rates may be stated in terms of dollars per thousand or they may be stated in mills. One mill is equal to 1/1,000 of a dollar or 1/10 of a cent.

If the tax rate is $6 a thousand, what is the mill rate?

Dollars	Rate
$1,000	$6.00
100	.60
10	.06
1	____ mills

Review the tax rates shown in Exercise 6-16 and figure the mill rate in Carolton for this year, last year and the previous year.

Year	Mills
This year	_____
Last year	_____
Previous year	_____

144

EXERCISE 6-27

Edit these sentences so that hyphenation conforms to rules given in "News Writing," pages 390 through 394 and pages 472 and 473. You may also want to consult Webster's New World Dictionary. Use standard editing marks to insert or delete punctuation.

1. The expresident called the action unAmerican and said that it was unbecoming to a well known political figure.

2. The seven year old girl traveled alone on a nonstop transAtlantic flight.

3. The chairman was reelected despite the charge that he was antiintellectual.

4. "I'm 7 years old," the boy said. "And in 69 years I will be seventy-six."

5. The 11-year-old child was gravely ill but rallied when she was given an antivirus vaccine.

6. Everyone has a right to work, but in some states the right is spelled out in right to work laws.

7. The antiBritish elements in the audience booed at the speaker's off-the-cuff remarks.

8. The accused, a two time loser, was quickly sentenced to a ninety nine year prison term.

9. Northwest won 21 to 7 in the final game of the season.

Number Correct _____

Student's Name _____

EXERCISE 6-28

Rewrite these sentences to avoid using *alleged* or *allegedly*. For example:

> The utility was fined $5,000 after the commission
> determined that it had *allegedly* violated safety
> regulations.

> The commission determined that the utility had
> violated safety regulations and fined it $5,000.

1. Police arrested the man they saw allegedly attacking two
   women students.

2. Police said they found that the man's alleged address
   was false.

3. Police said drug deals were allegedly discussed in the
   conversations they recorded.

4. A prisoner who allegedly fled from the county jail was
   recaptured two hours later.

5. John Doe went on trial Monday for an alleged attack on
   a guard at the county jail.

6. A nurse at Carolton General Hospital was charged with
   murder Friday for allegedly injecting a patient with a
   fatal dose of potassium chloride.

7. A 23-year-old woman was indicted Wednesday for her
   alleged role in a statewide drug ring.

8. The FBI has launched an investigation of alleged misuse
   of Family Court funds.

Number Correct _____

Student's Name _____

147

EXERCISE 6-29

Edit this news story. Correct errors in style. Use standard editing marks and practices. Do *not* rewrite. There may be errors in spelling, grammar, usage or punctuation.

01   Three heavily armed men burst into O'Flynn's last

02   night, robbed some 50 customers of the popular nightclub,

03   took 2 hostages, and escaped in a limousine driven by a

04   uniformed chauffeur.

05   One man was shot, apparently accidently, during the

06   holdup.

07   John T. (Knuckles) Shonsky, state middleweight boxing

08   champion in the 1960's, is at Carolton General hospital.

09   His physician says he has a subdural (ok) hemmorage.

10   A four man team of detectives headed by police

11   Lieutenant Jacob C. Bernstein is directing the search for

12   the holdup men and their hostages.

13   Taken hostage were Kermit Frogge, sixty, a retired

14   industrialist and the inventor of scotch tape, and Rodney

15   King, 18, an employe of the nightclub. King had worked

16   at the club for only ten days.

17   O'Flynn's is at 104 River Rd. in a renovated brick

18   mill overlooking the Indian River.

19   Harold Hill, manager of O'Flynn's, said the robbers

20   took about ten thousand dollars from club customers.

Number Correct _____

Student's Name _____

EXERCISE 6-30

Edit this news story. Correct errors in style. Use standard editing marks and practices. Do *not* rewrite. There may be errors in spelling, usage or punctuation.

01   The husband of a Carolton woman who was killed

02   yesterday in a shootout between police and a trio

03   suspected of selling drugs has asked for an inquest.

04   Dr. John E. Boomershine said he wants a complete

05   investigation into the death of his wife, Madeline, 27.

06   Boomershine is a veteranarian. He has an office in

07   the Oglethorpe building at 17 West Main Street.

08   The shooting occured in front of The Morning Record

09   Publishing Co. offices at 312 E. Main Street.

10   Boomershine, a "Morning Record" bookkeeper, was on

11   her way home from work. She was crossing the street when

12   the gunfire started. She was the only person on Main

13   St. to be hit.

14   The Morning Record Publishing Co. occupies a

15   three-story building in the heart of the cities historical

16   preservation district.

17   Dr. W.T. Door, Washington County Coroner, will

18   perform an autopsy tomorrow.

19   Carl Manners, 40, the Fla. man who was wounded in the

20   shooting is in serious condition at Carolton General

21   hospital. The police balistics lab is testing the gun

22   used by Manners.

Number Correct _____

7 Second-Day Stories

Spelling

predator, dumbbell, sizable, salable, vacuum, picnicking, parallel, minuscule, miniature, inaugurate, embarrassment, admissible, innocuous

Usage

ravage/ravish, relic/relict, rend/render, delegate/relegate, doctoral/doctorate, complement/compliment, connote/denote

Newsroom Vocabulary

spot news, round-up, follow, second-day story, background, backgrounder, shirttail, sidebar, add, insert, Fourth Estate, Guild, wire, editorialize

Second-Day Stories

These topics are treated in detail in George A. Hough 3rd, "News Writing," fourth edition:

Backgrounding
Chapter 11, "Second-Day Stories and Other Organizing Devices," pages 209 through 222.

Second-Day Stories
Chapter 11, "Second-Day Stories and Other Organizing Devices," pages 210 through 215.

Follow-up Stories
Chapter 11, "Second-Day Stories and Other Organizing Devices," pages 215 through 217.

Round-ups
Chapter 11, "Second-Day Stories and Other Organizing Devices," pages 217 through 219.

Before you begin work on assignments in this section, review these topics: summary leads, identification, attribution, obituaries, quotation, paired commas, hyphens.

EXERCISE 7-1

You were on rewrite this morning when the Record's police reporter called in a story. The city editor asked you to take the call, and you learned:

Police records show an ambulance run from 347 West Arizona to Carolton General. Time: 9:45 this morning. Patient: Harriet Ormsby.

You call the hospital and learn:

Mrs. Ormsby admitted today. She is in the cardiac care unit. No other information.

You check the directory, get a phone number for the Ormsby residence and talk to Mrs. Ormsby's husband. He tells you:

She has been in ill health for a couple of years. Since the fire yesterday, she hasn't felt well. She collapsed this morning after breakfast, and I called the ambulance. She's got a bad heart.

Look up the story about the fire (Exercise 6-7) and write a brief story for tomorrow's paper.

EXERCISE 7-2

You were on rewrite today and during the day took calls from the funeral homes in charge of arrangements for the teen-agers killed day before yesterday in the accident at the grade crossing (Exercise 6-22). Pull the three stories together under one lead. Obituaries with biographical material and lists of survivors ran in today's paper, so the only new information is the funerals. The three services will be held day after tomorrow.

From Door Brothers:

Carew services — 11 a.m. at First Congregational church. Nightingale to officiate. Body will be at church from 8:30 a.m. until the services. Burial in Forest Lawn.

From Jenkins:

Dawson services — Liberty Baptist church — Duttweiller — 10 a.m. — burial in Evergreen cemetery.

From McKay:

Ferreira services — rosary tomorrow at 7 o'clock at McKay. Services at 11 at St. Thomas. Father Flynn — burial church cemetery.

Write your story. Provide adequate background.

155

EXERCISE 7-3

You were on rewrite this morning when the Record's police reporter called in with a follow on the robbery at O'Malley's. You recall the earlier story (Exercise 6-4) that you wrote, which was published last week. The police reporter told you:

Police have a suspect in the O'Malley robbery. He was arraigned this morning in municipal court. Charge is armed robbery and assault with a deadly weapon. He pleaded not guilty, and Judge Hughes ordered him held for a preliminary hearing. He's got a public defender.

His attorney asked for bail. Hughes set it at $5,000, and Wood has no hope of raising it.

Name: Milford Wood. Age 30. No address.

You ask the police reporter how Scissors is getting along. She tells you:

I just checked at the hospital. He's in good condition now. He's going home tomorrow.

Check the clips on the earlier story and bring things up to date for tomorrow's paper.

EXERCISE 7-4

After you had written your holdup story (Exercise 6-24), you got a call from your police reporter, who has new information about the holdup.

Blaine just died. Hospital called Maher, who told your police reporter.

Watson is back in the hospital. He has a concussion and is being held for observation.

Swift is also in the hospital. He says his back was injured when he was shoved by one of the robbers. Hospital says he may also have a broken rib.

Your police reporter has also learned that police think the robbers escaped in a stolen car. A hotel guest, Hubert Hawkins, 35, of Phoenix City, Alabama, told the hotel that his 1988 Olds is missing. He had left it parked in front of the hotel.

Police have disseminated a description of the car as well as the descriptions of the robbers.

Write a new lead on your holdup story. Slug it *new lead holdup*.

If you have to revise another paragraph, write the paragraph and slug it *insert 1 holdup*. Indicate on your copy where the new copy should be inserted by marking *insert 1* in the margin where the insert is to go.

EXERCISE 7-5

You are on rewrite today and taking calls from the Record's suburban and rural correspondents. A few minutes ago, your stringer from Brewster called. She had just been to the sheriff's office, where she got the following:

Barbara Helen Johnson — age 17 —

She was driving home from a dance at West Branch with Harold Faver, also 17. Car left the road and struck a tree. Barbara was thrown out of the car. She was dead when sheriff's road patrol arrived. This was about one a.m. Faver was alive. He is at Carolton General in serious condition. Multiple fractures of both legs, possible internal injuries.

Accident was on County Trunk D about five miles east of Brewster. Sheriff doesn't know what caused the accident. Faver hasn't been able to make a statement.

Your correspondent also told you:

Barbara is the daughter of Mr. and Mrs. John L. Johnson. He is cashier at the First National Bank of Brewster. Faver is son of Mr. and Mrs. Charles Faver. He is Brewster high school principal. Besides her parents, Barbara leaves one brother, John Jr., a lieutenant in the Marines. He is stationed at Parris Island, South Carolina. He is on his way home.

Funeral services day after tomorrow — the Rev. Eli Baker will officiate — 1st Methodist Church in Brewster — burial in Mount Olivet cemetery —

Your correspondent has no other information. Write the story. First edition deadline is approaching. Put a Brewster dateline on the story.

FYI: Brewster is the county seat of Madison County, just west of Washington County. The Record has a substantial circulation in the region between Carolton and Brewster.

EXERCISE 7-6

While you were on rewrite today, you got a call from the Door funeral home with a late death. You learned:

Died at hospital this morning — Harriet Ormsby — address is 347 West Arizona. No arrangements made yet.

The name seems familiar, so you check this morning's paper and find a story (Exercise 7-1) that fills in a few details. You are on deadline, so write what you have.

EXERCISE 7-7

You were on rewrite this morning and were asked to follow up on the Clarke fatal (Exercise 6-15). You made a few calls and learned:

From the coroner:

A pathologist called in to perform an autopsy has decided cause of death was drowning. Coroner says both he and the pathologist believe an electrical shock contributed to her death.

From Deputy Medford:

Girl was knocked into the water by a shock from an electrical charge she received when she touched a metal ladder on the dock.

Not sure yet of the source of the electrical charge. Sheriff's detectives and DNR are still investigating.

Quote another swimmer said he felt a tingling sensation in the water a few seconds before the girl fell unquote.

We're pretty sure there was enough electricity running through the ladder to knock the girl off her feet.

You must provide enough background in your second-day story to fill in readers who did not see the accident story in this morning's paper.

EXERCISE 7-8

The Record's police reporter has just called you with news that a prisoner is missing from the county jail.

Man apparently walked out of the jail this morning with a group of visitors. He wasn't missed until a few minutes ago.

Sheriff says he is sending description to police and sheriff's departments in nearby counties and expects to have the man back in custody before long.

Description: white, five 10, 170 pounds, blond hair cut short. Mustache. Wearing blue shirt and blue denim pants. Red and black running shoes. Age 30.

Name: Milford Wood.

He was in jail waiting a preliminary hearing. Not armed, but may be dangerous.

You have only a few minutes to catch the first edition with this story.

EXERCISE 7-9

When you returned from lunch today, the city editor handed you a memo. It reads: Follow this up. Ormsby has been at city hall this morning, raising hell. He told the mayor the city is responsible for his wife's death.

A clipping was attached to the memo (Exercise 7-6).

You call Mr. Ormsby and he tells you:

She'd be alive today if the ambulance hadn't taken so long to answer my call.

Slow service by the ambulance is directly responsible for my wife's death.

You're the cautious type, so you call the Record's police reporter and ask her to check on the ambulance call. She does and tells you:

Police department records show the ambulance responded in 50 minutes. This is average — according to the records — for non-emergency service.

Write your story. Explain the background carefully.

EXERCISE 7-10

Here is another accident story. Your editor suggested that you combine it with the earlier accident story you have been working on (Exercise 7-5).

BREWSTER — (today's date) — Two elderly Brewster brothers were killed yesterday when the car in which they were riding was struck by another car near Spring Green in Madison county.

Dead are:

John Storm, 75, and his brother, Nels, 72, both of Rural Route 1, Spring Green.

They were thrown from their car when it collided with a car driven by William Bergman, 25, of Brewster.

Bergman was taken to Cottage Hospital in Brewster, where he is reported to be resting comfortably. He has a slight concussion and a wrenched back, the hospital said.

The accident occurred about 4:40 p.m. on a gravel road near the brothers' farm. They were returning home from visiting a neighbor.

Sheriff's road patrol officers said Bergman's car came over the top of a hill on the wrong side of the road and struck the Storm car head-on.

The brothers were thrown from the car by the impact. They apparently were killed instantly. Bergman, who was wearing a seat belt, was not seriously hurt.

Bodies of the two brothers are at the Hagenbeck Funeral Home in Spring Green. There are no survivors. Arrangements are not complete.

EXERCISE 7-11

You are on rewrite this morning when the Riley funeral home calls with the Blaine obit. Write it for tomorrow's paper.

Blaine was a native of Carolton. Born here. Parents Harold E. Blaine, on Northwest faculty, professor of history, and Marilyn (Love) Blaine. Parents live at 708 West California.

Age 48. Home was in Oak Park, Illinois.

Blaine a graduate of Central high and Northwest college. Majored in business. He has an MBA from Georgia State.

He is a veteran of the Viet Nam war. Served four years in Air Force. Released from active duty as a major. Has Air Medal and Silver Star.

After war, Blaine went to work for General Motors in Detroit. In 1980 he left GM and went to work for International Harvester. Now works for Great Lakes International in Oakbrook, Illinois, as a regional representative.

His wife, Analoyce Spaulding, also native of Carolton. They were married in 1976. They have two children: John, age four, and MaryBeth, age seven.

Blaine has two brothers, Albert, who lives in Kansas City, Missouri, and Randolph, who lives in Honolulu, Hawaii. He also has a sister, Susan, who lives in Atlanta. She is married to Belmont E. Downs.

Blaine will be buried here in Evergreen cemetery. There will be a service at the First Methodist Church the day after tomorrow at 3 o'clock. The family has always attended this church. Rev. Hardy C. Boise, the 1st Methodist minister, will officiate at the services.

The funeral director tells you that Blaine's family will be at the funeral home from seven to eight tomorrow night.

Memorials: college scholarship fund at Central high.

Other: member, VFW, Northwest College Alumni Society of Chicago, 1st Methodist Ch., Oak Park, Illinois, World Trade Club (Chicago), Chicago Press club.

Write the obit. It requires a second-day lead.

EXERCISE 7-12

The Record's police reporter called in with this story. Your city editor asked you to take the call and write the story for tomorrow's paper. You talk with the reporter and learn:

Carolton fire department got a call at 7:45 about a fire in a building near the airport. Fire was in the Acme Fire and Accident Insurance Co. building. Building has six stories. Fire apparently started in an office on first floor, according to the fire marshal. There was smoke damage throughout the building. Loss was substantial on first floor. Nothing but offices on first floor.

The fire marshal thinks the fire was set. Some physical evidence, he says. He also thinks it was a professional job. He has the description of a man seen near the building early this morning shortly before the fire was reported. He has sent the description to authorities in six nearby states.

Firemen fought the fire for two hours before they had it out and were sure it would not start up again.

Fire equipment from West Side station responded. Central Station equipment went to scene when second alarm sounded.

Fire chief estimates damage as quote possibly hundred thousand dollars unquote.

Night watchman named Peters turned in the alarm.

Company spokesman Harold Spizman, vice president for public relations, says building closed today. No idea when mess will be cleaned up and employees can return to work. Lost time will add to fire and smoke damage loss.

EXERCISE 7-13

Your editor reminded you that earlier in the day you wrote a story (Exercise 5-22) about a fatal accident in which a Carolton man was killed east of the city. "Get that story back," she tells you, "and add it to the other fatals."

You now have three fatal accidents to handle in one story. Use an itemizing lead.

161

EXERCISE 7-14

A story you wrote yesterday about the auto accident on Highway 30 was in today's paper.

This morning your city editor had a call from a local attorney, Sue Dendramis. She was upset about the story. Roger Willoughby is her client. She has been to see him in the hospital and says your story about the accident does not jibe with the facts.

She told your editor:

After Willoughby was given first aid at the hospital, a blood sample was taken at Willoughby's request. No trace of alcohol in his blood.

Willoughby has had the flu and has been taking medication ordered by his doctor. He says the medication makes him drowsy. He had taken medicine just before leaving home yesterday. He says he fell asleep at the wheel and that was the cause of his accident.

Willoughby has been taken out of the police ward and is in a private room. He will be released this afternoon. He has minor cuts and bruises and a bump on the head. No concussion.

Your editor tells you:

She's talking libel and she may have a case. Drunk driving is taken pretty seriously right now. I think she'll be satisfied with a correction. Fix something up. And for gosh sakes, don't believe everything you're told.

Write a correction for tomorrow's paper. Read page 51 in "Practice Exercises." Follow the model for correcting errors in Figure 20.3 on page 419 of "News Writing." See also "News Writing," pages 32 and 33 and 411 through 414 on accuracy and verifying information and pages 447 through 451 on libel and privacy.

EXERCISE 7-15

While you were on rewrite today, the Record's police reporter called in with a story. Your city editor asked you to take it. You were told:

The coroner's office has the toxicology results on the teen-agers killed a couple of weeks ago in an automobile accident at a grade crossing here (Exercise 6-22).

No evidence of drugs.

No report on the survivor. Hospital took blood sample but will not release results.

Blood alcohol content of the three who were killed:
Ferreira, .11 percent; Carew, .07 percent; Dawson, .06 percent.

162

continued on next page

Under state law, a driver is considered impaired if blood alcohol content is .05 to .09 percent, and under the influence if blood alcohol content is .10 percent or higher. You check the clips before writing your story (Exercises 6-22 and 7-2). You find another story published several days after the accident, in which family members were quoted. You can use these quotes if you wish:

Richard Ferreira, father of driver:

Ricky used to drink beer at home while he watched television with his friends. I don't think he was a heavy drinker. Just an occasional beer. He didn't drink much away from home. He never touched hard stuff.

Frances Ferreira, mother of the driver:

He would have a few beers at the house. But you don't know what they do when they are out.

The Morning Record has been campaigning against drunken driving, and your editor wants a complete story on this. Background your story.

EXERCISE 7-16

You took another call from the Record's police reporter and were told that she had an odd accident story that you might be interested in. Use these notes to write a story for tomorrow's paper.

Accident about 9 a.m. on Airport Road in front of the Acme building. Road is narrow here — two lanes — and fire trucks were parked along side of the road, blocking one lane. There's a lot of early-morning traffic on this road — people on their way to work in the city and on the campus.

Two cars collided. One driven by John Ely, age 40, of Madison. He was alone. Other car driven by William Sears, age 37, of rural Carolton. His son Richard was in the car with him. Richard is ten. He was injured and taken to Carolton General hospital by ambulance.

Richard's father went to the hospital with him. Boy was treated for abrasions and contusions and a sprained left knee. Released after treatment.

Carolton police accident prevention bureau officers investigated the accident. Officers arrested Ely after they found a .32 pistol in the glove compartment of his car. Pistol was loaded. Penalty in Washington county for an unregistered gun is 12 months in jail or a $500 fine or both. Police are checking to see if gun is registered.

Police also found a bundle of marijuana weighing 25 pounds in the trunk of Ely's car.

Ely is being held for investigation.

EXERCISE 7-17

You were on rewrite again today and have been taking calls from funeral homes and writing obits. The last call was from the Jenkins Funeral Home with the Boomershine obit. A story about Mrs. Boomershine's death was in the paper yesterday (Exercise 5-33). Write the obit for tomorrow's paper. The facts:

Boomershine, Madeline Mary, born January 30, 1959. Services tomorrow at 11 at St. Thomas church. Father George Flynn will say a mass of Christian burial. Burial in church cemetery. Rosary at funeral home tonight at 7.

Survivors: mother, (Mrs.) Bridget Murphy, Winston-Salem, North Carolina — sister, Margaret Murphy, Ashtabula, Ohio — two brothers — Ian and Jack Murphy, North Andover, Massachusetts — husband, John E. Boomershine, Carolton — two sons, Brian, age six, and John, Jr., age eight.

Mrs. Boomershine died day before yesterday.

She was born in North Andover, Mass. Graduate of Holy Cross College. Majored in accounting. She worked here for The Morning Record.

Member daughters of the American Revolution, the St. Thomas church PTA. She did volunteer work at Holy Cross hospital.

Boomershine family lived at 386 West Nevada. They have been in Carolton five years. Came here from East Lansing, Michigan. Dr. Boomershine studied vet medicine at Michigan State.

You check with the Record's business manager and learn that Mrs. Boomershine's job title was assistant controller.

You review the clips on the shooting in which she was killed.

You check with the coroner and are told that the cause of death was a single gunshot wound to the head and that the coroner considers it a homicide.

EXERCISE 7-18

While you were on rewrite today, the Record's police reporter called in these stories. The times referred to are this morning. Pull all three stories together into one story. Be concise. This is for tomorrow's paper.

8:05 a.m. Carolton police received a call from Don Waldron, 115 E. Main. He is owner of Duke's Shell Service, 511 Territorial Road. He reported that his station had been broken into during the night. A cash drawer in the station office was pried open and some change is missing. About $35. The cigarette machine was also pried open and about $50 worth of cigarettes is missing. Waldron says he can't find a .32-caliber pistol, which he keeps in the top drawer of his desk.

164

continued on next page

He thinks the back door was pried open with a crowbar. He left the station at 11 last night and locked up himself. Everything was okay then. He opened at 7:55 this morning and discovered the burglary.

8:15 Police get another call. From Jack Snell, 252 West New York. He says that his Texaco station at 585 S. Grant — at the corner of Lexington Road — has been broken into. He's on his way over there now.

8:20 Police car calls in from 585 S. Grant. Officer says he has talked to the station attendant who discovered the break. Her name is Paula Simpson. She found the back door to the station open when she arrived about 8:00 o'clock. Officer says Mr. Snell has just arrived. He closed up last night and everything was secure when he left at midnight. Snell says $100 is missing from the cash register. Ms. Simpson says she called Snell as soon as she discovered the open back door.

8:30 Desk sergeant at police headquarters says he had a call a little earlier from College Standard Service, corner Newton Road and Territorial Road, report of an attempted robbery. Call was from station owner, Jack Delnay, 202 Maple. He said that when he opened up this morning he found evidence that someone had tried to pry open the back door of the station. There are pry marks on the door and door frame, he said. Station was not broken into. Nothing missing.

EXERCISE 7-19

While you were on rewrite this morning, the Record's police reporter called with word that the getaway car in yesterday's bank robbery had been found. She told you:

Car recovered in Green county this morning. Was parked at side of a dirt road a mile or so off U.S. 210 about 20 miles east of Carolton. State police have taken car to state police station here.

You ask about fingerprints:

Nothing on that yet. Police crime lab technicians are going over the car now.

You ask if there is anything in the car that might identify the bank robbers:

Lieutenant Begg says a ski mask was found under front seat that appears to match description of masks the men were wearing when they robbed the bank.

You'll have to check the original robbery story before you write (Exercise 6-9).

EXERCISE 7-20

This morning you are working on the rewrite desk when Door Brothers calls with an obit. Write this one for tomorrow's paper. It will require a second-day lead, since there was a brief story in this morning's paper about Mrs. Ormsby's death.

Deceased: Mrs. Harriet Ormsby — died at Carolton General — yesterday — in ill health for some time

Survivors: husband

two daughters: Mrs. Otto Twardzynski, Carolton

Mrs. James J. Sullivan, Carolton

one son: Harold, Cincinnati, Ohio

granddaughter: Laura Twardzynski

sister: Mrs. Henry Quill, Carolton

Services: First Congregational church — tomorrow — 2 p.m. with Rev. H.L. Nightingale in charge of service — burial in Forest Lawn cemetery

Other:

Mrs. Ormsby lived in Carolton all her life. Public schools, Carolton Central grad, Northwest college grad. Was a public school teacher 32 years. Retired in 1982.

Mrs. Ormsby born May 15, 1917. Member VFW Auxiliary, Professional Women's club, Carolton Senior Citizen's Organization, attended Congregational church.

Husband retired vice president of First National Bank.

You recall that she was hospitalized a day or so after the fire in the apartment building where the Ormsbys lived. She was in the cardiac care unit at the hospital. Her husband complained about delay in ambulance service when she was taken to the hospital. Because of his complaint, there was an autopsy. Medical examiner decided death was from natural causes.

EXERCISE 7-21

You took another call from the Record's police reporter. She gave you facts on a minor accident that happened this morning at the airport. Your city editor told you to shirttail it to the accident story you have been working on (Exercise 7-16).

At 9:15 there was a minor accident at the Washington county airport.

A light plane overshot the east-west runway and tipped over in a ditch.

No one was hurt. Two people in the plane.

Occupants were Marshall Parks and John O'Byrne.

First accident of any kind at the airport this year.

EXERCISE 7-22

Revise these sentences so as to avoid the use of the present participle. For example:

> They contended the meeting was one-sided, *refusing* to participate.

> They contended the meeting was one-sided and *refused* to participate.

1. Fire broke out in the basement, filling the building with smoke.

2. The emphasis on rules eliminated debate, making participation a passive activity.

3. A man poured paint thinner on a woman and set her on fire with a match, critically injuring her.

4. A storm spread snow and freezing rain over the area last night, contributing to at least four deaths.

5. High winds and blinding snow battered the area yesterday, leaving hundreds of people stranded in cars or trapped in their homes.

6. A severe thunderstorm rolled across the Carolton area last night, causing one pedestrian to be struck by a falling tree.

7. A freight train carrying toxic chemicals was wrecked near Carolton today, forcing nearly 1,000 people from their homes.

Number Correct _____

Student's Name _____

EXERCISE 7-23

Many editors object to the offhand creation of verbs from nouns. Although this is a normal and useful way of creating words, sometimes the results are awkward. Objections have been raised to the verbs underlined in these sentences. Revise the sentences to get rid of the underlined verbs:

1.   Mrs. Smith was taken to the hospital and <u>sedated</u>.

2.   The television personality <u>hosted</u> a late-night talk show.

3.   New technology has <u>antiquated</u> many practices.

4.   The company is <u>headquartered</u> in New York.

5.   The candidate <u>motorcaded</u> through downtown streets.

6.   The prisoner <u>suicided</u> in his cell at the city jail.

7.   Smith <u>guested</u> on the network talk show.

8.   The pilot <u>messaged</u> her destination to the control tower.

9.   The judges <u>medaled</u> the winners of the track meet.

10. They <u>elevatored</u> to the top floor of the new hotel.

Number Correct _____

Student's Name _____

169

EXERCISE 7-24

Edit this news story. Correct errors in style. Use standard editing marks and practices. Do *not* rewrite. There may be errors in spelling, grammar, usage or punctuation.

01   Two Carolton residents were injured yesterday in a

02   one car accident at Lexington Rd. and Scott Street.

03   They are:

04   Michael Blodgett, nine, of 215 S. Grant Street.

05   Helen M. Hays, 70, of 109 East Ohio Avenue.

06   The two were passengers in a car driven by Mrs.

07   Marianne Blodgett, 215 S. Grant Street.

08   Police said Mrs. Blodgett lost control of her car

09   when a bicycle ridden by Sally E. Walker, 11 swerved in

10   front of her. The accident occured at 9:00 a.m.

11   Mrs. Blodgett braked to avoid striking the bicycle.

12   Her car struck the curb and hit a 60 foot utility pole.

13   A crowd collected, but police managed to disperse them

14   before they became unruly.

15   Mrs. Hays at first refused medical attention but was

16   eventually convinced to go to the hospital. She was

17   taken to St. Luke's Hospital, treated, and released.

18   Sally Walker did not seem effected by her narrow

19   escape from injury.

20   "I'm alright," she told police Lt. James Smith, Jr.

Number Correct _____

Student's Name _____

EXERCISE 7-25

Edit this news story. Correct errors in style. Use standard editing marks and practices. Do *not* rewrite. There may be errors in spelling, grammar, usage or punctuation.

01   Walter Bettencourt, Jr., 84, former publisher of

02   The Morning Record, died yesterday (Nov. 20, 1986) in

03   Bal Harbor, Florida. He had been ill for some time.

04   Mr. Bettencourt retired in 1970. He made his home

05   here but spent the winter months in Fla.

06   Services will be held tomorrow at 11:00 a.m. at All

07   Saints Episcopal Church at 680 North Jackson Street.

08   Rev. Edward E. Evers, pastor of all Saints will

09   officiate. Burial will be in Evergreen Cemetary.

10   Survivors include his wife, the former Elizabeth

11   Morley Wilson; two daughters, Anne Courtwright and

12   Mrs. John (Margaret) Cowles; a son, Walter E., of

13   La Jolla, California; and a sister, Mrs. Harriet Wills,

14   of Dallas, Tex.

15   Mr. Bettencourt attended the Lenox School and earned

16   a B.A. at Harvard college. He was a veteran of WW II.

17   He enlisted after Pearl Harbor, went on active duty as

18   a sergeant and retired from the United States Army

19   Reserve in 1955 as a lieutenant general. He was recalled

20   to active duty for ten months in the early 1960's.

21   He started his newspaper career in Chicago, Illinois.

22   He bought "The Morning Record" here in 1961.

Number Correct _____

Student's Name _____

8 Speeches

Spelling

skillful, sacrilege/sacrilegious, permissible, miscellaneous, dissertation, deity, colloquium, bizarre, awful, commitment, disastrous, lien

Usage

tenet/tenant, tortuous/torturous, uninterested/disinterested, venal/venial, after/following, couple of, type of, allege, allegation

Newsroom Vocabulary

paraphrase, Q. and A., partial quotes, no-news lead, bridge, swing paragraph, print, publish, broadsheet, tabloid, optical character reader, scanner

Speeches

These topics are treated in detail in George A. Hough 3rd, "News Writing," fourth edition:

Speech Leads
Chapter 12, "The Speech Story: Leads," pages 225 through 240.

Speech Story Development
Chapter 13, "Writing the Speech Story," pages 243 through 279.

Quotation
Chapter 7, "Quotation," pages 111 through 132.

Panel Discussions
Chapter 13, "Writing the Speech Story," pages 264 through 266, Figure 13.5 on pages 265 and 266 and Figure 13.6 on page 267.

Public Meetings
Chapter 13, "Writing the Speech Story," pages 272 and 273 and Figures 13.9 and 13.10 on pages 273 through 276.

EXERCISE 8-1

1. Using this statement and speech tag, write a Type A and a Type B lead in the blanks.

   statement: The Administration is going to see that U.S. cities get more federal aid.

   speech tag: HUD Administrator Urban T. Beach said today.

   Type A _____ (that) _____

   _____

   _____

   Type B _____

   _____

   _____

2. Using this statement and speech tag, write a Type A and a Type B lead in the blanks.

   statement: The ability to read is the most basic and essential ingredient in education today.

   speech tag: State Superintendent Harold North said here today.

   Type A _____ (that) _____

   _____

   _____

   Type B _____

   _____

   _____

   How do Type A and Type B sentences differ? Is the connector *that* essential to a Type A sentence? What is the purpose of the comma in the Type B sentence?

Student's Name _____

EXERCISE 8-2

1. Using this statement and speech tag, write a Type A and a Type B lead.
    Note that the statement appears as a direct quotation. Change it to indirect
    and edit to make it more concise.

    statement: I strongly believe that we in government have an obligation
    to monitor our own advertising as carefully as we review the
    advertising of the private sector.

    speech tag: Henry E. Hopgood, director of the state consumer affairs
    department, said here today.

    Type A _____

    _____

    _____

    Type B _____

    _____

    _____

2. Using this statement and speech tag, write a Type A and a Type B lead in
    the blanks.

    statement: I think that all Americans must be allowed to vote, even if it
    means registering illiterate persons.

    speech tag: Dorothy Knowles, Washington County Democratic chairman,
    said here today.

    Type A _____

    _____

    _____

    Type B _____

    _____

    _____

Student's Name _____

EXERCISE 8-3

Indicate in the blanks at right whether the lead is a Type A lead, Type B lead or neither. Use the letter A, B or N to indicate your choice.

1. The print media are alive and well and in no danger of demise, John H. Sitco said here today.   _____

2. John H. Sitco gave a talk here today about the problems of the print media.   _____

3. The print media are in no danger of imminent death, the publisher of Flags magazine told the Adcraft Club today.   _____

4. John H. Sitco said here today that the print media are in no danger of demise.   _____

5. "The Print Media: A Healthy Industry" was the subject of a speech given here today by the publisher of Flags magazine.   _____

6. John H. Sitco, publisher of Flags magazine, discussed the health of the print media here today at a meeting of advertising executives.   _____

7. The print media are in no danger of imminent demise — they're alive and well, John H. Sitco, publisher of Flags magazine, said here today.   _____

8. We should hang on to our better-educated workers and retrain those who are poorly educated, the state labor commissioner said here Monday.   _____

9. The state labor commissioner said here Monday that the state should hang on to its better-educated workers and retrain those who are poorly educated.   _____

10. The state labor commissioner discussed employment in a speech here Monday.   _____

11. "Full Employment Now" was the title of a talk given here Monday by the state labor commissioner.   _____

12. The state labor commissioner told the directors of the Washington County Chamber of Commerce here Monday that the state must hold on to its better-educated workers.   _____

Number Correct _____

Student's Name _____

Speech Lead Form

Use this form for the lead for Exercise 8-4. Read the text of the speech in Exercise 8-4 and tailor it to this three-paragraph form.

First paragraph: a concise summary statement, a paraphrase — your own words.

Second paragraph: details that add to what was said in the first paragraph — again, in your own words.

Third paragraph: a follow-up of the first two paragraphs, with a direct quote that adds to and completes the ideas expressed in the first and second paragraphs.

    Charles E. Lafferty, professor of economics at Northwest College,

said here Monday that _____

_____

_____

    Lafferty said that _____

_____

    " _____

_____

_____," he said.

(more)

Student's Name _____

EXERCISE 8-4

Charles E. Lafferty, professor of economics at Northwest College, gave a talk last night on employment policy. You may say that he spoke to faculty and students of the School of Business on campus. Write a three-paragraph speech lead based on this excerpt from Lafferty's speech.

Despite the passage of the Equal Pay Act of 1963 and the ban on sex-based discrimination in employment in 1964, the female-male earnings gap remains significant and pervasive. Demands for pay equity will continue, therefore, to be heard in the courts, in the halls of state legislatures and the Congress, and at the bargaining table.

Since 1955, the median earnings of women working full-time throughout the year has fluctuated between 57 percent and 64 percent of the median for men.

Occupation appears to account for more of the earnings gap than any other factor, and the level of pay in any given occupation appears directly related to its sex composition. Overall, "women's work" pays an average of roughly $4,000 less per year than "men's work."

EXERCISE 8-5

Using this text, write a three-paragraph lead for a speech story. Follow the format shown in the speech-story blank on page 183. You may write a naming lead or a blind lead.

The speaker is Aaron Blakewell, executive director of the state Chamber of Commerce. He spoke last night at a meeting of the Rotary Club.

The text:

We in the business community have got to assume more aggressive leadership if we are going to improve the nation's educational system.

Business and industry must, of course, continue to invest heavily in research and development. But business and industry must put even more dollars into education.

There's no point in developing a higher technology and a more sophisticated means of production if we won't have educated workers.

We can improve our schools and our educational system. We can have a better educated work force.

Education is a local matter. And business and industry have a great influence on the local level. Let's act now. It will be too late when we can't find qualified people for new and replacement jobs.

EXERCISE 8-6

Using this text, write a three-paragraph lead for a speech story. Follow the format shown in the speech-story blank on page 183. You may write a naming lead or a blind lead. The speaker is Robert J. Wussler, president of Turner Broadcasting System. You can say he spoke on campus last night. The text:

Publishers who ignore the lessons television can teach them do so at their peril.

If I were a newspaper publisher, I'd apply many of the same principles at my newspapers that are being applied to television coverage of the news.

Your daily package needs concise organization. The audience has a low threshold for boredom. They have become used to fast flashes of information on the television screen.

I'd give sports a higher profile. The public has an insatiable interest in sports. Newspapers have been late in exploiting this interest.

EXERCISE 8-7

Barber B. Conable Jr., president of the World Bank and a former Republican congressman from New York, was on campus yesterday to speak at a meeting of the Young Republican Club. Write a three-paragraph speech lead based on this excerpt from his talk. The meeting Mr. Conable addressed was held in the Student Union.

I personally believe that representative government is alive and well and functioning the way it was intended to function: not very well. I really believe that our whole system of diffusion of powers was designed to build some impasse in the Government and to make it difficult for the Government to accumulate the necessary power to make major decisions.

I think we are a pluralistic society and are likely to stay that way until such time as the Government becomes more efficient. And it can't become more efficient unless it changes its basic outline, simply because we have spread its powers so broadly that it takes a crisis to bring it together.

We are really a crisis-activated institution. And that has all kinds of interesting implications. It means that we don't do anything unless there's consensus out there that unless we do something, something very bad is going to happen. And that means we're almost inevitably behind the curve.

EXERCISE 8-8

Write a news story based on this excerpt from a talk given on campus yesterday by Dr. Bernard Lown. Dr. Lown is on the faculty of the School of Public Health at Harvard. He is founder and co-president of International Physicians for the Prevention of Nuclear War. He spoke at a symposium on nuclear disarmament sponsored by the college's Alumni Association.

Nuclear testing is one of the motor forces which drive the arms race. It is the key to the development of new nuclear weapons systems, systems more destabilizing, less verifiable and more provocative than their predecessors. A ban on nuclear testing is the first step in reversing the steady march toward the brink. It is not a panacea. It is a first step. Why can't my government take that first small step?

EXERCISE 8-9

This is the text of an essay by Dr. Sissela Bok. Dr. Bok, a philosopher, is on the faculty of Brandeis University. The essay was written to coincide with publication in early 1983 of Dr. Bok's book "Secrets: On the Ethics of Concealment and Revelation." You can treat this like the text of a speech and write a news story for tomorrow's paper.

Never, except in wartime, has America experienced such a rapid, extensive buildup of government secrecy as in the last few years. The increase has come about through changes so disparate, often inconspicuous and at times so sudden as to elude adequate public debate. Together, these changes signal a sharp reversal of the last two decades' movement toward greater public access to government information. It is time to assess the cumulative impact and to decide whether they truly serve the nation's best interests.

In the name of national security, federal officials have moved to bring about not only sweeping increases of secrecy about government activities, but also new forms of control over the private sector. They have sought to curtail access to information in several ways: by limiting the scope of the Freedom of Information Act, by giving administrators greater power to classify documents as secret and by expanding covert activities of the Central Intelligence Agency and Federal Bureau of Investigation both at home and abroad.

The government has also moved to exercise greater control over scientists, educators, students and business employees. It is pressing for new restrictions on commerce and exports. It has asked for closer oversight over scientific research and publication beyond what is already in the domain of classified information. It has sought to exercise stricter control over the foreigners' access to university courses, libraries, laboratories and scientific symposiums. (Thus, in 1982 the Pentagon blocked the presentation of about 100 papers at an international convention on optical engineering — doing so, to the authors' consternation, just before the papers were to be delivered.)

continued on page 188

187

To some extent, such efforts are understandable. Governments feel more vulnerable as ever fewer military and other secrets are safe from the new technologies of intelligence. Measures such as the Freedom of Information Act have at times been used for purposes sponsors never expected, such as corporate espionage. Leaking adds to the growing amount of information openly available. Leaders of democracies perceive a dangerous imbalance between the relative openness of their societies and the extensive controls exercised by the Soviet Union and other countries. International tensions and the arms race increase the vulnerability still further. In response to growing fears that commercial, scientific and military secrets will be stolen or simply drift abroad, the call goes out for ever stricter and more extensive measures of control.

While understandable, such policies risk weakening, not strengthening, any nation that adopts them, for they rest on two illusions.

The first is misplaced confidence in the power of traditional methods of official secrecy — censorship, for instance, or crackdowns on leaking. (New techniques, from ever more sophisticated devices for eavesdropping to miniature cameras and cryptography, have vastly expanded the amount of information at the disposal of those with the resources to acquire it.) Short of turning an open society into a garrison state, it will not be possible to restrict trade, scholarship, scientific exchanges and news reporting enough to achieve the desired security. (Even if such controls could somehow be imposed domestically, they would hardly stop the continued flow of scientific and technological information between countries.)

The second illusion is the notion that increased government secrecy carries no risks — that it is innocuous, much like a blanket that can be put on for protection or taken off at will. No democracy can afford such complacency. Secrecy almost invariably comes to conceal far more than was originally planned. And the appeal to national security offers a handy reason to avoid public scrutiny of neglect, mistakes and wrongdoing. It has been invoked to cover up matters the public has every right to know: military blunders, cost overruns, White House "plumbers," enemies lists.

The growth of official controls over information in the private sector, in addition to its political dangers, also risks damaging trade, innovation of every kind and research. Already, scientists warn that many will turn away from fields threatened with censorship. Paradoxically, the controls officials impose to buttress national security may wear it down.

Given such dangers, the presumption against increased government controls is strong. Advocates of stricter controls owe it to the nation to show where existing provisions for administrative and military secrecy fall short. They must demonstrate that each new measure serves indispensable and attainable purposes, and provide convincing safeguards against risks that it may do harm, spread and invite abuse.

EXERCISE 8-10

These are excerpts from remarks made today by President Miguel de la Madrid Hurtado of Mexico. President de la Madrid is on campus for a symposium sponsored by the Cordell Hull Center for International Programs. He spoke at a plenary session in the Law auditorium on the Northwest College campus.

Today, Latin America demands a new understanding between its countries and the industrialized countries of the hemisphere. The profound changes that have taken place make it imperative to open new channels of cooperation and trade that will insure effective political communication and that will meet the development needs of our region.

The countries of Latin America seek, in conditions of equality and mutual respect, a new kind of relationship with the United States. They want to do away with any shadow of subordination while preserving sovereignties and national identity. For us, independence is not a part of our past but a daily conquest. It is the supreme value of our history.

Promising democratic developments that are evident in various Latin American nations call for the full acceptance of pluralism. A uniform style of democratic life cannot be imposed on anyone. Democracy, by definition, cannot use the arms of tyranny.

For us, peace and development have been and continue to be fundamental issues. The necessary cooperation with the countries of the north should be free of any political conditions, discriminatory criteria or demands for impossible reciprocity. Justice and well-being are the only effective guarantees for warding off the dangers of instability and a wide-spread conflagration in Latin America.

Unfortunately, there has been a steep decline in the region's economic activity in recent years, and the standard of living of the Latin American people has seriously deteriorated.

It is true that our difficulties derive from domestic factors, but there are also decisive elements that lie within the structure of the international economy.

External indebtedness, high interest rates and the growing protectionism practiced by the advanced economies are, at the same time, the cause and the effect of the crisis.

Developing nations seem to be trapped in an iron circle of indebtedness and the cancellation of progress. High rates of interest decrease investment, reduce export capacity and thus make a greater inflow of foreign exchange impossible. An essential remedy will be for the raw materials and manufactured goods of our countries to have greater access to international markets and for protectionism to be eliminated.

continued on page 190

189

We are convinced that the Central American conflict is a result of the economic deficiencies, political backwardness and social injustice that have afflicted the countries of the area. We therefore cannot accept its becoming part of the East-West confrontation, nor can we accept reforms and structural changes being viewed as a threat to the security of the other countries of the hemisphere.

The United States must uphold its ideals both at home and abroad. It should insure that the future of its people is based on tolerance, understanding, recognition of foreign identities and respect for the wishes of others.

I am confident that the American people will invariably prefer the limited exercise of power to the use of force, and reason to domination.

EXERCISE 8-11

The Rev. Jesse L. Jackson spoke on campus last night. His speech in the Student Union was sponsored by the All-College Student Association. Write a three-paragraph lead based on this excerpt from Jackson's speech.

In life Martin Luther King Jr. projected himself as "a drum major for justice." In death he is being projected by the media as a non-threatening "dreamer."

We must resist this weak and anemic memory of a great man. Why is it that, even though Dr. King was perhaps the greatest practitioner of applied theology of our era, President Reagan cannot honor his memory without qualification — implying he was a Communist agent instead of a prophet in the Judeo-Christian tradition? Why is it that so many politicians today emphasize that Dr. King was a dreamer and add, almost by accident, that, oh yeah, his dreams became reality?

I submit that they want to project him as a dreamer because they wish us to remember this great leader as an idealist without substance, not as the concrete reality he was. Dr. King was a realist with ideals, he was not an idealist without reality. The only way to honor him is to make his memory a continuing concrete reality and be driven by his spirit. We honor him by challenging the Justice Department to enforce the Voting Rights Act and end denial of voter access and participation. We honor him by increasing voter registration and fighting to make the poor visible again. We dishonor him by propping up a system that is killing and maiming thousands in South Africa and the Philippines and practicing violence in Central America.

Dr. Martin Luther King Jr. was not assassinated for dreaming. He was assassinated for acting and challenging the Government.

We honor Dr. King most by action for justice. His birthday should be celebrated by action, not just speeches and songs about action.

EXERCISE 8-12

Don Edwards, chairman of the House Judiciary Subcommittee on Civil and Constitutional Rights, spoke on campus last night. His appearance was sponsored by the Carolton chapter of the American Civil Liberties Union. Write a story for tomorrow's paper, using this advance copy of his text.

From reading recent news stories on disagreement within the United States Commission on Civil Rights over the meaning of equality, one might think it is fine for the commission to be a debating society for its members and that the debates are based on factual research. Nothing could be further from the truth.

The commission was established in 1957 to serve as the Federal Government's independent watchdog over civil-rights matters and to monitor Federal laws and policies with respect to discrimination or denials of equal protection of the laws. For 25 years, the commission met its mandate well, exposing discrimination throughout the country and evaluating administrations both Republican and Democratic.

In 1983, when President Reagan insisted on firing commissioners who criticized his enforcement policies not just in affirmative action, but also on such issues as the tax exemption for Bob Jones University and his opposition to strengthening the Voting Rights Act, the real issue was whether the commission would retain its independent watchdog function. We have our answer. Not a single monitoring report or statement on enforcement in any Federal agency has been published since the commission was reconstituted in 1983. One of its major functions has simply ceased.

As we examine the handiwork of the reconstituted commission, keep in mind that it is no longer an independent body, but is now simply an arm of the Reagan Administration. As Clarence M. Pendleton Jr., commission chairman, told the Eagle Forum, the Phyllis Schlafly group, recently: "I am proud to be on President Reagan's team. It is an honor to develop civil rights policy with other distinguished Americans, gentlemen like Brad Reynolds, Clarence Thomas and Edwin Meese."

Consistent with the policy goals of the Administration, the commission has replaced state advisory committee members who insisted on reporting on civil-rights problems in their states that called Administration policy into question. On the rare occasion when the commission does issue statements, they coincide with Administration policy, including opposition to the Civil Rights Restoration Act and pay equity as a means of ending wage discrimination.

Perhaps most tragic, the commission has abandoned its role as a fact-finding investigatory agency on civil rights. The majority of the commission has developed a habit of announcing conclusions on subjects under consideration before any investigation takes place. We know what the results of studies will be before they've even

continued on page 192

begun. For example, Chairman Pendleton, Vice Chairman Morris B. Abram and Linda Chavez, staff director, first announced their opposition to comparable worth and then commissioned a study. Not surprisingly, the study also rejected comparable worth.

It strains reason to claim intellectual rigor for the single report issued by the commission over the last 20 months. Such a claim flies in the face of such objective assessments as that done by the General Accounting Office on the comparable-worth report. After a lengthy analysis, the G.A.O. found that the commission defined comparable worth differently from advocates of comparable worth, and rejected the concept based on that different definition. Furthermore, G.A.O. found that the report was filled with inconsistencies and mistakes of fact.

The American taxpayers deserve a Civil Rights Commission that will be an independent watchdog to see that the laws are enforced so that we may someday achieve true equal opportunity in our society. Our nation also deserves a commission that will restrain its penchant for announcing conclusions until some honest fact gathering is done. Unfortunately, we now have neither, and a debating society, however eloquent the debaters, is no substitute for a strong, independent Civil Rights Commission.

FYI: Edwards is a Democrat and represents the 10th Congressional District of California. His home is in San Jose.

EXERCISE 8-13

James Vorenberg, dean of the Harvard Law School, was on campus yesterday to give the Law Day address at Northwest College. He spoke in the LaFollette Auditorium to Law School faculty and students, but his remarks, as you can see, were directed primarily to the students. Write a story for tomorrow's paper based on this excerpt from his speech.

As lawyers, you will be the objects of admiration and cynicism. The legal profession today offers ample justification for both. One thing is clear: It needs the best you can give it. Those to whom being a lawyer is just the means to personal wealth and power may gain both, but they will miss many of the satisfactions the profession offers.

Think about yourselves as lawyers in three different, but closely related, roles.

First, you will represent people with difficulties and fears that overwhelm them and who will turn to you for help in making their way through a maze of rules and institutions. For the poor, this means confronting the landlord who will not provide heat or remove lead paint, the local welfare office that has cut off benefits or a social service agency that threatens to remove a child from a parent who lacks the knowledge or strength to fight back. Even for those who can pay a fee,

continued on next page

the events that call for a lawyer can be intimidating — a nasty lawsuit, the potential loss of one's business, a marital breakup or trouble with a government agency. Whether you are in private practice, government or a legal service office, you will have the special responsibility of dealing with people when they are most vulnerable, and will enjoy the special satisfaction that comes from providing help when it is most needed.

Second, as a lawyer you can be an adventurer, or joint venturer with others, in seeking needed changes in laws, legal processes, the legal profession — and in society. Almost every major public issue involves law, and some of your predecessors have played heroic roles in such quests as those for racial equality, for arms control, for children's rights, for environmental protection and for international human rights. None of those issues is behind us.

Within the legal system, your generation must deal with courts that are increasingly overwhelmed by caseloads and with the need, as a matter of simple fairness, to provide legal assistance to the poor. And the legal profession itself is undergoing fundamental changes as large law firms get larger, the competition for legal business gets fiercer and pressure increases to find alternatives to litigation for resolving disputes.

Third, think of yourselves as intellectuals who bring creative abilities and imagination to the solution of difficult problems. One of the great pleasures of being a lawyer is seeing hard thinking translated into the results you are seeking for your clients. Whether you are planning a complex corporate merger, writing a brief for an appellate court or seeking to persuade a judge to place a convicted defendant on probation, you should bring to your task all the intellectual power and craftsmanship of which you are capable.

I hope your life in the law will enable you to see yourselves as respected and independent professionals. During the recent controversy about whether a lawyer must divulge a client's commission, or planned commission, of a crime, it was asked whether a lawyer is just a "hired gun." That expresses the issue too narrowly.

What is really at stake is your integrity. You will have to develop your own standards of what you will and will not do, and be ready to be judged by them. Some of the issues will be agonizingly difficult. In particular cases, you may find that the interests of a client conflict with your view of the public interest or your sense of justice. More broadly, you will have to decide to what you are willing to devote your talents.

Whether you are working in private practice or public service, in small or large offices, you will share responsibility for the processes of justice that are a measure of the decency of a society. It is only fair that you carry this responsibility, for if lawyers who build their livelihoods on those processes are not morally obliged to serve as their guardians, who does have that obligation?

EXERCISE 8-14

Write a news story based on this speech by Edward T. Foote 2nd, president of the University of Miami. He spoke today to the faculty of the School of Education at Northwest College.

Higher education is becoming increasingly commercialized. Colleges and universities are big business. That much is clear. What is not clear is how they will survive as educational institutions.

Until recently, higher education occupied a special, quiet place in our culture. A college education, after all, was central to the American dream. The decade of the 1960s burst this cocoon, spun for generations by a respectful public. The developing commercialization of higher education has its roots in the politicization of higher education during those years.

Students became the focus of political resistance to the Vietnam War; campuses swirled in controversy. The older generation winced. Even without the social upheavals of the 1960s, universities would have commanded more public attention because of their swelling size. With those upheavals, they got a lot more than they wanted.

Meanwhile, higher education became a magnet for new laws and increased litigation. Such issues as affirmative action, draft registration, and faculty tenure gave lawyers a field day in academe. Federal auditors swarmed over university research accounts. The Supreme Court decision that the National Collegiate Athletic Association violated antitrust laws in negotiating television rights for football games is only the most recent example of the trend. The net result of all this has been to draw the university even further into the marketplace.

Along with Government penetration came the conviction that colleges and universities, now immensely complex institutions, were outgrowing the old ways of doing business. Computers, among a host of technological advances of the 70s, opened new worlds to educators and changed traditional management practices. Trustees, often from the arena of big business, exerted more control. Professors formed unions to win more economic power. Their innocence fading, universities flexed their own muscles in the larger world.

Thus, on the eve of Ronald Reagan's 1980 victory, educators had become concerned with almost everything but education. Mr. Reagan's election did not make the educator's task easier.

Astonishing many who recalled Sputnik only too well, he pledged drastic cuts in Federal scholarship and loan programs and in support for basic research, asking industry to pick up the slack.

Coincidentally, he was elected just as the number of college-age students declined for the first time in a generation, a trend expected to continue until the 1990s. The shrinkage of the student market and Federal support forced higher education into a spirited search

194

continued on next page

for new sources of funds, accelerating further the drift toward commercialization.

There is now a fierce competitive scramble for the available students. At a gathering of college presidents, one is likely to hear more talk of marketing techniques than of Shakespeare. Educators turn increasingly to "commercial" practices like advertising. Universities undertake joint ventures with entrepreneurs. Scientists become rich from patents. Trustees experiment with venture capitalism.

The demand for marketable skills presses heavily on the curriculum. Threatened increasingly are rigorous courses in the arts and sciences, the core knowledge of what has traditionally been considered the educated person. "Professional" programs proliferate at lower and lower levels, channeling interest too early for truly educating anyone, including professionals, well.

Some changes, such as sophisticated strategic planning, are beneficial, but many are not. Temporary market conditions should not dictate the curriculum. An education is for life, for a person's last job as much as his first.

The question for most colleges and universities is not one of survival. Most are tough survivors. Education itself is not. It is a fragile process requiring not only constant attention, but deep reverence for its root principles. Among these principles is the requirement that thinkers — students and scholars — be free to experiment, create, learn, dream in their own way.

The marketplace cannot afford such short-term luxuries. Yet America cannot afford to abandon them, for long-term they are not luxuries. Learning is not to be rushed. Research leading to new discoveries takes time. Profitability is fundamentally incompatible with the essence of a university. A department of philosophy will never be profitable, but without one there is no university.

Maintaining a strong, independent system of higher education is a task too important to leave to the whims of the marketplace. This is no time to be preparing half-educated leaders or failing to invest for the 21st century, whether the challenge is cancer, robotics or a weapons system. Much needed — and soon — is a national commitment to rebuild our strapped universities, buy the necessary computers, bring our outmoded laboratories up to date, encourage our students to learn to the limits of their capacity. The commitment must include private philanthropy and collaboration with industry, of course, but it will fail if it does not also include sustained, heavy investment of public funds.

EXERCISE 8-15

You covered a speech last night by Ronald E. Rhody, now senior vice president and director for corporate communications, Bank of America, San Francisco. Mr. Rhody was here for a regional meeting of the Public Relations Society of America. His talk was one of several on the relations of business and the press. The text:

I believe an unfettered press is absolutely essential to the survival of democracy. I believe in the role of the press as a watchdog of our freedoms. But I also believe in responsibility. And I fear that the excesses and irresponsibility being practiced by a few highly visible segments of the press — and being recognized by a public becoming increasingly sophisticated in the ways of the media — are eroding the public faith, support and credibility the press absolutely must have to do its job. Not in its best interests, but in ours — as free citizens in a free society.

The broad claim that journalism has had for its position in our society is that it does — or is supposed to — provide us with a powerful, largely incorruptible, impartial third party —one that speaks for the general interest. Walter Lippmann saw journalism as an institution standing apart, charged with supplying society with reliable, impartial information.

When the reliability of that information becomes increasingly suspect and when the facade of impartiality erodes, that claim is put in jeopardy — and so are we.

Unfortunately, the reliability of much of the information we're receiving is becoming increasingly suspect and the facade of impartiality is crumbling as people become more and more aware that what they see and hear every day — in media that they trust — may be manipulated by the reporter to make his or her case, or fabricated out of whole cloth entirely, to advance a particular career or point of view.

We do a considerable disservice to ourselves, the public and the press when we fail to insist on two simple but absolutely critical requirements for responsible journalism — fairness and accuracy.

Most of us have on our staffs people whose reportorial skills are as good, whose writing talent is as bright, whose intelligence is as high, and whose ethics are as lofty as any with whom we deal in the media.

There is no reason, then, to settle for anything less than accuracy and fairness.

The responsible journalists I know feel the same way.

I say these things constructively, because nobody has a bigger stake in a strong and healthy press in this country than business.

continued on next page

I have to say now that most of the misimpressions, or errors, or unfairness that so many are so concerned about is business's own fault.

The fact that the public may be misinformed on key economic or business issues, may be misled about our respective operations and intentions, is largely our own doing. We have permitted this because, either out of fear of criticism or controversy, we have failed to take the initiative.

There is no question in my mind that the business and financial press in this country understands business better than business understands the press.

There is also no question in my mind that many business managers are suffering, unnecessarily, from a "the press is out to get us" complex.

There is no anti-business bias among journalists per se. It's a matter of reference. The press tends to be liberal. Business tends to be conservative. The press does have a bias — a populist bias — and is inclined to see the world divided into two groups: "special interests" — read "big institutions" — and "the people." There is a good guys/bad guys mentality at work here.

Rather than fume and pout about reportage that is wrong, misleading, or just downright insulting, we should take the initiative and correct it.

If it is the nature of the news business that complex information must be simplified — even oversimplified — and packaged in a form that interests and entertains — we should get with the program. It seems to me that simplification is too important a job to leave to an uninformed reporter. We should do it ourselves.

To do so, we may have to overcome, within our own organizations, the objections of attorneys that all possible caveats be present, or of technicians that all possible details be included, or the insistence of senior managers that it isn't possible to understand fact A unless it is seen in context with number B.

We need to be prepared with understandable, concise, and interesting explanations of our actions and intentions. We should not continue to leave this critical responsibility to an uninformed reporter in hopes he or she will be willing — and able — to interpret our message correctly to the public.

I believe there is such a thing as the public's right to know. Not everything and not instantaneously, but I believe people do have a right to know about those things which affect their health, or safety, or well-being, or the quality of their lives.

We in business and industry conduct ourselves, however, as if government and the media have the exclusive franchise to serve

continued on page 198

197

that right. I don't believe that is, or should be, the case. I believe we own a large share of the franchise, too — and must take the initiative to use it.

That may mean — probably will mean — that in the future we will begin to stop relying so heavily on the media as "distributors" of information about us, and instead, will start taking our information directly to the publics we serve and who touch us. Developing technologies will allow us to do so.

I believe we, in our institutions, have as much right and responsibility to serve the public's right to know as do media or the government, and I believe we should take the initiative, by whatever means are necessary, to insure that full and fair information about our activities is made available to the publics we touch. In the public interest, nothing less is acceptable. In the public interest, nothing more is necessary.

EXERCISE 8-16

You covered a speech last night on the Northwest College campus. The speaker was John B. Parrish, professor emeritus of economics, the University of Illinois. The occasion was the annual faculty and student convocation of the School of Arts and Sciences. Write about 400 words for tomorrow's paper. The text of Parrish's speech, given to you in advance, follows:

Critics argue that women, despite strong gains in the business world, have been kept out of the board rooms by continuing male prejudice. They usually point out that of the 500 largest industrial companies, only one has a woman as top executive (Katharine Graham of the Washington Post Company).

That picture may be accurate, but it hardly tells the whole story. It takes a generation for a man who starts at the bottom of the corporate hierarchy to reach the top. It has only been 10 years since women began entering the business world in large numbers. Clearly it is too early to say how far — or high — they can go.

But other things are changing, too. Now, when they find the ladder to the top blocked, women are increasingly leaving to start their own businesses. The estimated 20 newly minted, self-made millionaires who are women would seem to offer proof that the switch is being accomplished with considerable success.

President Reagan has called this the "Age of the Entrepreneur," and he might well have added — "especially for women." Their participation in the most dynamic segment of the United States economy — small entrepreneurial businesses — is particularly impressive.

In 1960, women owners accounted for only about one of every ten start-up companies. By 1985, their share of these enterprises had risen to one in three, and if present trends continue, women will

continued on next page

start half of all new businesses by 1995. For a number of reasons, it seems likely that the trend will continue.

First, women today exercise much greater control over the timing and number of children they have. In addition, it is now much safer to have children after the age of 30. These two developments enable women to pursue several paths — marriage, childrearing, school, a career — and to a greater extent than ever before.

Second, more women are getting college degrees, which tends to enhance upward economic mobility. In 1950, women made up about 30 percent of college students. In 1982, 52 percent of the nation's college students were women. This trend has been reinforced by a shift away from the liberal arts toward business and professional training.

In addition to being better prepared, women who run their own businesses today can also find more supporting services than they could a decade earlier. Dozens of "women in business" books and magazines are now available. A number of professional associations, such as the National Association for Female Executives, have been created to provide special counseling to women.

Federal equal credit laws and changing attitudes have given women greater access to credit by making it easier for women to borrow money and to establish credit in their own names. And the activities of women's equal rights organizations, although difficult to quantify, have probably encouraged women to strike out on their own in business.

The final development that should accelerate women's participation in business involves the changing structure of the American economy. Women have been attracted particularly to service industries, which have enjoyed a robust expansion in jobs since World War II.

Women's start-up businesses will be concentrated in the service areas, thus expanding this sector even more. Most college women will marry, and have children as well as careers. Their husbands will probably also have demanding careers. These high-income, low-time families will need and be able to pay for an ever widening range of services — child care, travel, cleaning, investment and accounting — creating more demand for new service jobs and businesses.

These portents may be ironic. The high-income, two-earner families will enjoy a rising standard of living, leaving behind the poorly educated, single-earner families. The new freedom for women may create a wider spread between the haves and have-nots.

EXERCISE 8-17

You were assigned last night to cover a panel discussion at the annual Press Institute on the Northwest College campus. Panelists were Charles T. Brumback, president of the Chicago Tribune; Lloyd G. Schermer, president of Lee Enterprises; and Joel H. Walker, publisher of the Troy Daily News in Troy, Ohio. The topic of the panel was "The Future of American Newspapers." Write a story for tomorrow's paper based on these excerpts from the discussion.

Walker:

I'm optimistic about this business. There'll be newspapers in some form for as long as any of us are alive. And there'll be radio, television, cable, home video, computers and a lot of other information systems that aren't even developed yet.

Schermer:

I believe the daily newspaper occupies a unique and essential place in our society but will continue to do so only if we as publishers and managers act rather than react. The challenge for newspapers in the next decade will be the battle for revenues.

Brumback:

I see nothing but promise in the future of big city newspapers. I do not see a major threat from video text or the newspaper-in-the-home concept. Within the next 20 years, I don't see computers developing to the point where electronic data bases will be more useful than print data bases. Your investment in new press equipment is safe.

Walker:

If the small newspapers in this country are going to survive into the next century — and it's only a few years away — they are going to have to produce compelling, interesting, truly informative products.

Schermer:

High on our priority list must be a better quality product, but perhaps not in a traditional sense. We have to get much closer to what our readers want — not what our editors want. Furthermore, I believe our mission is going to change. We can no longer just be observers and reporters of the news. We will have to get out and create events, news and advertising. We have a unique role to play in our communities by becoming a catalyst for change.

Brumback:

Content, quality and packaging of the big city newspaper will change with the times. Reproduction quality will improve significantly as

200

continued on next page

a result of new technology. Advertising revenues will improve as newspapers once again are recognized as a mass medium.

Walker:

If publishers are going to try to survive with undereducated writers and correspondents, with low-quality photos, with sloppy graphic design and poor presswork, they're kidding themselves. We can't make it with ad people who are merely pick-up clerks rather than aggressive, innovative salesmen. And survival will be difficult with editors and reporters who aren't tuned in — tuned not only to the community, but to the area, state, the U.S. and the world.

Schermer:

We must strive to make our newspapers a place where all our employees are turned on every day by their jobs. Newspapers where people come to work not because they have to, but because they want to.

How do we find the people we will need to reinvent our newspapers for a more secure and fulfilling future? Well, we are not going to be able to go out and hire that kind of talent off the street. We are going to be required to develop them from within our organizations. Our success will be determined by how effective we are as managers and leaders.

Brumback:

I think you will see newspapers following the lead of USA Today. They will be more colorful, with better graphics and tighter editing. The responsibility to inform readers on local, regional and national issues will continue to require in-depth coverage as in the past.

Walker:

Our primary mission is to provide our readers, our community, with good, solid local news coverage. And local news coverage, no matter how you define it, must not be shortchanged. Local news needs strong writing and capable people to report it. It can't be left to clerks and stringers. Good reporters and good editors are essential. Readers are becoming more sophisticated every day. They know when a story is covered and written correctly or when it is just left to a nonprofessional. Our scope must be broader. Local news is more than covering council and school board meetings. It's more than running the photo of the homecoming queen. It's more than covering Friday night high school football games.

(The panelists answered questions from the audience at the end of their presentation.)

Brumback: (In response to a question about the future of USA Today.)

continued on page 202

201

USA Today is one of the most significant influences on newspapers today. It represents the first major change in newspapers since the introduction of color. Its punchy, TV style of writing and editing is being copied by many in the industry. Every day there are fewer and fewer skeptics about the future of this innovative product.

Walker: (In response to a question about skimpy coverage of world affairs in smaller newspapers.)

For three consecutive years during the Vietnam war, we sent a reporter there to interview and take pictures of servicemen from our area.

Just this spring, our managing editor spent two weeks in Russia, traveling with a group of citizen diplomats from our area. Her subsequent series of stories and photos — and a special section we produced — evoked as much response from readers as anything we've ever done.

EXERCISE 8-18

Albert Shanker, president of the American Federation of Teachers, was in town yesterday to speak to the annual meeting of the Washington County Teachers Association. He spoke in LaFollette Auditorium on campus. Write a story about his talk for tomorrow's paper.

In the last few years states have passed laws and issued regulations requiring students to take math, English, science and social studies. In many states students can't graduate without passing competency tests in these areas. But it is easier to pass laws and issue regulations than to implement them. How will the students master these subjects unless there are teachers who can teach them? The warning signals are everywhere. In spite of talk about tougher and higher standards, more and more uncertified and unqualified teachers are being hired across the country. Tens of thousands of classes are taught by misassigned teachers — teachers qualified in one subject teaching a different subject in which they are not qualified.

Unless there are major changes, schools across the country will employ more and more teachers who cannot pass minimum competency tests themselves. Once hired, such teachers will have to be carefully watched and supervised, thus making the job even less attractive to the competent.

The recent report of the California Commission on the Teaching Profession is revolutionary. While it calls for major improvements in teacher salaries and working conditions, it goes far beyond. It calls for turning teaching into a true profession by making it self-governing in the same way other professions are. It would create a teaching standards board, with a majority of teachers, which would establish standards for entry and advancement in the profession and establish requirements for creating new categories of teachers

continued on next page

such as mentors, peer evaluators and staff developers as part of a career ladder plan. It would establish standards for suspending or revoking teaching credentials. In addition —

It calls for a radical alteration of teacher preparation and training by requiring all teachers to have a four-year liberal arts education with subject-matter majors and minors, followed by a year of graduate study in professional education and a one-year residency.

It creates a "board certified" classification, so that teachers with added study and outstanding demonstrated skills can gain recognition and earn more on the basis of objective statewide procedures.

Teachers would get full salary credit if they moved from one district to another, giving them the same opportunity as other professionals — or anyone else — to move within a career from one location to another.

It calls on the legislature and school boards to establish a widespread system of sabbaticals.

The report restructures the teaching career, since under the plan teachers would not only perform their usual classroom functions, but would also help train new teachers and have sufficient time to conduct research and to share ideas with colleagues. Teachers would not be mere hired hands doing what they were told by supervisors. They'd be more like senior partners in a law firm. In a recommendation on how to "involve teachers in school decision-making," the commission said teachers should be involved in a "range of responsibilities," including selection of new teachers, evaluation of teachers' performance, helping establish goals for the school, development and coordination of curriculum across grade levels and within departments, design and conduct of inservice education at the school site, and the organization of the school for effective instruction, among other items.

Another major change called for is that schools would be required to publish an index to inform the public at least every two years of the conditions for learning and teaching in every school in the state. Among the items that would be reported on in such an index, the commission said, should be class size, teacher assignments outside the area of competence, time spent by teachers on non-teaching tasks, availability of qualified personnel to provide counseling and other special services for students, availability of well qualified, adequately compensated substitutes and teachers' assessment of the quality of school leadership.

The commission had the courage to state that there's a high price tag on what it recommends, but it believes that the alternative — failing to educate youngsters well or even adequately because the state has not been able to attract and keep good teachers — will be even more costly in the long run.

What is true in California is also true for the rest of the country.

EXERCISE 8-19

Here is an excerpt from a speech given on the Northwest College campus last night by Gilbert Fite, professor of history at the University of Georgia. He was on campus to address the college's annual alumni dinner. The text:

Higher education has a function that goes beyond that of providing professional competence, however important that may be. At least we talk about those other benefits and virtues that are somehow supposed to be connected with a college education. These include such things as love of learning, intellectual growth, cultural awareness, personal development and many other benefits. Indeed, if we surveyed college and university catalogues published over the last century we could make a long list of the outcomes purportedly associated with a college education, all in addition to preparation for a profession.

I submit, however, that the true function of higher education is to foster intellectual activity and creativity. College has to do with the mind, with thinking and with a student's thought processes. It should deal with the matter of how we look at problems and how we weigh and handle evidence. A college education should be concerned with gaining perspective on ourselves and the world around us. Let me repeat, the university experience should be concerned primarily with thought, with thinking.

It is clear enough that the activities that go on in the halls of colleges and universities have greatly increased our store of knowledge, but the important question is, have we achieved greater understanding, or to put it another way, do we use that knowledge in a rational and reasonable way? Are college graduates more rational, more reasonable, more understanding, more analytical in their approach to problems, more humane, more civilized and cultured in the best sense, more decent in human relationships, and do they have a greater love of learning than those who have never had a formal course in history, literature, science or mathematics? In short, has college affected their behavior? Is there evidence that our graduates think better than non-college people?

During the years since the end of World War II literally millions of Americans have attended colleges and universities, and graduates have flooded into our society in ever increasing numbers. We are the most highly credentialed and degreed society in human history. What kind of leaven, so to speak, have these millions of college graduates provided in our society? Have they led the way toward a better political, social and economic system, and improved the standard of human relationships? Have these college graduates been an influence in raising the level of civility, refinement, reason and culture? Have they brought wisdom and enlightenment to the affairs of men? I think the answer to these questions is fairly obvious. It is mainly "no," and at the most "maybe."

College trained individuals seem to be as emotional, indeed even at times hysterical, and as lacking in rationality and reason in dealing

continued on next page

with other people, and with various problems, as individuals who have never been exposed to higher education. They act on emotion rather than reason, which is just the opposite of what we think we are teaching in our mathematics, science, history and other courses where we apply reason to objective evidence. A decade or so ago, many college students even turned to mysticism and spiritualism of one kind or another. They were more concerned with feeling than with thinking. While such people may find a certain amount of personal relief and satisfaction sitting under a banyan tree in contemplation, it is no substitute for thinking and reason.

There is, of course, nothing wrong with emotion. It is important in our lives. But as Gordon N. Ray, [former] president of the Guggenheim Foundation, wrote some years ago, "Powerful emotional responses become socially valuable only when they are combined with trained intelligence and a firm grasp of reality, and it is precisely these things that students should get from the university."

What I am getting at is simply this: universities have become the center of a great knowledge industry, and in our highly technical society knowledge is the basis of power. The people who hold knowledge and power are mainly college graduates. But knowledge and power, uncontrolled and ungoverned by reason and by decent human values and high moral standards, are a source of terrible danger to us as a people and to a free society.

It is not enough for our universities to produce knowledge, a task at which they have been remarkably successful. They and their constituencies must point the way for the best use of that knowledge. Besides promoting reason, self-restraint, humane and civilized behavior, the University must always operate itself in promoting high moral and ethical principles. You may say that the University can only be a reflection of the society in which it operates. I say that the standards, principles and behavior on a university campus should be higher than those in the general society. Why? Because we claim to be educated. The same should be true of a society with large numbers of college graduates.

Somehow higher education needs to make a greater difference in human affairs than it has in the past. In producing knowledge we have achieved huge successes; in applying that knowledge to human relationships, in providing the leaven for a more just society, and in supplying a humanizing and civilizing influence our record is poor. This is the challenge before us. I do not pretend to know how this is to be done, but I know that it must be done. Believing in the rational approach to problems, I believe that our first task is to identify the problem. Somehow we must combine the vast knowledge that students are accumulating on campus with appreciation of, and commitment to, the highest humanistic and social values.

EXERCISE 8-20

You were assigned last night to cover the monthly meeting of the Carolton planning board, the city board that is responsible for planning and zoning. All members of the board were present: Richard Daggett (chairman), Harold Gold, Nancy Johnson, Lorraine Worthington and George Rogers. Rogers is an ex officio member.

Your notes:

Bob Dwight appeared to talk about his plans for a subdivision on West Wisconsin.

Dwight wants approval of his sub/div plans: quote I don't want to go to all the expense of submitting an application if the board is going to turn the plan down unquote.

Sub/div will include 40 single-family, brick veneer homes on half-acre lots — land he wants to develop contains about 50 acres — expenses mean site plans, architectural renderings and so on.

Dwight wants a waiver to allow all the houses to be built in one year. (City now limits building in any new subdivision to 20 units a year.)

Worthington: On what grounds do you want a waiver?

Dwight: Too expensive to stretch building out over 2 years. The city needs housing now. I'd like to get this all done in one operation.

Rogers: We've got to have some limits on growth. We can't accommodate that many new homes in one year.

Dwight: I can't see phasing in this project. It doesn't make any sense to do it over 2 years. If you can see your way clear to granting a waiver, I'll include eight units of affordable housing in the project.

Daggett: That's not going to qualify under the state program.

(To qualify for the state Housing Opportunity Program, the number of affordable housing units in a development must be 25 percent.)

Gold: Can't you increase that to ten units?

Dwight: Can I get a waiver?

Daggett: Can we get the affordable units? Without those ten lots, I'm opposed to the plan.

Dwight: I'll guarantee it. What kind of a guarantee do you want? I'll work with the board.

continued on next page

(Issue here is the affordable housing. Under state guidelines, families with incomes of $17,000 to $35,000 can qualify for five and one half percent mortgages.)

(After some discussion, Dwight says he'll include ten units of affordable housing.)

Worthington: You are suggesting five units to be sold for no more than $80,000 and five for no more than $110,000. I think that should be cut to no more than $100,000.

Dwight: I can't do it. You're asking me to lop $50,000 off the top. That's a lot of money.

Rogers: I don't think $110,000 homes are affordable housing.

Daggett: I think we have to see a site plan and some drawings before we can do anything for you.

No vote, but board members told Dwight they wanted to be helpful, and would be as cooperative as possible when he brings in a concrete subdivision proposal.

Dwight: (to reporters after the meeting) I've tried to work with the board — I'll continue to work with the board — but I can't just pour money into this thing until I know where I stand.

The board told Dwight it needs to see:

> plans for improvement of the intersection of
> Wisconsin and Territorial road —
>
> designation of units that will be affordable
> housing —
>
> building plans, architectural renderings and
> landscape plans —

Daggett, Gold, Johnson, Rogers indicated they would go along with Dwight. Worthington holds out — says quote I'm not willing to waiver the phasing unquote.

Write your story. Your lead ought to summarize the results of the meeting. Use direct quotes where you can. Zoning is a touchy question in Carolton, so this is a story with high reader interest.

EXERCISE 8-21

Many editors object to the off-hand creation of verbs from nouns. Although this is a normal and useful way of creating words, sometimes the results are awkward. Objections have been raised to the verbs underlined in these sentences. Revise the sentences to get rid of the underlined verbs.

1. Smith <u>authored</u> the novel "Home in the Islands."

2. He said the college would be glad <u>to host</u> the conference.

3. The members <u>balloted</u> for a new president.

4. Smith, as president, <u>chairmanned</u> the meeting.

5. The theater company <u>repertoried</u> through the state.

6. The strike settled, the company and union <u>inked</u> a revised contract.

7. Smith shared custody, so he <u>parented</u> only on weekends.

8. The bride chose a single color <u>to theme</u> her wedding.

9. The candidates <u>handbilled</u> the entire city.

10. The senior class dance <u>featured</u> the music of Stan Jones.

Number Correct _____

Student's Name _____

EXERCISE 8-22

Eliminate the *redundancies* or wordiness in these items. You may *X* them out on the typewriter, draw a line through the unnecessary words or write or type a revision in the space at the right. Some of the items may be acceptable as written.

1.   tendered his resignation   _____

2.   told her listeners that   _____

3.   was able to escape   _____

4.   was taken to jail   _____

5.   once in a great while   _____

6.   on one occasion   _____

7.   went on to say   _____

8.   in the near future   _____

9.   at the present time   _____

10.   united in holy matrimony   _____

11.   brought to a sudden halt   _____

12.   at that time   _____

13.   all of a sudden   _____

14.   is of the opinion that   _____

15.   gave its approval   _____

16.   in the event that   _____

17.   refer back   _____

18.   canceled out   _____

19.   another alternative   _____

20.   made an investigation of   _____

Number Correct _____

Student's Name _____

EXERCISE 8-23

Edit this news story. Correct errors in style. Use standard editing marks and practices. Do *not* rewrite. There may be errors in spelling, usage or punctuation.

01   Northwest College (NWC) announced Wednesday that they

02 will change to a semester system effective next June.

03   Pres. John R. McKay said the change would benefit

04 faculty and students but not effect taypayers

05   McKay said that in his judgment the change would

06 enhance the college's reputation.

07   "We have considered all aspects of our academic year,

08 he said, "I am sure we are doing the right thing."

09   Faculty members have expressed some reservations.

10   Dr. Henry Huxtable, professor of veterinary medicine,

11 called the move radical.

12   Dr. Granville Holmes, Professor of Journalism, said

13 he welcomed the change.

14   McKay said, however that the change would require

15 additional computer capacity in the registrar's office.

16   Alumni have "mixed feelings" about the semester plan.

17   Mrs. Louise Baxter, president of the Northwest

18 college Alumni Assn. said that many former graduates

19 oppose the plan.

20   "I am an alumni myself, Mrs. Baxter said, "and I don't

21 like the idea."

Number Correct _____

Student's Name _____

EXERCISE 8-24

Edit this news story. Correct errors in style. Use standard editing marks and practices. Do *not* rewrite. There may be errors in spelling, usage or punctuation.

01   The Chairman of the Washington County Planning and

02   Zoning commission yesterday charged that the commission

03   can't enforce its own regulations.

04   Charles Miller, the commission chairman said that

05   unless the commission increases the size of its staff,

06   there is little chance that the situation will change.

07   "I wonder if all the regulations are really worth it,

08   said Miller.

09   Miller said homeowners object to zoning in any form

10   and pay very little attention to the zoning ordnances.

11   In an interview with "The Morning Record," Miller said

12   he was "astonished" at the violations of zoning

13   regulations coming to his attention.

14   "At least 10% of the violations," Miller said, "are

15   deliberate and willful."

16   "We can't begin to get a handle on the situation."

17   "We're working on redrafting our regulations."

18   Miller said the five member planning commission may

19   come up with new guidelines to improve enforcement.

20   "Its up to the members," he said.

Number Correct _____

Student's Name _____

9 Broadcast News

Spelling

desiccate, accommodate, ax, phony, naive, drunkenness, questionnaire, paraphernalia, tendon/tendinitis, argue/argument, lighten/lightning, nuclear

Usage

principle/principal, kudos, destroy/demolish, unique, court martial/courts martial, a number of/the number of

Newsroom Vocabulary

AP Broadcast News Handbook, RTNDA, news peg, stringer, journeyman, summary, ombudsman, new journalism, hard copy, play up

Broadcast News

This topic is treated in detail in George A. Hough 3rd, "News Writing," fourth edition:

Broadcast News
Chapter 14, "Broadcast News," pages 281 through 297.

While you are working on exercises in this section, assume that you have been asked to fill in for a news writer at the radio station owned by The Morning Record Co.

You will be writing copy for news broadcasts that are carried the first five minutes of each hour and for the longer newscasts that are carried at noon and 6 p.m.

EXERCISE 9-1

Write 100 words on last night's storm for the noon news broadcast (see Exercise 3-3).

EXERCISE 9-2

Write 25 to 30 words for an hourly news broadcast on the appointment of the new education association director (see Exercise 3-8).

EXERCISE 9-3

Write 25 to 30 words for an hourly news broadcast on the closing of a portion of the interstate (see Exercise 3-9).

EXERCISE 9-4

Write 25 to 30 words for an hourly news broadcast on the appointment of the new librarian (see Exercise 3-15).

EXERCISE 9-5

Write 25 to 30 words for an hourly news broadcast on the appointment of a Northwest College faculty member to the state banking board (see Exercise 3-23).

EXERCISE 9-6

Write 50 to 60 words on the train accident for the noon news broadcast (see Exercise 3-18).

EXERCISE 9-7

Write 30 to 40 words on the new industrial plant for the noon news broadcast (see Exercise 3-7).

EXERCISE 9-8

Write 25 to 30 words on the automobile safety award to the city for an hourly news broadcast (see Exercise 4-9).

EXERCISE 9-9

Write 50 to 60 words on the Special Olympics for the 6 p.m. news broadcast (see Exercise 4-10).

EXERCISE 9-10

Write 25 to 30 words for an hourly news broadcast on the speech to be given Wednesday by Carl Sagan (see Exercise 5-17).

EXERCISE 9-11

Write 25 to 30 words for an hourly news broadcast on the Northwest College commencement speaker (see Exercise 5-7).

EXERCISE 9-12

Write 50 to 60 words on the auto fatality for the upcoming hourly news broadcast (see Exercise 5-22).

EXERCISE 9-13

Write 150 words on this morning's bank robbery for the noon news broadcast (see Exercise 6-9).

EXERCISE 9-14

Write 100 to 125 words for the noon broadcast on the fatal accident at Indian River Park last night (see Exercise 6-15).

EXERCISE 9-15

Write 100 to 125 words on the state tax revenue story for the noon news broadcast (see Exercise 6-2).

EXERCISE 9-16

Write 150 words for the 6 p.m. news broadcast on the rescue of the 7-year-old boy this morning (see Exercise 6-3).

EXERCISE 9-17

Write 75 to 100 words for an hourly news broadcast on the holdup last night at O'Malley's (see Exercise 6-4).

EXERCISE 9-18

Write 150 words on the triple fatality last night for the noon news broadcast (see Exercise 6-22).

EXERCISE 9-19

Write 50 to 60 words for an hourly news broadcast on the city treasurer's accident in Rogers City this morning (see Exercise 6-17).

EXERCISE 9-20

A well-known Carolton woman, Carolyn Dwight, died yesterday. Write a 100-word obit for the noon news broadcast (see Exercise 6-10).

EXERCISE 9-21

Write 100 words for the noon news broadcast on the holdup and shooting this morning at the Holiday Inn (see Exercise 6-24).

EXERCISE 9-22

Write 50 to 60 words for an hourly newscast on the arrest of a suspect in the O'Malley's holdup (see Exercise 7-3).

EXERCISE 9-23

Write about 100 words for the noon news broadcast on the charges Zelig Ormsby made this morning (see Exercise 7-9).

EXERCISE 9-24

Write about 75 words for the 6 p.m. newscast on plans for services for three Carolton youths who were killed in an auto accident earlier this week (see Exercise 7-2).

EXERCISE 9-25

Write about 100 words for the noon news broadcast on the shooting yesterday in which a Carolton woman was killed (see Exercise 5-33).

EXERCISE 9-26

Write a 75- to 100-word obit for Madeline Boomershine for the noon news broadcast (see Exercise 7-17).

EXERCISE 9-27

Write 35 to 50 words for the upcoming hourly news broadcast on the death of the man shot in the Holiday Inn holdup this morning (see Exercise 7-4).

EXERCISE 9-28

Write 50 to 60 words on the Acme fire for an hourly news broadcast (see Exercise 7-12).

EXERCISE 9-29

Write 25 to 30 words for an hourly news broadcast on the plane accident at the airport this morning (see Exercise 7-21).

EXERCISE 9-30

Write 25 to 30 words for an upcoming hourly news broadcast about the prisoner who walked out of the jail this morning (see Exercise 7-8).

EXERCISE 9-31

Write 50 to 60 words for an upcoming hourly news broadcast on the recovery of the bank-robbery getaway car (see Exercise 7-19).

EXERCISE 9-32

You covered last night's speech by the president of the University of Miami. Write 125 to 150 words on the speech for the noon news broadcast (see Exercise 8-14).

EXERCISE 9-33

Write 50 to 75 words on the Foote speech for an hourly news broadcast later this afternoon (see Exercise 8-14).

EXERCISE 9-34

Write 100 words for the noon news broadcast on the fake night-deposit box at the Farmers and Merchants Bank (see Exercise 10-18).

EXERCISE 9-35

Write 75 to 100 words for the 6 p.m. news broadcast on the bomb scare at the Federal Building this morning (see Exercise 10-15).

EXERCISE 9-36

Write 25 to 35 words for an hourly news broadcast on the thief who tried to steal a policewoman's purse (see Exercise 10-3).

EXERCISE 9-37

Write 100 to 125 words for the 6 p.m. news broadcast on the elderly woman who nearly lost her purse to a petty thief (see Exercise 10-22).

EXERCISE 9-38

Write 75 to 100 words for the noon news broadcast about the fire early this morning at the Liberty Baptist Church (see Exercise 10-6).

EXERCISE 9-39

Write 100 to 125 words for the 6 p.m. news broadcast on the tree theft at the Anderson home at 641 N. Sherman (see Exercise 10-13).

EXERCISE 9-40

Eliminate the *redundancies* in these items below. You may *X* them out on the typewriter, draw a line through the unnecessary words or write or type a revision in the space at the right. Some of the items may be acceptable as written.

1. at a speed of six knots an hour _____

2. a cousin of his _____

3. the exact same _____

4. is currently working at _____

5. was positively identified as _____

6. is already in the process of _____

7. is required to _____

8. a new recruit _____

9. broke a past record _____

10. along with _____

11. the sum total is _____

12. a coroner's inquest _____

13. in the field of journalism _____

14. ink pens _____

15. located at _____

16. completely destroyed _____

17. appointed to the position of _____

18. doomed to failure _____

19. is currently _____

20. four different kinds _____

Number Correct _____

Student's Name _____

EXERCISE 9-41

Edit these sentences so that hyphenation conforms to rules given in "News Writing," pages 390 through 394 and pages 472 and 473. You may also want to consult Webster's New World Dictionary. Use standard editing marks to insert or delete punctuation. Some of the sentences may be correct as written.

1. The city-county reporter blamed the rainy weather on the H-bomb his father-in-law built in his newly-renovated garage.

2. No one can jump higher than the 7 foot, 6-inch center on the Northwest College award winning basketball team.

3. The pilots climbed into the two man craft and plied their six foot long oars.

4. The coach said the players were second rate performers.

5. Most French Canadian nationals speak English, but not all Mexican American citizens speak Spanish.

6. He had a know it all attitude and had always been filled with self pity.

7. The transAtlantic voyage was an anti-climax to the tour.

8. "Turn to the next chapter," the instructor said, "and study the three- to four-year contracts."

9. The team scored a first quarter touchdown but trailed at the end of the third quarter.

10. Tom Thumb was a little man, but he was not little-known.

Number Correct _____

Student's Name _____

EXERCISE 9-42

Edit this news story. Correct errors in style. Use standard editing marks and practices. Revise, but do *not* rewrite. There may be errors in spelling, usage or punctuation.

01   The Chairman of the Washington County zoning

02 commission said in an interview yesterday that the

03 commission is so tied up in red tape it can't get it's

04 work done.

05   "People tell us "You people have too many regulations"

06 -- and their correct," Miller said.

07   Miller said the commissioners have been accused of

08 acting like "dictators" when they do try to enforce

09 zoning ordnances.

10   "We're just enforcing zoning requirements," Miller

11 said, "We are not policemen."

12   Miller said he agrees with critics that there may be

13 "too many" regulations.

14   "But the fact is, we have to enforce them (zoning

15 regulations) if we are to do it (the job) right," Miller

16 said.

17   Miller said the commission does not have the manpower

18 it needs.

19   "We need more people or less regulations," he said.

20   Even when violations are found, said Miller, there is

21 no guarantee of punishment.

Number Correct _____

Student's Name _____

EXERCISE 9-43

Edit this news story. Correct errors in style. Use standard editing marks and practices. Revise, but do *not* rewrite. There may be errors in spelling, usage or punctuation.

01   A statewide alarm has been issued for the men who held

02 up O'Flynn's yesterday, took two hostages and fled.

03   The trio shoved their hostages out the door and into a

04 car with Ga. license plates. The car left the club

05 parking lot in the general direction of Columbia,

06 South Carolina.

07   Detectives are interviewing witnesses in an attempt to

08 get descriptions of the holdup men.

09   "One resembled the six-foot-two-inch tailback on the

10 Northwest team," detective Lieut. Jacob Bernstein said.

11   "The similarity just occured to me," he said. "I hope

12 that is not an unfortunate inuendo."

13   O'Flynn's may lose their liquor license because of the

14 holdup. Bernstein said the nightclub was supposed to

15 close at 12 p.m. It was still open when the holdup men

16 entered the building at 1 A.M.

17   Mrs. Helen Shonsky, whose husband was wounded during

18 the holdup, screamed nonstop after he was shot. A

19 bartender had to hit her on the head with a coke bottle

20 to quiet her.

21   Sheriff Abel Look was at the nightclub yesterday

22 seeking any evidence that might be admissable if the

23 bandits are tried.

Number Correct _____

Student's Name _____

10 Features

Spelling

kindergarten/kindergartner, impostor, goodbye,* exacerbate, aesthetic, plagiarize/plagiarism, politicking, provocateur, malfeasance, synchronize/synchronous, erudite, separate

Usage

discreet/discrete, complacent/complaisant, capital/capitol, reluctant/reticent, pathos/bathos, title/entitle

Newsroom Vocabulary

feature, featurize, bright, page brightener, human interest, suspended interest, tube, video display terminal, cold type, hot type

Features

This topic is treated in detail in George A. Hough 3rd, "News Writing," fourth edition:

Features
Chapter 15, "Features," pages 299 through 317.

EXERCISE 10-1

Finals week is always an occasion for a news or feature story on students and how they are coping with their examinations. Your editor asked you to work up a feature, so you checked with the news bureau at Northwest College. Bill Morrissey suggested that you talk with Dr. Hirsch in the medical school. He is a nationally known expert on stress. You interview Dr. Hirsch:

You: Dr. Hirsch, what can you tell me about the effect of finals on students?

Hirsch: Well, finals are a little tough on students, but not really more than any other week of the term.

You: No extra stress?

Hirsch: Well, yes, but it's what you might call an escapable stress. If you are studying, you can get up and take a break. You have a feeling of being in control.

You: Has there been any research on this subject?

Hirsch: Yes, a number of animal studies have shown that stress is damaging only if it's inescapable.

You: Do you find more illness during finals than at other times during the term?

Hirsch: Actually, no, though there is a well-known relationship between stress and illness. But it's not true of college students. At least it doesn't show up during finals.

You: Any data on that subject?

Hirsch: Yes, we have reviewed the record of student visits to the health service over the past 10 years, and we found that, oddly enough, students visit the health service less during finals week than during other weeks of the term.

You: I wonder why.

Hirsch: Well, we think it's because students just won't take the time to trek over here to the clinic.

You: But there's sort of a tradition that students tend to get tired and sick a lot during finals.

Hirsch: That's something of a myth. Students talk a lot about how tough they're having it, how late they study and how sick they feel, but that's not the same as being truly ill.

You: Any advice for students about how to cope with finals?

Hirsch: Sure. They ought to start studying before the last minute, and they ought to get a good night's sleep before taking an exam. A good night's rest is a sure cure for stress.

EXERCISE 10-2

Ted Davis, the Record's advertising manager, stopped in the newsroom today to tell you about a classified ad that appeared in this morning's paper.

The ad, you learn, was placed by Horace Gilmore, vice president of a local construction company. He runs the ad every year on his wife's birthday. The ad asks readers of The Morning Record to telephone Mrs. Gilmore and wish her a happy birthday. Mrs. Gilmore always gets lots of calls, Davis tells you.

You call Mrs. Gilmore and ask her about the ad. She tells you:

The calls never stop. I have to take the phone off the hook long enough to take a bath or have a cup of coffee. I'm getting a little weary of this kind of birthday. Why, I get a couple of hundred calls every year. I hope he'll think of something different next year.

One year he was going to put a birthday message on a billboard down on Main street, but my daughter talked him out of it. My god, that would have been up there a month.

You thank Mrs. Gilmore, wish her a happy birthday and then call her husband. He tells you:

He's run the ad for the past five years. It costs about $50 for the ad. He thinks it's a great idea, but admits that his wife is getting a bit tired of the gag.

The calls start coming as soon as the paper is out and go on all day. Most of the people who call are complete strangers. They are all very nice. Some even sing "happy birthday to you."

This story has feature possibilities. See what you can do.

EXERCISE 10-3

While you were on rewrite today, the Record's police reporter called in. The city editor was laughing as she asked you to take the story. Make it bright. You could make page one.

Police are holding John Jewell, 31, Mobile, Alabama, at headquarters — charge is attempted theft — he was arrested by police on West Main a block from headquarters — he had attempted to grab a purse from a police officer — Sergeant Gail Ivory — attached to juvenile division — she was just going up steps of headquarters when Jewell grabbed at her shoulder bag — she held on to the bag and he ran.

A couple of police officers who were on their way into the building ran after him — Ivory yelled at him to stop and fired two warning shots in air — officers caught him about a block from headquarters — Ivory works in plain clothes — Jewell apparently didn't know she was a cop — happened about 7:45 this morning.

EXERCISE 10-4

You were on rewrite today when your city editor asked you to take a call from the Record's police reporter. "Here's a good one," you were told. "Write something funny. We need a little humor for page one."

Reporter: This is a funny one. A prisoner tried to escape from Joe Marshall this morning.

You: What happened?

Reporter: Joe was walking the guy from police headquarters over to municipal court when he broke loose and ran.

You: He get away?

Reporter: Naw. Marshall's too fast for him. Heck, when he caught up with him, Joe had hardly hit his stride.

You: How far did the guy get?

Reporter: A block or so. He was winded and just quit running.

You: What happened to him?

Reporter: Oh, Joe just took him on over to court. The poor guy was too winded to say much. Judge Hughes gave him 30 days. He was charged with d and d.

You know that Marshall runs the mile on the police track team and holds a number of records. He also competes in road races. He plans to enter the Peachtree road race in Atlanta next summer. *D and d* means *drunk and disorderly*.

EXERCISE 10-5

While you were on rewrite today, the Record's police reporter called with a story he thinks is funny. He told you:

The robbery squad just nabbed a guy who must be the dumbest thief in the world. Listen. They had a burglary the other night at the Copper Kettle restaurant. No big deal. The burglars got about a hundred bucks from the cash register and broke open a cigaret machine and took maybe fifty bucks worth of cigarets. They caught the guy this morning. Found his fingerprints in the restaurant. He was on file because he'd been arrested before. He got hungry while he was in the restaurant and fixed himself a bowl of chili. Left his fingerprints all over the bowl and the spoon he used. Name is Pete Rigsby. Arrest last year was for theft. He served 30 days. Detectives just went over to his house, and there he was.

You can quote Lieutenant Begg if you want to.

FYI: Rigsby's prints were on file in the police identification bureau.

237

EXERCISE 10-6

While you were on rewrite today, the Record's police reporter called with a fire story. He told you:

Three-alarm fire — 5:45 this morning — church at 911 Grant — pretty bad damage — fire trucks didn't return to station until after 8.

You check the city directory, find the name of the church, call the pastor, John Duttweiler, and ask him about the damage. He tells you:

This is a terrible blow to the congregation. We just last week finished renovation of the sanctuary. Members of the congregation have been raising money, and we have taken up special collections for two years to pay for the renovations. We paid for it ourselves because we didn't want to mortgage the church.

You press Duttweiler for details and learn:

Duttweiler has been pastor for five years.

The renovation just completed was the first phase of a three-year program to renovate the church and parish hall.

The entire interior of the church was burned out in the fire. Church has some 600 members. Work so far has cost $40,000. Loss only partly covered by insurance.

Work had included new wiring, refinishing the pews, new stained-glass windows, wall-to-wall carpeting and a new baptismal font.

Congregation had been planning to hold special services this Sunday to mark the 50th anniversary of the founding of the congregation and to celebrate completion of the first phase of the renovation project. Services will be held somewhere else now.

Duttweiler says:

I've been a member of this congregation all my life. This hurts.

This is more than a routine fire story. Give it feature treatment. Use the best direct quotes.

EXERCISE 10-7

You were covering the police and fire beat today, and while you were at the downtown fire station, you picked up this story:

Rescue squad called to 503 East Vermont yesterday afternoon at 4:15. Child stuck in chimney.

Rescue squad had to get help from firemen. They used hammers and chisels to get the kid out. He was so far down the chimney you couldn't see him from the roof.

continued on next page

Finally got him out. Kid's story is that he got home from school and found the house locked. Figured he could get in by shinnying down the chimney. He's a little guy. Only 8.

Mother came home about four o'clock and heard him screaming. When she finally figured out where the kid was, she called the fire department.

Lt. Strauss tells you:

Kid looked like a little old chimney sweep when we got him out. He was scared, but he's a tough little guy. He'll be all right. Good thing we've got a couple of bricklayers in the department. They told us how and where to cut and chisel to get him out.

We started in the fireplace and worked up. All we could see of him from the fireplace were the bottoms of his feet.

It took us about four hours to get him out.

You call the boy's home and talk to his mother. She tells you:

It was Jimmy, James. He's our youngest. He's all right. Just got a chipped tooth.

I asked him why he tried to go down the chimney, and he said it was a mistake.

EXERCISE 10-8

While you were in the office this morning, the Record's county building reporter called with what he thinks is a funny story. Here are your notes:

A stenographer in the county clerk's office wrote a letter to a friend the other day, using a computer terminal in the clerk's office. She forgot to clear the letter out of the system when she finished and somehow it got into the central computer, and the next day it was printed out with a lot of official memos and circulated around the entire building.

In the letter she had told her friend that she was finding Carolton pretty quiet — said her love life was dull. Quote I'd sure like to meet a good-looking guy unquote.

The county clerk laughed it off. Said it was just a technical error in the computer system. He doesn't think anyone in his office will write personal letters at work after this.

The woman has taken a lot of kidding, but she says it has been worth it. Most of her free evenings and weekends for the next several weeks have been spoken for.

There is no need to use the name of the woman in this story.

239

EXERCISE 10-9

The Record's stringer on campus called this morning with a story that you might be able to do something with. Here are your notes:

From the stringer:

Students managed to put all the plumbing in Hallowell hall — the new residence hall on campus — out of commission last night.

College maintenance crews can't fix it and college has had to call in a plumbing contractor.

Students synchronized their watches last night and at exactly ten o'clock flushed every toilet in the building. Nothing has worked since.

You want to get a little more background on the story and call the college public relations office and talk with Terry Dawson. He doesn't really want to see the story published, but he gives you a little background.

From Dawson:

Students have been agitating for longer break between terms. The synchronized flush was part of the protest. Students thought college would give in, postpone final exams and let them go home early. President McKay has issued a formal notice that the college's exam and vacation schedule will remain unchanged.

The college is going to bill residents of the hall for the damage, too.

About 450 students live in Hallowell hall. It's one of the co-ed halls — it houses both men and women students. You ask, and he tells you that there are 237 toilets in the building.

EXERCISE 10-10

Your federal beat reporter called this story in this morning. Your city editor liked it. "Give me a bright for the front page," she told you.

One of the stamp machines at a self-service postal unit on campus had to be repaired today because it jammed. The postmaster had a visit this morning from a student who handed him a whole roll of stamps that came out of the machine. She put in enough money for one stamp and got a whole roll. The postmaster said he was glad to get the stamps back. The roll had 250 stamps. The stamps can go back in another machine.

Student is Helen Fraser.

Postmaster didn't offer her any reward. He just said "thanks."

Postmaster wouldn't say which stamp machine was at fault but did say that the malfunction was not likely to re-occur.

EXERCISE 10-11

When you came into the newsroom today, you found Bill Jones, one of the Record's copy editors, passing out cigars and accepting congratulations on the birth of twins.

His wife, Betty, went into Carolton General last night and the babies were born this morning.

Bill tells you his wife is pretty upset in some ways, though she is terribly pleased with the twins — girls — who haven't been named yet. They were a week or so early, and Betty didn't get to finish the bar exam.

Betty has been going to the law school at Northwest since their first child started school three years ago. She got her degree last June. She took the first part of the state bar examination last week. She was supposed to take the second part today, but instead she's in the hospital.

Your editor thinks there's a story here, so you call Mrs. Jones and chat with her. She tells you:

I don't know whether they'll call me a flunk or a non-taker. They're beautiful babies, but I wish they had waited another day or so.

You ask her when she can take the exam again, but she says she isn't sure. She does want to practice law, even with three children to look after. She thinks she can do it but perhaps will have to set up her law office at home.

Write the story for tomorrow's paper. Keep it short.

EXERCISE 10-12

The Record's man at the courthouse called this story in just now. Your city editor wants it for tomorrow's paper.

In municipal court — before Judge Hughes — attempted theft case — Stanley C. Updyke — age 34 — gave address of city rescue mission — sentenced to 30 days in county jail on plea of guilty.

City cops nabbed him about 2 this morning — outside bank at 604 West Main.

Complaint said he was trying to fish night deposits out of the bank's night-deposit chute.

He had a fishline with hooks and a sinker — cops spotted him and made arrest — before he had been able to haul anything out.

Bank says about a dozen deposits were in the night depository, but as far as they know nothing is missing.

EXERCISE 10-13

The Record's police reporter turned this story up today. He told you:

Complaint this morning — theft of a tree from residence at 641 North Sherman — sawed down and removed — probably last night or early this morning — Canadian spruce — valued at five hundred dollars — complainant is H.C. Anderson.

You know that in the days before Christmas a lot of trees are stolen. There might be a feature angle to the story, so you call the house and talk with Mrs. Anderson. She tells you:

I cried all morning. That tree meant the world to us. How could anyone hurt us like that?

We're both 80 years old. We won't live long enough to see another tree grow up to be so beautiful.

We planted that tree when we bought this house 15 years ago. It was the most beautiful tree.

She also tells you:

The tree was about fifteen feet high and broad at the base. A perfect Christmas tree. They will have a Christmas tree indoors, but they have always put lights on this tree at Christmas time. They were going to get the lights on it today.

Not all feature stories are humorous. This one certainly isn't. But write the story carefully. There's a fine line between sentiment and sentimentality.

EXERCISE 10-14

The Record's city hall reporter called this in this morning. Write it for tomorrow's paper.

Tax office at city hall is a madhouse. Tax bills went out last week, but lots of people didn't get them and the tax office has been getting phone calls from all over town.

They've been blaming the mail. Joe Thompson even went over and raised cain with the post office.

Then this morning they found that the mail chute in city hall was plugged up. When they finally got it cleared, they had a couple of thousand letters. Some had been in the chute a week. About half of them were tax bills. Tax office is on third floor at city hall, and clerks had been putting the bills in the mail chute.

Joe says he's going to send the tax clerks over to the main post office with mail after this. Postmaster says all the delayed mail is being hand stamped and handled as a priority.

EXERCISE 10-15

You were on rewrite today. The Record's reporter at the Federal Building called with a story about a bomb scare. The city editor asked you to take the call and to write the story. Here's what the Federal beat reporter told you:

Federal building was evacuated this morning — bomb scare — clerks in the Internal Revenue Service office called police — said they had a suspicious package in the office — package was leaking an unidentified liquid —

Carolton police bomb squad went to federal building — ordered building evacuated — several hundred persons had to go out to the street while the bomb squad went into the IRS office —

Package was a gym bag — it was leaking — bomb squad took it to city landfill off Territorial road and blew it up.

Turned out package was only someone's lunch. From what was left of it, police identified a bologna sandwich wrapped in aluminum foil, a thermos of coffee and several chocolate chip cookies.

FBI agents learned later lunch belonged to an IRS agent. He had left it in a gym bag under his desk while he went out to do some errands.

Bomb squad officer-in-charge, Sgt. Hal Floyde, says it was quote just a little case of nerves up in IRS unquote.

EXERCISE 10-16

The Record's courthouse reporter called this in today. Today is Valentine's Day, so this is a timely story.

Employees at the courthouse got into the spirit of the day. In the county clerk's office, they had red hearts plastered all over the place. Also had a big sign: "Congratulations and Best Wishes for a Long Life Together."

Miss Williams says they thought they ought to do something for couples who apply for a marriage license on Valentine's day.

Employees in clerk of court's office didn't have any signs up, but they kept a tally on the number of divorce actions filed today. There were five.

Miss Williams says only three couples applied for marriage licenses today.

It may be difficult to get in the mood for this story unless you are asked to write it in mid-February. If the season is right, perhaps you can give it a light touch. Be creative.

EXERCISE 10-17

In court this morning, you ran into Don Meyers, Judge Hughes' clerk, who told you about an incident in the judge's court during early morning arraignments.

Meyers: You should have seen the judge's face when he saw that tee-shirt. He was pretty upset.

You: What was on it? A dirty word?

Meyers: You can say that again. It said: "I'm so happy I could ... er, uh ... defecate," only it didn't say that.

You: You mean it said ... ?

Meyers: Yep.

You: What did the judge say?

Meyers: Hughes told the guy — he was in court to be arraigned on a possession charge — marijuana — that there was a dress code in municipal court and that tee-shirts aren't proper dress.

You: That all?

Meyers: No. Then he said that if that was his idea of happiness, he'd accommodate him.

You: What did he mean by that?

Meyers: He accepted the guy's not guilty plea, held him for a preliminary hearing and set bond at a thousand bucks. The guy couldn't post the bond, so he's going to be in the county jail for a while. Hughes told him he'd like the county jail. It's got new plumbing.

You check Judge Hughes' docket and find the man's name: Eric Leonard, no known address, age 22. Pleaded not guilty to a charge of possession of one-quarter ounce of marijuana. Bond set at $1,000. Unable to post bond. Remanded to jail to wait for preliminary hearing.

Write the story for tomorrow's paper. Before you write, however, check the policy section of the Style Guide. What does it say about four-letter words?

EXERCISE 10-18

Write a feature story based on this information. Your city editor wants it for tomorrow's paper.

From the local FBI office:

Robbery last night at the Farmers and Merchants bank downtown. Loss about $15,000 so far.

One or more persons unknown rigged a fake night-deposit box at the bank. Fake box was a standard metal mail drop box of the type the postal service places on streets for deposit of mail. Fake box had been repainted — white with green lettering that said "Farmers and Merchants Bank" and "Temporary Night Depository."

Box placed in front of opening of regular night depository. Piece of plywood used to seal off regular depository.

Box apparently set in place after dark last night. Removed before daylight this morning.

From Washington county sheriff's office:

A sheriff's road patrol car found the repainted box in a ditch alongside Old Meetinghouse Road about 9 this morning.

From Farmers and Merchants Bank:

Robbery discovered this morning when several customers came into the bank and told bank tellers they had decided not to use the temporary box. So far the bank has identified 7 customers who put deposits in the fake box.

From Carolton postmaster:

Mailbox is one that was reported missing last week from in front of a postal sub-station on the Northwest college campus. He says that he notified campus police and Carolton police about the missing box. He says he thought it had probably been taken by students as a prank.

From the FBI:

No prank. No clues. Special agents are investigating.

EXERCISE 10-19

This morning while you were at work, you got a call from Dalton Arnold at the college public relations office. He wanted to set the record straight on a story that appeared this morning in the Daily Student, the college newspaper. Arnold was upset. He said he'd been getting phone calls all morning. He told you:

President McKay has stopped answering his phone. He's had calls from UPI and AP and the Times.

You hadn't seen this morning's Daily Student, so Arnold explains:

The paper carried a front-page story reporting that the college had been sold for $250 million to a consortium of Middle East businessmen who plan to turn the campus into an Islamic studies and research center. The story said the businessmen considered the purchase a tax shelter.

Arnold says:

The story is a hoax. The college has not been sold. It is not for sale. You can't sell the college, for god's sake, it's a state institution. It belongs to the taxpayers.

Arnold also tells you that President McKay had a talk with the editors of the student newspaper this morning.

You ask whether the student editors are in trouble.

Arnold says:

No, not really. McKay does have a sense of humor, you know.

The college may want a straightforward story explaining the hoax and reassuring the public, but your story ought to be more than a correction notice. See what you can do.

EXERCISE 10-20

One of the clerks in the Record's classified department told you about a couple of odd classified ads that ran in the Record during the past few days. Here's what she said:

A woman came in and placed an ad under "for sale" — for her husband. It ran three days, then she came in and ran a second ad under "notices," canceling her offer.

You sense a story here and ask for the name of the advertiser. Her name is Tina Lewis, and she lives in Carolton.

continued on next page

You look up the ads:

> Husband for sale: cheap. Comes complete with hunting and fishing equipment, one pair jeans, two shirts, boots, black Labrador retriever, and 50 pounds of venison. Pretty good guy, but not home much from October to December and April to October. Will consider trade. Phone 846-3111.

> Retraction of husband for sale cheap. Everyone wants the dog, not the husband.

You call Mrs. Lewis. She tells you:

I had no idea I would get any reaction. It was just a joke, though my husband wasn't too pleased about it. I got more than 60 phone calls, and, you know, some of the women who called were real serious.

I think he spends too much time hunting and fishing, but I guess I'll keep him.

Mrs. Lewis also tells you that she and her husband have been married for 25 years. They celebrated their 25th wedding anniversary last month.

Write a page brightener for tomorrow's front page.

EXERCISE 10-21

Everyone in the newsroom has been kidding Jim Sullivan, the news editor, about his wife's allergy. She's allergic to newsprint and news ink. Jim thinks he may have to get another job. Every night he brings home enough ink and newsprint dust to make his wife ill.

His wife didn't know she was allergic to printer's ink and newsprint when they got married last summer. But ever since, she has sneezed constantly. Her doctor didn't know what was wrong, so he sent her to an allergist.

Sullivan says:

She had more than 100 tests before they found out what it was that made her sneeze.

She can't even pick up a newspaper without sneezing.

Worse yet, she sneezes when she gets too near me.

Jim isn't amused, but a lot of people in the newsroom think it's funny. There are elements of humor in the situation. See if you can write this as a page brightener in the suspended-interest format.

EXERCISE 10-22

The Record's police reporter called just now with a story about a mugging. Here's what he told you:

Victim was a woman, age 75, lives in an apartment over on Arizona — 347 West — she was on her way to a bingo game at the senior citizen center when a guy grabbed her purse — right in front of her building — you'll like this — he took off and she ran after him — nearly caught him, too, but a cop saw what was going on and went after him — caught him behind a building going through her purse.

Woman's name is Louisa May Booker.

Before you begin writing your story, the police reporter calls back with more. He tells you:

I just talked to Miss Booker. You'll like this. Listen to these quotes —

> That guy took off like a deer, but I was right behind him. I was so angry I wanted to kill him. I chased him to hell and gone. Then that nice policeman caught him.

> I didn't give him a chance. He picked on the wrong old lady.

I talked to the cop, too, John Chin, a patrolman. He said he was on foot patrol when he saw a guy running and an old lady chasing him. Here's a quote — Boy, did she run. I finally overtook her and went after him.

Chin says he caught up to the guy and put the cuffs on him — man's at police headquarters now. Chin says he's been booked for unarmed robbery. Name is Sam Walker.

I asked Chin what she had in her purse and he says not much, about ten bucks and her house keys.

You call Miss Booker and verify the story and the quotes. She adds one more:

> I'm a tough cookie. I don't take any guff from anybody.

She says the Carolton police are great, but she has one regret. She never got to the bingo game.

Write your story. Take advantage of the quotes. Give the story light treatment.

EXERCISE 10-23

Make any changes in these sentences that may be necessary to make them conform to the standards of informal American English.

1. He said he would only talk with the president.

2. None of the boys were hurt in the accident last week.

3. Everyone in the room seems to be happy, the teacher said.

4. The board of county commissioners was dismayed at the vote.

5. The large number of accidents was attributed to the snow.

6. Neither they nor he is going to get away with it.

7. No one in the class is going downtown for the parade.

8. The board of regents reluctantly announced its decision.

9. Each student's classroom work and exam grade was figured in.

10. The speaker of the house only criticized the governor.

11. Board members reported on their spring vacation plans.

12. Everybody on board said his prayers when the engine failed.

13. All the boys and all the girls were going.

14. We'll give everyone credit for his many contributions.

15. Neither of his short stories was published.

Number Correct _____

Student's Name _____

EXERCISE 10-24

Edit these sentences to improve punctuation. Use standard editing marks to insert or delete punctuation. Do *not* rewrite.

1. Perry Jackson, 81, of 231 Oak St., was confined to a nursing home in Monroe, La. where he died on March 11, 1983 without regaining consciousness.

2. Darrel Smith, the Northwest College football coach has signed an agreement with WOOK-TV for a series of post-game programs this fall.

3. The Felch Lecture will be in the LaFollette Auditorium Monday at 8 p.m. the college has announced.

4. John Jones, 18, of 311 Market St. was arrested early Monday.

5. The surgeon excised the liver, spleen, and gall bladder.

6. Classes will be held in Room 203, Mondays, at 4 p.m.

7. Jones, a freshman quarterback has a large collection of medals, trophies, and awards.

8. Military service is not all it's cracked up to be the soldier told his mother, an elderly, miserly, but loving matriarch.

9. Jones was inducted at Fort Benning on Jan. 12 at noon.

10. Eating, drinking and sleeping aren't enough, he said.

Number Correct _____

Student's Name _____

251

EXERCISE 10-25

Edit this news story. Correct errors in style, spelling, punctuation, grammar and usage. Use standard editing marks. Do *not* rewrite.

01   A major earthquake jarred the southeastern United

02 States early yesterday.

03   The quake measured 7.5 on the Richter scale, according

04 to the National Oceanic and Atmospheric Administration.

05   Charlotte, North Carolina, was the epicenter, the

06 weather service reported. The tremblor caused extensive

07 damage in Charlotte and the surrounding area.

08   Charlotte Mayor Henry Schulz said he was shocked by

09 the damage.

10   "It's like WW II," he told the AP. "Everything is

11 gone."

12   Shortly after the quake, the North Carolina highway

13 patrol set up road blocks on Interstate 85 South of

14 Charlotte.

15   Hundreds of homes were leveled at Charlotte and the

16 five story Hilton hotel at the Charlotte airport was

17 heavily damaged. Another hotel was totally destroyed.

18   In other parts of the southeast, the weather service

19 said, damages ranged from light to moderate.

20   Heavy rains were an added problem through the south.

21   "Its a tragedy," Mayor Schulz said. "Its awfull."

22   Emergency shelters are sheltering hundreds of

23 homeless people the mayor said.

Number Correct _____

Student's Name _____

EXERCISE 10-26

Edit this news story. Correct errors in style. Use standard editing marks and practices. Do *not* rewrite. There may be errors in spelling, grammar, usage or punctuation.

01   Hundreds of people whose homes were damaged or

02   destroyed in yesterday's earthquake in the southeast were

03   crowded into undamaged public buildings - high schools,

04   city halls and auditoriums.

05   Red Cross volunteers served the hungry refugees hot

06   dogs, french fries, and coke.

07   "A dietician would be horrified at the things I'm

08   eating," one homeless man said.

09   The hardest hit areas were placed under martial law as

10   a deterent to looting.

11   At Charlotte, bodies of those killed by the quake

12   were taken to improvised morgues in schools, churches,

13   and warehouses.

14   The National Guard and police were keeping badly

15   damaged public buildings under surveillence.

16   Flags in Charlotte flew at half mast in memory

17   of those who lost their lives in the quake.

18   A heat wave swept over the region after the quake,

19   and the temperature rose to 32 degrees celsius.

20   Public health authorities plan to innoculate all

21   residents of Charlotte to avoid any outbreak of disease.

Number Correct _____

Student's Name _____

11 Public Relations

Spelling

rhetoric/rhetorical, accede, pejorative, eleemosynary, coroner, subpoena,* wisdom, caricature, fluorescent, rarefied, phenomenon, excerpt

Usage

exotic/erotic/esoteric, because/since, sight/site/cite, oriented/orientation, averse/adverse, amend/emend

Newsroom Vocabulary

public relations, public information, media, press release, handout, advance, release date, embargo, hold

Public Relations

For the most part, public relations requires the same sort of factual, understandable and interesting writing that you find in newspapers.

In this section of "Practice Exercises," you will write the same kinds of stories you have written before: simple news stories. These will be about coming events, about honors and awards, about programs and about speeches. Some of these you will write for use in The Morning Record, some for distribution as press releases or as news stories intended for trade publications.

While you are working on exercises in this section, you will consider that you have been assigned to The Morning Record's promotion department, an in-house public relations department, as a staff writer.

The promotion department handles all public relations and promotional activities for The Morning Record. It publishes a monthly employee publication called Newsline, develops community programs and each year plans and holds a Press Institute in cooperation with the School of Journalism at Northwest College. The promotion department also does some market research and conducts readership surveys.

Unless you are given other instructions, set up your copy in the manner shown in the model on page 259.

your name
Promotion Department

For Immediate Release

CAROLTON -- (today's date) -- Fred W. Nelson, city editor
of The Morning Record since 1984, has resigned to join Graham
Associates, a public relations firm.

Nelson joined the Record staff as a general assignment
reporter in 1976 immediately after his graduation from the
School of Journalism at Northwest College.

He spent the past year in Washington on an American
Political Science Association fellowship. He returned to the
Record in August.

##

EXERCISE 11-1

This morning Debbie Williams, promotion manager of the Record, gave you a press release and asked you to write a story about it for tomorrow's paper. The press release came from the Central State Chapter of the Society of Professional Journalists, Sigma Delta Chi. Debbie Williams is a member and chairman of the chapter's Freedom of Information Committee.

Text of the press release:

The Central State Professional Chapter of the Society of Professional Journalists, Sigma Delta Chi applauds the recent Supreme Court decision that the Securities and Exchange Commission lacks authority to stop publication of a financial newsletter.

Although the court decided the case on technical grounds, it is a major First Amendment victory for the public and the press.

The case involved Christopher L. Lowe, a financial adviser who continued to publish a newsletter after he was convicted on charges that he misappropriated a client's funds. The decision means that while the SEC can continue to prosecute any financial adviser who gives fraudulent advice — as it should — the commission will not be able to prevent any publication from publishing.

The decision also should serve as a warning to other federal agencies that might be tempted to try to impose prior restraint on publications. The Supreme Court's decision clearly is in keeping with the spirit of the First Amendment.

The publication in question is the Lowe Investment and Financial Letter. The court ruled eight to nothing against the SEC.

EXERCISE 11-2

Walter Bettencourt, former publisher of the Record, died yesterday, and his obit was published in this morning's paper (Exercise 7-25). You have been asked to write an obit for Editor & Publisher. In the obit, you will have to emphasize Bettencourt's newspaper career and play down other details. Use a Carolton dateline and today's date.

You check the clips in the reference library and find additional information about his newspaper career and his association with the Record:

Started as reporter on Chicago Daily News 1927. Went to Chicago American in 1932. Became city editor and managing editor. Came to Carolton in 1961 and bought the Record from the Benjamin Ames family, owners since 1920. Majority owner of stock in The Morning Record Co. Son-in-law, Fred Courtwright, present publisher, and his wife, Bettencourt's daughter, own rest of stock. Bettencourt was: President ASNE 1962; president state press association 1965 and 1966; president ANPA in 1970. Gave Northwest college million dollars in 1975 to establish Bettencourt professorship in journalism.

EXERCISE 11-3

You have just been given a copy of the program for the annual Press Institute. The Record is one of the sponsors of this program, and the promotion department is responsible for publicity.

Write a story on the program for tomorrow's paper. Just hit the high spots. The Friday and Saturday referred to in the program are the last weekend of this month.

EXERCISE 11-4

The Morning Record and the Central State Chapter of the Society of Professional Journalists, Sigma Delta Chi are planning a public relations workshop for local organizations. The publicity chairmen of the local clubs and organizations will be invited to attend. The workshop will be held next Thursday at 5:30 p.m. at the Civic Center.

The workshop will cost $10, and this will include a box supper.

These Morning Record staffers will take part: Carter, Irving, Latham and Ellenburg.

Write the story for tomorrow's paper.

Include the promotion department's telephone number in the story, so people can call to register for the workshop. The number is 355-6568.

EXERCISE 11-5

At the Press Institute luncheon Saturday, you picked up the list of winners in the College Press Association writing contest. Two of the winners have local ties:

Jane Jackson	third place
John Medford Jr.	second place
Eleanor Fiore	first place

Write a story and see that it gets to the Record's city editor in time for tomorrow's paper.

Medford attends Ferris Institute and is managing editor of the Ferris Flyer, the Ferris student newspaper. His father is a Washington county sheriff. Eleanor Fiore is local, too. She's a student at Northwest College and writes for the Daily Student. Jane Jackson has no local ties. She attends Southeastern State in Brookfield and writes for the Brookfield Booster.

EXERCISE 11-6

One of your responsibilities while you have been working in the promotion department has been the Press Institute. One of the speakers yesterday was John Chancellor, senior commentator for NBC News. You were at the dinner when Chancellor spoke, and you obtained a copy of his speech. The Record's city editor has asked you to write a story based on this excerpt from the text:

Ideas need careful care and feeding, and that has never been as true as it is today. We live in a world stuffed with information, groaning and creaking under the biggest load of facts and statistics in history. Can good ideas get lost in all this? They certainly can.

It is hard these days for an idea to get a hearing — from the university or the press or a foundation. There is a clamor of ideas — a cacophony. There is intense competition for chances to develop ideas. We have reached a stage in this country where we are generating ideas at a faster and faster rate, and society's ability to deal with the flow and pay for the development of the ideas is in danger of being overloaded.

Ideas, especially in the sciences, are expensive. Long ago in history, ideas came virtually without cost. Newton didn't have much of an expense account. By the time Tom Edison and Henry Ford came along, the ideas cost a little more, but not much. Yet I wonder how much money went into the discovery of DNA, which contains our genetic code. DNA itself — the acid — was discovered in 1870 in a process that cost little. It was almost 100 years later when Watson and Crick began to break the code. I wonder how much money went into that.

We need ideas more than we ever did before. Things are changing. The kind of changes we're going through requires a steady, uninterrupted supply of fresh ideas and innovative techniques. Americans are as good at that as any people in the world.

One of the challenges we face is to sustain that great American momentum in the discovery of the new, in the finding of new ways to do things and make things. It's not going to be easy. It is a contest with other countries that may be decided by the end of this century. Its outcome will shape the United States in the next century.

EXERCISE 11-7

Miss Williams has suggested that you do another advance story on the Press Institute. Build this one around Jim Polk, the NBC reporter. You don't have a bio sketch, but Polk is listed in Who's Who. Include something on the writing contest.

EXERCISE 11-8

The promotion manager wants another advance story on the Press Institute. Write this one around the Saturday luncheon speaker. He hasn't provided a biographical sketch, but he is listed in Who's Who.

40th Annual Press Institute

Friday

9:00 a.m.   Registration, Center for Continuing Education

10:00 a.m. Welcome
John R. McKay, President
Northwest College

11:00 a.m. Panel: "Careers in Journalism"
Moderator: William A. Irving, The Morning Record
Panelists: Elliott Brack, Marietta Daily Journal
and Neighbor Newspapers
Marion Higginbotham, Daily Student
David J. Bishop, Ann Arbor News

1:00 p.m.   Luncheon
Speaker: John Chancellor, NBC News
"A More Competitive America"

2:30 p.m.   Panel: "Effective Use of Wire Services"
Panelists: Conrad C. Fink, University of Georgia
John Doe, AP Bureau, Detroit
Richard A. Oppel, Charlotte Observer

4:00 p.m.   The Wilbur Fisk Storey Lecture
Speaker: Thomas W. Jobson, Asbury Park Press

6:30 p.m.   Hospitality Hour at the Carolton Country Club

7:30 p.m.   Dinner at the Carolton Country Club
Speaker: the Hon. Robert E. Moore, Lieutenant
Governor

Saturday

8:00 a.m.   Breakfast
Speaker: Jane Fields, editorial page editor, The
Somerset Post

10:00 a.m. Panel: "Is Anybody Out There Reading Us?"
Panelists: Charles Carter, New York Daily News
Linda Miller, Morning Record
Henry Hill, School of Journalism

11:15 a.m. Panel: "Improving Newspaper Content"
Panelists: Neal Shine, Detroit Free Press
Mark Matthews, Denver Standard
Michael R. Fancher, Seattle Times

1:00 p.m.   Awards Luncheon
Speaker: Robert Clark, consultant for news,
Harte Hanks Newspapers,
San Antonio, Texas
"The Three Blind Mice of Journalism"
Awards to Newspapers
Nominations to Hall of Fame

2:30 p.m.   Press Institute Workshops
Room 110   Generating Story Ideas
Room 204   Editing
Room 210   Managing the Newsroom

4:00 p.m.   Panel: "Investigative Reporting"
Moderator: James Polk, NBC News, Washington
Panelists: Michele Fleet, Post-Tribune,
Crown Point, Ind.
John DeMott,
Memphis State University
John Ullmann,
Minneapolis Star and Tribune

7:00 p.m.   Hospitality Hour at the Carolton Country Club

8:00 p.m.   Annual Press Institute Banquet,
Carolton Country Club

State College Press Association

Writing Contest

Members of the College Press Association who wish to enter the writing contest are to report on the speech by John Chancellor, NBC News, Friday noon.

Typewriters will be available in Room 204 of the Journalism Building. Report to the journalism office, Room 250, for your contest number. Contestants will be allowed one hour and twenty minutes to complete a story.

The contest will be judged by faculty of the School of Journalism. Winners will be announced at the awards luncheon on Saturday.

40th Annual

Press Institute

Northwest College Center for Continuing Education

Northwest College

Carolton

Co-Sponsored by

Northwest College School of Journalism

The Morning Record

EXERCISE 11-9

You were assigned to cover the annual Chamber of Commerce dinner last night. Write a story for tomorrow's paper. Here are the facts:

The Chamber made a special award to a member of the Record staff.

Chamber president Lawrence MacClure presented the award. About 150 chamber members were at the dinner. The dinner was held at the Hotel Lenox.

The award was given for quote helpful criticism unquote of the Carolton and Washington county business community.

The award was given to Marilyn Carter, the Record's executive editor.

MacClure said quote We feel that while we don't always agree with everything the Record says, this is more than offset by the Record's thorough and accurate reporting about the business community unquote.

Carter has been executive editor of the Record for the past two years. Before that she was managing editor and still earlier was city editor.

FYI: MacClure is the outgoing Chamber president. The new president, installed last night, is Nancy Johnson (Exercise 2-10).

EXERCISE 11-10

The Morning Record, the Washington County Human Rights Commission and the Carolton Community Relations Association make an award once a year to someone in the community who has contributed to the community through volunteer work. Because the Record is one of the sponsors of the program, the promotion department handles the story for the city desk. The volunteer of the year was named yesterday. Write the story.

He is a member of the Carolton Rotary club, a member of the board of directors of the United Way, a deacon at All Saints Episcopal church, president of the PTA at the Harvey O'Higgins junior high, and scoutmaster of Boy Scout troop 43 of Carolton.

He is an insurance agent, with offices in the Wirtz building.

His name is Randolph M. Spooner, age 42, married, three children.

He will get a $2,000 check. Check doesn't go to him, but to a local charity or community group of his choice. He has designated the Boy Scouts.

The money is donated by the First National Bank, the Record and the Washington County Foundation.

EXERCISE 11-11

The Record wants a story on the Clark speech at the Press Institute. Since you were to be at the luncheon on assignment for the promotion department, you have been asked to do the story. Write a story based on these excerpts.

There are three problems of journalism that to me resemble the three blind mice. They are problems we must not be blind to. If we as editors are blind to them, we are in trouble with our readers — with the public.

The first of these blind spots is minorities.

Over half our newspapers still have no minorities in their newsrooms. If our newsrooms are to reflect the general population in racial balance — we have a very long way to go.

I see this as a moral issue, yes. But I also see it as an economic one. By 1990 minorities will be 25 percent of this country's population. By the year 2000, 29 percent. And here we stand in our newsrooms at something over 6 percent.

We have a responsibility to inform all Americans about all of America — about race relations as well as business triumphs, about poverty as well as wealth. The problems of race affect us all. And I am convinced that we cannot report, even in the hinterland, what is happening in this country without the help of a cross-section of Americans in our newsrooms.

I am greatly heartened by the steps many of our newspapers have been taking to improve the situation.

Let's not let minorities be one of our blind spots. If we do, I am convinced that our future is in real jeopardy.

My second blind mouse is credibility.

It has become fashionable in the past few months to say that the media have no credibility crisis. I quote from the recent Times Mirror/Gallup study: "There is no credibility crisis for the nation's news media. If credibility is defined as believability, then credibility is, in fact, one of the media's strongest suits."

That study showed that established news organizations — the TV news networks, the leading newspapers, several news programs on radio and TV, even quote the daily newspaper you are most familiar with unquote — came out with flying colors when people were asked how much they thought these institutions could be believed.

However, I don't think we have any reason to become complacent about credibility. I would urge that you do not have a blind spot about credibility. No one is suggesting that we slack off on quality journalism or hard-hitting reporting. We simply have to be tuned in better to the needs and feelings of the public. If we do not, we run the risk, again, of getting our tails cut off.

My third blind mouse is education for journalism.

I doubt if any editor would disagree that we want educated, well-rounded people on our staffs. We want people who can go right to work, yes, but we also want them to have backgrounds in economics and history and political science and other things that become more and more important as society generally becomes more educated and more sophisticated. This is especially true, it seems to me, in a society that

continued on next page

relies on television for spot news, for generally superficial information about events, but that relies on newspapers to give them depth and understanding.

We need to insist on educated people in our newsrooms. If we are blind to that need, in today's world, again we run the risk of losing credibility and put ourselves in jeopardy.

The public will not accept shoddy journalism for long, in my view. I suppose trash will always sell, but it's not journalism. We all know the basics of our business. We know how to report, how to edit, how to display pictures, how to write convincing editorials. But we need to remember the things that give us depth, give us quality, that maintain our heritage as public servants dedicated to the public good.

We have no guarantee that the First Amendment will be with us forever and ever. We in journalism hold it sacred, but a huge segment of the public is not even aware of what it is. The press does not have a divine right to exist. We must deserve our place in society and carry it out responsibly. Only then will the public feel that the press indeed is a credible, honorable institution worthy of support.

Only if we take seriously the problems that face us, and address them earnestly, can we be assured that we are playing our rightful and responsible role in a free society.

EXERCISE 11-12

You have been given this press release and asked to write a story about the awards for tomorrow's paper. The Record publishes a teen page once a month, and the students who won the NCTE awards have been on the staff of the teen page this year. They attend Central High. The press release:

CHAMPAIGN-URBANA — The National Council of Teachers of English has named winners in its annual writing contest.

Awards will go to 750 high school juniors who entered the NCTE Achievement Awards in Writing program.

The NCTE is a professional organization of individuals and institutional members at all levels of instruction. Its goal is to increase the effectiveness of the teaching of English language and literature in the nation's schools and colleges.

Winners include:

Look, Ann, Carolton. Parents: Stanley and Helen Look.
Warren, Richard, Carolton. Parents: Richard and Evie Warren.

Over 6,000 juniors were nominated this year for Achievement Awards in Writing. Each piece of writing submitted by a nominee was read and evaluated by two judges. A third judge produced the final list of students. About 13 per cent of those nominated were singled out for awards. The winners are among the best student writers in the country.

Winners receive a special plaque and a certificate.

EXERCISE 11-13

You covered the awards lunch Saturday at the Press Institute and picked up the list of winners in the better newspaper contest. The Morning Record and several of its staff have won awards. You sift these from the long list of winners.

General excellence: Morning Record, first place.

Editorial writing: Eric Latham.

Spot news photo: John Timulty, Morning Record, for photos taken during a student demonstration on the college campus last spring.

Investigative reporting: Deborah Brown, Morning Record, for a series of stories on bank failures in the state.

Best feature story: James Look, Record police reporter, for a story on a lost child.

Write the story for the Record's employee publication, Newsline.

EXERCISE 11-14

Write a news story for Editor & Publisher based on these facts:

The Morning Record has a number of incentive programs for its employees including one called the Bettencourt award, which is awarded annually to one or more employees who have been active in community affairs.

Two employees will get Bettencourt awards this year. Each will get a check for $1,000 and a commemorative plaque.

The two are Linda Miller, the Record's city editor, and Don Peters, the Record's production manager.

Peters has worked with the Washington county Little League since he came to Carolton eight years ago. He is treasurer of the league, coaches a team in the senior division and umpires in the junior division.

Miller has served on the boards of Carolton General hospital and the Carolton Day Care Council. She is a member of the Carolton Professonal Women's club and was one of the first women members of the Central State Professional Chapter of Sigma Delta Chi. For the past two years she has been president of the SPJ/SDX chapter.

EXERCISE 11-15

Make any changes in these sentences that may be necessary to make them conform to the standards of informal American English.

1. The student missed only a couple lectures last term.

2. The student's home was adjacent of the campus.

3. When the class ended, everybody picked up their books.

4. Police said the bomb contained a new type explosive.

5. The grant was awarded from the University of Texas.

6. The student only passed the test after three attempts.

7. The City Council will meet Monday to review their bylaws.

8. Each student picked up his books and quietly left the room.

9. A number of voters were waiting in line to cast their ballots.

10. Everybody in the class was expected to do their own project.

11. The trustees will meet tomorrow to elect their new chairman.

12. Not one of the students considered that they might fail.

13. Neither of them was willing to give up their seat.

14. The Bill of Rights deal with fundamental American liberties.

15. Ten tons are too much for a wheelbarrow to carry.

Number Correct _____

Student's Name _____

269

EXERCISE 11-16

Make any changes in these sentences that may be necessary to make them conform to the standards of informal American English.

1. Each of the prisoners took his rations and walked away.

2. "If I was able," he said, "I would be the first to volunteer."

3. John was not absent often. He only missed a couple of lectures.

4. Smith is presently superintendent of schools in Carolton.

5. "I'm not hurt," he said. "I'm perfectly alright."

6. The number of things one shouldn't do is enormous.

7. The money was divided between the three boys.

8. Everybody thought that they played the game well.

9. Neither John, Bill or Henry were accepted by a college.

10. The sound of the bells mingle with the voices of the choir.

11. Two weeks are not long enough for a restful vacation.

12. Sloppy sentences or careless grammar are not acceptable.

13. "Get up!" he said. "You can't lay around all day like this."

14. Smith was awarded for his bravery. He was given a medal.

Number Correct _____

Student's Name _____

271

EXERCISE 11-17

Edit this news story. Correct errors in style. Use standard editing marks and practices. Do *not* rewrite. There may be errors in spelling, grammar, usage or punctuation.

01   Two Cleveland, O., residents have filed suit in

02 Washington county circuit court against the Territory

03 and Western Railroad.

04   The suit was filed as a result of an accident last

05 May in which Rev. Edgar D. Callahan was killed at the

06 rail crossing on Territorial Rd. just north of Perimeter

07 Road.

08   The suit seeks $8,000,000 in damages, $7500 for

09 medical expenses and $1000 for pain and suffering.

10   Attorneys for Callahan's daughter, Mrs. Consuela

11 O'Byrne, 40, and her son, Mark, four, filed the suit

12 yesterday.

13   Their suit accuses the railroad of negligence and

14 alleges that crossing signals weren't operating that day.

15   Callahan, Mrs. O'Byrne and Mark were on their way to

16 visit Callahan's mother on Mother's day when the

17 accident occured. Callahan, 70, was the former church

18 editor of The "Morning Record."

19   Mrs. O'Byrne said yesterday that she still is not

20 well.

21   "Every time I think of the accident," she said, "I

22 feel nauseous. Its been weird."

23   The railroad has retained legal council.

Number Correct _____

Student's Name _____

EXERCISE 11-18

Edit this news story. Correct errors in style. Use standard editing marks and practices. Do *not* rewrite. There may be errors in spelling, grammar, usage or punctuation.

01   Bank robbers yesterday blasted open a two foot thick

02   concrete wall at the back of the First National bank and

03   took $2000 from an open safe.

04   The bank, at 16 West Main St., is the oldest bank in

05   the city.   The principle stockholder is Mrs. Helen

06   Overkampf, a former resident of Carrolton, who now lives

07   in Portland, Oregon.

08   The bank is usually not open after three in the

09   afternoon.   John C. Elmer, the bank's vice president,

10   said 7 customers and fourteen bank employes were in the

11   bank yesterday afternoon.

12   Mr. Elmer said the bank's losses are covered by

13   insurance.   The bank is insured for losses up to fifty

14   million dollars.

15   A bank customer, Alice Short, 27, of 604 Washington

16   Rd. was injured by the blast.   She was standing by the

17   24 inch thick back wall.   She was taken to Holy Cross

18   hospital by ambulance.

19   The Carrolton police bomb squad is investigating.

20   Police Sergeant Alex Cordoba said he believed the robbers

21   used plastic explosive in coke bottles.

22   Police have issued an eight state alarm for the

23   robbers.   The money taken was mostly in $5.00 and $10.00

24   bills.   Number Correct _____

Student's Name _____

12 The Rewrite Desk

Spelling

defunct, acknowledgment, catalog,* colloquial, hurricane, straightforward, asphyxiate, egregious, homicide, credible/credibility, athlete/athletic, canvass

Usage

adopt/approve/enact/pass, average/mean/median/norm, citizen/resident/native, accuse/charge/indict, comprise/compose/constitute, perquisite/prerequisite

Newsroom Vocabulary

editor, copy editor, edit, update, trim, boil, cut, rewrite, rewriteman, Ed & Pub, journalism reviews, box

277

The Rewrite Desk

This topic is treated in detail in George A. Hough 3rd, "News Writing," fourth edition:

Rewrite
Chapter 20, "Be Clear, Complete and Accurate," pages 403 through 418.

Chapter 21, "Editing, Revising and Rewriting," pages 421 through 439.

EXERCISE 12-1

You were on rewrite today when the Record's police reporter called in with several stories. You took them and then asked the city editor for instructions. "Lead with the Williams shooting," she said, "and shirttail the others."

(williams shooting)

Police are holding James Williams, 57, for investigation of murder — he's an insurance adjuster — lives at 700 W. Utah — arrested last night — at his home — neighbors called the cops — they found him in the kitchen with a .45 pistol — he took a couple of pot shots at the officers — quite a little shoot-out before he gave up — he has a flesh wound in the left arm — cops took him to Carolton General emergency — then to headquarters —cops found his wife in bedroom upstairs — four bullets in her chest — dead on arrival at Carolton General — detectives said neighbors heard them quarreling and then heard shots — there was a record of trouble between them — cops called there once or twice before — Det. Sgt. O'Neil is in charge — he says Williams will probably be arraigned tomorrow — wife's name is Marcia — she's an accountant — kept books for a lot of businesses in town — she's pretty well known — used to be on the city council — no children.

You check the reference library and find that Mrs. Williams served two terms on the City Council, 1980 through 1984, and did not seek re-election. She was admitted to the bar last month.

(robbery)

shooting at 103 E. Main — liquor store — attempted robbery — owner winged a guy trying to hold him up — cops looking for the guy now — about 30, maybe five ten and about 180 — wearing army jacket — work pants — combat boots — sandy hair — white — scar on left cheek — may have a bullet wound in his right arm — guy went into store about closing time last night — ten or so — and pulled a gun — owner — Clyde Morris — sixty-eight — ducked behind counter and the guy shot at him — Morris fired back with a .38 he had under the counter — police car going by heard the shot and investigated — the guy ran, but the cops shot at him and they swear he was hit — cops are Bill Sturdevant and Tom Rickles.

(body)

cops found a guy in the parking lot behind post office last night — dead — bullet wound in the head — Robert Turkington — about 30 — lived at 601 E. Main — had a social security card on him — and that was about all — cops say he was a wino — probably rolled for his last buck — no clues.

EXERCISE 12-2

Rewrite this press release. Use as much as you think necessary, but be sure that your story is a news story, not a sales pitch for the candidate.

News Release

From: Ms. Lillian Leamy
        211 S. Sherman St.
        Carolton

For Immediate Release

A long-time advocate of equal rights for women and minorities, Ms. Lillian Leamy today announced that she will be a candidate for Washington County Clerk.

Active in community affairs, Ms. Leamy is a member of the Executive Board of 11th Congressional District Democrats, the NAACP, the Women's Caucus of the Washington County Democratic Party, the Carolton Democratic Committee, and the Washington County Chapter of the National Organization for Women.

In announcing her candidacy, Ms. Leamy pointed out that she was instrumental in obtaining the first mobile registration unit in Washington County. Ms. Leamy went on to say — "I drove that mobile registration unit countless miles throughout the county, the city of Carolton, and nearby communities in an effort to register voters. And from this experience I found out how hard it is to get people to register. As such, I have decided to run for county clerk. If elected, I will do whatever is necessary to make registering to vote easier.

Turning her attention to Carolton, Ms. Leamy vigorously attacked the existing situation. She said: "Every means possible must be employed to make voting simpler and more convenient."

Ms. Leamy, formerly a lobbyist for the Washington County Education Assn., was a strong supporter of the Equal Rights Amendment. She was also the first woman in the state to be registered as a lobbyist.

##

EXERCISE 12-3

The metric system, if it is ever adopted in this country, would require us to get used to very precise measurements. And metrics would make obsolete a lot of interesting old words, words long used in specifying sizes, weights, measurements and distances.

The following are interesting old words and terms. Look them up. Explain their etymology. Cite the reference work you used to do this exercise.

mill (a term used in tax stories); fathom; furlong; pica; ream; quire; knot; stone; hand; chain; acre; cable's length; agate line

EXERCISE 12-4

Your city editor handed you this story with instructions to rewrite it. The story originally appeared in yesterday's paper. "Rewrite and cut it," your editor said.

The story, as you can see, has a feature lead and is told chronologically. Rewrite, use a summary lead and organize the story in the inverted-pyramid format.

For a time Branson Potter had the upper hand in a classic game of hide-and-seek.

But about the time he figured he was well hidden, the police guessed just where he was.

As a result, Potter's sitting behind bars at Carolton police headquarters.

It all started about 11:40 a.m. today when Potter was in Municipal Judge Arthur B. Hempstead Jr.'s courtroom to stand trial for aggravated assault and battery.

Taking advantage of a momentary distraction in the courtoom, Potter ran into the hall. Police ran after him, but Potter eluded them.

Two police officers driving along Main Street saw Potter running from the courthouse and recognized him as a recent guest at police headquarters. They followed him as far as the 400 block on North Grant and called for reinforcements.

Four police cars and two teams of detectives converged on the 400 block. Diligent search failed to locate Potter.

Either it wasn't Potter they had been chasing, or he had found a secure hiding place.

Later in the afternoon, Potter was apprehended at his home at 506 South Sherman by Detective Sgt. Emil Crow. Potter was sitting in his kitchen reading a newspaper and eating a sandwich when Crow knocked at the back door.

He surrendered quietly.

EXERCISE 12-5

Your city editor handed you this story, from the first edition of today's paper. "Sharpen this up," she said. "I want it for the second edition."

Richard Higgins of Madison, a representative of the state Human Rights Commission, will speak at Sunday's meeting of the Huxley Institute for Biosocial Research.

The meeting will be from 3-5:30 p.m. in Room 112 of the Holiday Inn in Carolton.

He will discuss "Protecting Human Rights of Mental Patients."

The institute is a non-profit voluntary organization dedicated to educating persons about prevention and elimination of schizophrenia and hypoglycemia.

EXERCISE 12-6

This story was handed to you by the Record's state editor. He wants a rewrite. Give the story a strong summary lead and include an itemized list of the victims.

Special to the Morning Record

BREWSTER — He was trapped upstairs with his wife and four children as flames engulfed the first floor of their home, said Elmer Vernor, so he broke a window and jumped to safety. He told his wife to have the rest of the family follow.

But, Vernor told neighbors, his wife apparently was overcome by fumes and smoke. She and the couple's four small children perished in the flames early Monday.

Authorities identified the victims as Mrs. Renee Vernor, 26, her three daughters, Mary, 7, Margaret, 5, Marion, 3, and a son, Michael, 1.

Vernor, age 28, and his brother, Edward, age 25, who leaped to safety from another upstairs window of the two-story frame home, drove a pickup truck to the Warren Freitag home about a mile away to get help. Both were scantily dressed in the below-freezing weather.

Firefighters from Brewster found the flames out of control when they arrived. The house was destroyed.

Vernor told the Freitags that he, his wife and their four children made their way to a stairway landing but were unable to get through the smoke and fumes.

Vernor said he broke a window on the landing and told his wife he would jump to the ground, then she should toss the children to him, then jump. The rest of the family did not make it.

Vernor and his brother are self-employed loggers. The family moved to the Brewster area last summer from near Carolton.

EXERCISE 12-7

While you were on rewrite this morning, the Record's police reporter called in with a shooting story. It has a couple of good angles. Your notes:

Gardner Green — age 14 — condition critical — Carolton General — brought in from home — 714 North Jackson — gunshot — bullet in right chest — removed last night — police say accidental shooting — father shot him with 22 caliber target pistol.

Father cleaning pistol. Didn't realize it was loaded. Father is Virgil, age 35 — security guard — Farmers Bank — says they were going to go target shooting yesterday afternoon — he was pretty shaken up.

You call Green and ask about the shooting. He tells you:

I didn't know it was loaded. I was cleaning the pistol and turned around to put it back in the rack. It just went off. Gardner was standing a few feet away. I heard a kind of "pow" and he said, "Dad, you shot me." I didn't believe it until I saw the blood.

EXERCISE 12-8

While you were on rewrite this morning, the Jenkins Funeral Home called in the Clark obit. Write it for tomorrow's paper. Be sure you include background on the accident in your story.

Kim Clark, age 18, 608 East Ohio. Parents: John and Wilma.

Services Friday at 4 p.m. at Liberty Baptist church. Duttweiler to officiate. Burial — Evergreen cemetery.

Family: parents
           grandparents — m/m Harry Clark, Charlotte, N.C.
           brother — Arthur, student at U of Texas
           sister — Marilyn, student at Johns Hopkins
           sister — Anne (Mrs. John L. Natwick, Pittsfield, Mass.)

Kim a senior at Carolton Central — honor student — had been accepted at Bowdoin for fall — born in Carolton — on high school swim team — member National Honor Society — French club, Drama club and Science club — members of her high school class will be honorary pall bearers — parents want memorial gifts to go to scholarship fund at high school.

EXERCISE 12-9

This story was brought in by the engineers' publicity chairman. Your city editor thinks it should be rewritten.

How Northwest college is using computers in research and teaching will be discussed by Dr. Richard Verway, chairman of the college's computer science department and director of the college's computer laboratory, before a dinner meeting tomorrow night at 6:30 p.m.

Dr. Verway is responsible for all computer systems at Northwest college, including the system that has just been installed in the college library. Northwest will take delivery on a new computer system next month that will link all college departments and residence halls to the computer lab and the main library. Details concerning these computers will be presented by Dr. Verway. A discussion will follow.

The Washington County Society of Professional Engineers will meet at the Lenox Hotel in the Centennial Room.

EXERCISE 12-10

We live in an age of high technology. Here's a list of instruments or scales used for measuring. What does each measure or record? What is the etymology of each word?

clinometer; hydrometer; tachometer; taffrail log; Snellen chart; Beaufort scale; theodolite; stadimeter; tonometer

EXERCISE 12-11

You found a note on your desk this morning about a program scheduled on campus next week. From the note and whatever else you can dig up, write a story for tomorrow's paper.

The note:

Colloquium — Monday — faculty lounge — Mark Twain Hall — 4:00 p.m. — speaker — Luisa Flores — she will discuss the work of a Spanish novelist — Ana Maria Matute — colloquium is one held each term by the romance language department — Flores will speak in Spanish — you can get more from Don Harmon in the romance language department.

You call Harmon and he tells you:

Matute is a distinguished novelist — lives in Madrid — won a number of literary prizes — she writes novels and short stories — also some children's books — many have been translated into English — and other languages, including French, German, Italian and Portuguese.

Her manuscripts are at Boston University in the Ana Maria Matute Collection. She is a member of the Hispanic Society of America.

Flores is an assistant professor in the romance language department. She wrote her doctoral dissertation on Matute.

EXERCISE 12-12

This story was written for the Record's first edition. Your city editor thinks it could be improved if it had a better lead. Rewrite the story and give it an itemizing lead.

Two employees of the Shook Chemical Corp., 950 N. Meade St., were burned seriously and another was overcome by smoke yesterday in an explosion and fire in the plant's mixing room.

Fire Chief John Wiggins described the explosion as a "blowback" and said it apparently occurred because chemicals were not mixed in the proper order.

Edward Dean, 25, of 408 S. Meade, suffered burns over 60 percent of his body and Mark Diaz, 30, of 520 E. New York Ave., was burned over 70 percent of his body. Both are in critical condition at Carolton General Hospital.

Another employee, James Abrams, 31, of 422 E. Wisconsin Ave., and James Nixon, 32, of 217 S. Grant, a Carolton fireman, were overcome by smoke. Both are being treated at St. Luke's Hospital.

Fire Lt. Jacob Strauss said it could not be determined immediately what chemicals the employees were mixing or what went wrong. The mixing room, in a small building near the chemical company's main building, was badly damaged by the explosion and the fire that followed.

EXERCISE 12-13

Rewrite this story. Your editor wants something other than a direct quote lead. The story is a little long, too.

"This was just one of those things," June Price said Monday as she walked back from the firing line at the 80th annual Grand American Trapshooting Tournament.

The slim, 40-year-old Carolton secretary had shattered 200 straight targets to become the first woman ever to record a perfect score in Grand American shooting.

"I've never even had 100 straight before," she said. "Everything just seemed to fall into place."

Mrs. Price, the state women's champion, is a novice at the game. Her husband, Flynn, taught her to shoot just four years ago.

As state champion, she also competed Monday in the 100-target extra event for state champions only.

In that competition, she broke 97 of 100. She also had to pick her clay targets from among a flock of birds that picked a poor place to feed as the nation's best trapshooters were going about their sport.

"The birds didn't bother me," the attractive Mrs. Price said. "I'd just had it for the day."

EXERCISE 12-14

Professional users of words — news writers, public speakers, novelists, politicians, actors, poets and others — enjoy words and take pleasure in using them with effect.

A while back, a member of Congress was quoted as saying:

When we want anything, we have to go begging as sycophants to the nabobs of Squeedunk, to the pooh-bahs of Podunk.

I do not want CBS or NBC to continue to be the pooh-bahs or panjandrums of what the public may hear ...

Colorful and interesting words. What do they mean? Where did they come from? Look up the underlined words and write a brief report explaining their meanings. Cite your sources.

EXERCISE 12-15

These words and phrases are derived from names. What is their meaning in modern American English? How did these words acquire their present meaning? Who were the men and women whose names lie behind the present meanings?

(an) ananias; nimrod; magdalen; judas; jonah; methuselah; abigail; jezebel; doubting Thomas

EXERCISE 12-16

Your city editor handed you this story, a clipping from this morning's Daily Student. She wanted a quick rewrite for tomorrow's paper. "Boil it down," she said.

Although most of the dozen lectures scheduled at the Conference Center on campus during the term are open to the public without charge, the great majority of them are too technically oriented for most people. However, tomorrow evening's lecture by Sheldon Simms of the Population Council and the special lecture next Thursday by George Green of Harvard University will be of interest to the general public.

Tomorrow night Dr. Simms, one of the world's experts on population control, will speak on "Population Issues: A Timely Report." Dr. Simms plans to stress the societal rather than the scientific aspects of his subject. His lecture is scheduled for 8:00 in the Auditorium.

George Green's lecture, scheduled for 8:00 next Thursday night, will treat a subject that has become quite controversial. Prof. Green will lecture on "The Efficacy of Acupuncture." He has seen acupuncture practiced in China and will describe his observations of the technique and discuss recent evidence as well as his own views.

EXERCISE 12-17

This provocative passage appears in John McPhee's book "Basin and Range."

Imagine an E. L. Doctorow novel in which Alfred Tennyson, William Tweed, Abner Doubleday, Jim Bridger, and Martha Jane Canary sat down to a dinner cooked by Rutherford B. Hayes.

When could this interesting social affair have taken place? Cite your sources.

EXERCISE 12-18

Words derived from names are called *eponyms*. These are words like *boycott*, *watt*, *malapropism* and *sideburns*. The words listed here are not exactly eponyms, but they derive from names. What is the meaning of each? How did each expression originate?

Hansen's disease; Murphy's law; Hobson's choice; Parkinson's Law; Custer's last stand; Cleopatra's needle; shank's mare; Adam's ale; Montezuma's revenge

EXERCISE 12-19

Legal holidays are proliferating, and now that many commemorative days are observed on a Monday to provide longer weekends, much of the significance of some long-established observances, even their proper date, is forgotten.

What is the date of these holidays or special days? Is this the date originally established? If not, what was that date?

> Columbus Day, Memorial Day, Washington's
> Birthday, Arbor Day, Flag Day

What is the significance of these?

> The first Tuesday after the first Monday in
> November, Shrove Tuesday, February 2nd

When are these holidays observed and why?

> Patriot's Day, All Saints Day, Labor Day,
> Independence Day

How is the date of Easter determined?

EXERCISE 12-20

While you were on rewrite today, your city editor handed you a story turned in earlier in the day. "Here," she said. "Check this for me. The names don't follow style."

You read over the story, checked names against the city directory and supplied missing first names and initials. One name, however, was not in the directory, that of Danny Litwhiler, former head baseball coach at Michigan State University and a major league ball player.

Your city editor is waiting for the story. Is the name Danny or Daniel? Does Litwhiler have a middle initial?

EXERCISE 12-21

Your city editor handed you a memo with notes for a story. "Here," she said. "Fix this up."

New scholarship fund at high school — memorial to Kim Clark — started with ten thousand dollar gift from grandparents — Mr. and Mrs. Harry Clark — school also has about $2500 that came in after the funeral — memorials — to add to the fund. Fund will be called the Kim Clark Scholarship.

EXERCISE 12-22

Who said it? Identify the author, the approximate date and where possible, the circumstances that prompted the remark. *Type* your answer under each quotation.

1. Here I stand, I cannot do otherwise.

2. I shall return.

3. Ich bin ein Berliner.

4. This generation of Americans has a rendezvous with destiny.

5. War is hell.

6. I have not yet begun to fight.

7. The public be damned.

8. I have nothing to offer but blood, toil, tears and sweat.

9. History is more or less bunk.

10. Th' supreme coort follows th' illiction returns.

Number Correct _____

Student's Name _____

EXERCISE 12-23

Make any changes in these sentences that may be necessary to make them conform to the standards of informal American English.

1. During the exam, everyone must sit in their seat.

2. The instructor said that hopefully the exam would be easy.

3. "That's the most unique thing I ever saw," he said.

4. He will likely be elected president next year.

5. He's the type person no one really likes.

6. There were only a handful of people who attended the meeting.

7. He can only sing when he is inebriated.

8. The man was accused of allegedly embezzling bank funds.

9. Smith had a quiet day. He just laid around the house and read.

10. The City Council scheduled it's meeting for Tuesday night.

11. Ethics, he said, are an important part of the course.

12. "Try and be good," the mother said to the child.

13. "Of course I'll be there," Smith assured hurriedly.

14. The train derailed when it reached the open switch.

Number Correct _____

Student's Name _____

291

EXERCISE 12-24

Edit these sentences to improve punctuation. Use standard editing marks to insert or delete punctuation. Do *not* rewrite.

1. The new officers are: John Foster, president; William Cook, vice president; Henry James, secretary, and Helen Moody, treasurer. Warren Hobbs will be president elect.

2. Smith, a native of Washington, D.C. has enrolled at Northwest College.

3. District Attorney John Doe, a Democratic candidate for governor has failed to file his federal tax returns.

4. According to the almanac the sun will rise at 7 a.m.

5. John Doe, the president's deputy press secretary said he hoped consultations would come early next month.

6. Jones lost his way in the storm police said Monday.

7. He married a graduate of Smith College, a native of Albany, N.Y. and they moved to Athens, Ga. where she worked for the Daily News weekdays, Saturday, and Sunday.

8. Darrel Smith, the Northwest College football coach has signed with a publisher to write a novel, a play, and a history of college football the Daily News reported Thursday.

9. City Council will meet at City Hall, Monday, at 7 p.m.

Number Correct _____

Student's Name _____

EXERCISE 12-25

Rewrite the following sentences so that the numbers are changed as they are
in the following example:

> Ten inches of snow fell overnight and paralyzed the
> city.
>
> A 10-inch snowfall paralyzed the city overnight.

1. Firemen responded to two alarms and extinguished the
    fire.

2. Carolton police cars carry two officers at all times.

3. A Carolton boy, age 7, was injured in the accident.

4. The union approved a contract that will expire in two
    years.

5. The fire that destroyed the Barnes Hotel started on the
    first floor and spread through the other five floors.

6. Two Carolton residents were injured last night when
    their cars collided on Main Street.

7. Economists think the state must wait two more years
    before business conditions improve.

8. Police said the injured man was struck twice with a
    pipe three feet long.

Number Correct _____

Student's Name _____

EXERCISE 12-26

Eliminate the *redundancies* or wordiness in these items. You may *X* them out on the typewriter, draw a line through the unnecessary words or write or type a revision in the space at the right. Some of the items may be acceptable as written.

1. dead body   _____

2. brown colored cloth   _____

3. new innovation   _____

4. first of all   _____

5. announced his future plans _____

6. completely decapitated   _____

7. high school education   _____

8. started off   _____

9. on Easter Sunday   _____

10. perhaps it may happen   _____

11. in the year 1986   _____

12. at a meeting held here   _____

13. equilateral triangle   _____

14. past experience has shown _____

15. old adage   _____

16. consensus of opinion   _____

17. book of poetry   _____

18. uniformed chauffeur   _____

19. an invited guest   _____

20. small in size   _____

Number Correct _____

Student's Name _____

EXERCISE 12-27

Edit this news story. Correct errors in style. Use standard editing marks and practices. Do *not* rewrite. There may be errors in spelling, grammar, usage or punctuation.

01   Senator Ernest F. Higginbottom formally entered the

02   democratic presidential race yesterday.

03   Higginbottom, who lives in Carrolton, has been in the

04   United States Senate since 1978.

05   In a press briefing at the National Press club in

06   Washington, D.C. he told his staff, friends, and members

07   of the working press about his political aspirations.

08   He then flew from Washington National airport last

09   night to Carrolton where he is scheduled to speak at a

10   Law day convocation at the School of Law at Northwest

11   College. Higginbottom earned an M.A. and a J.D. at

12   Northwest College.

13   He will tell the Law day audience that he expects to

14   win in primaries in New Hampshire, Wis., and Minn.

15   Higginbottom, a spry 61 year old believes his party

16   can win the next election if they develop programs

17   for the '90's and later.

18   Higginbottom was governor from 1970 to 1976. He was

19   the first governor to serve a four year term. Rumors

20   of his candidacy have been published in "The Morning

21   Record." He is the 3rd Democrat to enter the race.

Number Correct _____

Student's Name _____

EXERCISE 12-28

Edit this news story. Correct errors in style. Use standard editing marks and practices. Do *not* rewrite. There may be errors in spelling, grammar, usage or punctuation.

01   Services for Alexander G. Bell, 72, a Professor

02   Emeritus at Northwest college, will be held at 12 p.m.

03   tomorrow at the First Baptist church, 602 West Florida

04   Avenue, Carolton.

05   The Rev. John Q. Lewis will officiate. Burial will be

06   in the church cemetary.

07   Bell was a native of Bangor, Me., and was educated in

08   the schools there and in Boston. He was a graduate of

09   Boston university and earned a Master of Arts degree

10   in history at Olivet College, Olivet, Michigan.

11   He is survived by his wife, Jane; two sons, John and

12   Alexander, Jr.; a brother, William, a well-known writer

13   who has authored a book on satelites; a sister, Anne,

14   Pasadena, Calif.; and a cousin, Arthur, Dallas, Tex.

15   He was a member of the Sons of the American

16   Revolution, the Carrolton Rotary Club, the Ohio Valley

17   Historical Assn., and Veterans of Foreign Wars.

18   He was a veteran of WWII. He served in the Air Force

19   in the Pacific Theater. He remained in the reserve and

20   retired as a United States Air Force colonel.

21   Bell joined the faculty at Northwest college in 1948.

Number Correct _____

Student's Name _____

301

Appendix

1 Reference Library

Newspaper Reference Library

The Morning Record's reference library has the following reference works available for use by newsroom staff:

The Associated Press Stylebook and Libel Manual

Webster's New World Dictionary of the American Language

Webster's Third New International Dictionary

The New Columbia Encyclopedia

Who's Who in America

Black's Law Dictionary

The World Almanac

Editor & Publisher International Year Book

State Press Association Directory

Statistical Abstract of the United States

State Statistical Abstract

Rand McNally New Cosmopolitan World Atlas

United States Government Organization Manual

Bulfinch's Mythology

The Careful Writer by Theodore Bernstein

Practical English Handbook by Watkins and Dillingham

The Baseball Encyclopedia

Maps
  State Highways
  City of Carolton and Washington County
  Northwest College Campus

The resources of The New York Times Index and The New York Times Information Bank are available through a terminal in the reference library. Much of the content of the Record since 1920 is also stored in a data bank, available for quick reference through a terminal in the reference library.

Appendix

2 Directories: City of Carolton and Northwest College

Directories

These directories, modeled on city and university directories, list in alphabetical order every person who lives or works in Carolton or who has some connection with Northwest College. The reverse directory lists people, buildings and organizations by street address.

If you detect any discrepancy between the spelling of a name, a person's occupation or an address given in an exercise and that given in the directory, follow the directory. The directory gives correct names and correct addresses. Use it.

Unless otherwise indicated on the maps of Carolton and the Carolton area, streets running north and south are *streets* and streets running east and west are *avenues*.

Carolton Residents

A

Abrams, James   *foreman*   434 E. Wisconsin
Anderson, H.C.   *retired*   641 N. Sherman
Anderson, Hattie (Mrs. H.C.)
Applegate, Charles O.   *book dealer*   714 N. Sheridan
Arnold, Dalton   *state employee*   84 Beech
Ashford, John   *bank teller*   157 S. Houston

B

Baker, Howard L.   *landscaper*   247 S. Jackson
Baker, William   *lawyer*   84 Oak
Baker, Mary (Mrs. William)   *accountant*
Baker, Harold   *student*
Banks, Charles   *book dealer*   510 E. New York
Barke, Willis   *detective*   602 W. Florida
Barth, Julius E.   *florist*   278 W. Ohio
Bates, Alpha E.   *physician*   311 Sycamore
Begg, John   *police officer*   570 W. California
Bell, Alexander Graham   *retired*   308 Beech
Bell, Jane (Mrs. Alexander G.)
Bettencourt, Walter Jr.   *retired*   87 Indian River Place
Bettencourt, Elizabeth (Mrs. Walter Jr.)
Blaine, Harold E.   *teacher*   708 W. California
Blaine, Marilyn (Mrs. Harold)
Blake, John   *bookkeeper*   104 E. Perimeter
Blake, Vivian (Mrs. John)
Boise, Hardy C.   *minister*   215 Beech
Booker, Louisa Mae   *retired*   347 W. Arizona
Boomershine, John E.   *veterinarian*   386 W. Nevada
Boomershine, Madeline M. (Mrs. John E.)
Boomershine, Brian
Boomershine, John Jr.
Boylan, Harold S.   *attorney*   587 E. Utah
Brackett, Marlene   *publicist*   782 N. Scott
Brewster, Alex   *salesman*   258 W. Oregon
Brewster, Helene (Mrs. Alex)
Brewster, David   *student*
Brown, Deborah   *reporter*   180 E. Arizona
Brown, Robert   *teacher*   301 Beech
Brown, Myla (Mrs. Robert)
Brown, Robert E.   *student*
Buchanan, H.L.   *contractor*   503 E. Vermont
Buchanan, Rose (Mrs. H.L.)
Buchanan, James
Buchanan, Robert

C

Carew, Alfred   *administrator*   146 Walnut
Carew, Luther   *painter*   210 W. California
Carew, Melanie (Mrs. Luther)
Carew, Lawrence   *student*
Carter, Dawson   *salesman*   212 E. Florida
Carter, Maura (Mrs. Dawson)
Carter, Anthony   *student*
Carter, Marilyn   *editor*   227 S. Calhoun
Chin, John   *police officer*   S. Western Avenue
Choate, Stephen P.   304 S. Jackson
Choate, N.L. (Mrs. Stephen P.)   *office worker*
Clark, John   *grocer*   608 E. Ohio
Clark, Wilma (Mrs. John)
Clark, Kim   *student*
Cleveland, William R.   *truck driver*   539 S. Grant
Cook, Gerald A.   *administrator*   604 N. Houston
Coolidge, Calvin R.   *building manager*   510 W. Lexington
Coolidge, Ethel (Mrs. Calvin R.)
Coolidge, John   *student*
Cooper, Herbert W.   *conservation officer*   304 W. Nevada
Cordoba, Alexis   *police sergeant*   512 S. Grant
Courtwright, Fred III   *publisher*   212 E. New York
Courtwright, Anne (Mrs. Fred)
Cristo, S.   *teacher*   109 S. Lee
Crow, Emil   *police sergeant*   412 Sycamore
Curtis, Raymond   *county employee*   618 Washington Road
Curtis, Eileen (Mrs. Raymond)   *beautician*
Curtis, Eileen   *student*

D

Daggett, Richard   *civil engineer*   380 E. Arizona
Daggett, Emma (Mrs. Richard)   *cartographer*
Davis, Theodore   *advertising manager*   875 N. Stuart
Dawson, Ronald   *printer*   308 S. Houston
Dawson, Gilda (Mrs. Ronald)
Dawson, Stephen   *student*
Dean, Edward S.   *chemist*   408 S. Meade
Delaney, John R.   *service station owner*   202 Maple
Dendramis, Sue Ellen   *attorney*   942 N. Grant
Diaz, Mark L.   *factory worker*   520 E. New York
Dickens, Henry   *county manager*   27 Maple
Dickens, Anne (Mrs. Henry)   *writer*
Donnelly, William T.   *college administrator*   307 E. California
Door, W.T.   *physician*   327 S. Houston

Duttweiler, John R., Rev.   *minister*   210
   Walnut
Dwight, Marion   *registered nurse*   810 N. Grant
Dwight, Robert   *contractor*   350 W. Arizona
Dwight, Carolyn (Mrs. Robert)

E

Ellenberg, Kellie   *editor*   216 N. Scott
Elmer, John C.   *banker*   408 W. Utah
Evans, Clayton   *fire marshal*   308 S. Calhoun
Evers, Edward E., Rev.   *minister*   683 N.
   Jackson

F

Feldpausch, J.   *teacher*   347 W. Arizona
Ferguson, Gerald S.   *bookkeeper*   Airport Road
Ferreira, Richard Sr.   *security guard*   127
   Maple
Ferreira, Frances (Mrs. Richard)
Ferreira, Elwyn   *mechanic*
Ferreira, Richard Jr.   *student*
Fiore, Emil Jr.   *restaurant owner*   581 N. Lee
Fiore, Carlotta (Mrs. Emil Jr.)
Fiore, Eleanor   *student*
Flores, Luisa   *teacher*   510 W. Lexington
Floyde, Halbert O.   *police officer*   622 S.
   Jackson
Flynn, George A., Rev.   *priest*   478 W.
   Maryland
Franklin, Ben   *printer*   18 Beech
Franklin, Charity (Mrs. Ben)
Franklin, Robert   *student*
Funderburke, James L.   *stockbroker*   418 S.
   Lee

G

Gibbs, Beverly   *teacher*   505 W. Florida
Gibbs, John   120 Indian River Place
Gibbs, Kathrine (Mrs. John)
Gillette, Ralph   *electrician*   437 S. Lee
Gillette, Helen (Mrs. Ralph)
Gilmore, Horace A.   *contractor*   335 W.
   Oregon
Gilmore, Sarah (Mrs. Horace A.)
Gilmore, Horace N.   *artist*   583 S. Grant
Gold, Harold S.   *accountant*   180 N. Calhoun
Gold, Morris   *jeweler*   408 W. Arizona
Gold, Esther (Mrs. Morris)
Gomez, Delores   *secretary*   184 Maple
Gomez, Luis   *student*
Green, Virgil   *security guard*   714 N. Jackson
Green, Rachel (Mrs. Virgil)   *clerk*
Green, Debra   *student*
Green, Gardner   *student*

H

Hall, Henry   *chauffeur*   301 S. Sherman
Hall, Myra (Mrs. Henry)
Handy, W.H. III   *banker*   306 E. Oregon
Hardy, James   *teacher*   97 River Road
Harmon, Donald   *teacher*   518 W. Lexington
Harris, Charles   *pharmacist*   216 N. Grant
Harris, Christine   *pharmacist*
Hawkins, Emma   *antique dealer*   411 N. Grant
Hazelton, William M.   *police officer*   704 W.
   Perimeter
Hazelton, Margaret (Mrs. William M.)
Hempstead, Arthur B. Jr.   *municipal judge*
   657 N. Sheridan
Henderson, Maurice   *medical technician*   462
   W. Florida
Hickock, Bruce B.   *banker*   371 E. Nevada
Hickock, Walter   *state police*   350 Sycamore
Higginbottom, Ernest F.   *U.S. Senator*   590 E.
   Nevada
Hillman, Walter   *sales representative*   240 W.
   Wisconsin
Hirsch, Dr. H.L.   *physician*   850 N. Stuart
Hoffman, Rita   *banker*   224 E. Florida
Holmes, Granville   *teacher*   15 Sycamore
Hope, Jonathan   *fire captain*   409 E. New York
Howe, George A.   *printer*   616 E. Wisconsin
Howe, Harriet (Mrs. George A.)
Huang, Charles O.   *state employee*   327 E.
   Florida
Hughes, Charles E.   *jurist*   540 E. Nevada

I

Irving, William H.   *editor*   710 W. Florida
Ivory, G.R.   *police officer*   550 W. Newton
   Road

J

Jackson, Terry   *teacher*   97 Oak
Jackson, Ella (Mrs. Terry)
Johnson, Harry O.   *insurance*   260
   Washington Road
Johnson, Mary (Mrs. Harry O.)   *teacher*
Johnson, Nancy   *hardware dealer*   111 E.
   Oregon
Jones, Myron   *computer programmer*   141 N.
   Meade
Jones, Ellen (Mrs. Myron)
Jones, Mary   *student*
Jones, William F.   *editor*   115 S. Sheridan
Jones, Elizabeth (Mrs. William F.)
Jones, Lydia

K

Kane, Wadsworth   *insurance*   599 W. Maryland

Kane, Hilda (Mrs. Wadsworth)

Kane, Brian   *student*

Kelly, James   *contractor*   S. Western Avenue

Kirby, Helen   *librarian*   211 Sycamore

Korth, Frank   *laborer*   Old Meetinghouse Road

Krug, Herbert   *state employee*   560 W. Newton Road

Krug, Jessie W.   *state employee*   215 River Road

L

LaFrance, Genevieve   *professor*   340 E. New York

Latham, Eric   *editor*   212 N. Calhoun

Leamy, Lillian   *attorney*   27 W. Ohio

Leavitt, Rollin R.   *teacher*   221 Maple

Lewis, Elwyn   *IRS agent*   345 W. Ohio

Lewis, Tina (Mrs. Elwyn)

Lewis, Edward   *student*

Lewis, John Q.   *minister*   550 N. Sheridan

Lodge, John A.   *county auditor*   197 River Road

Look, Abel   *sheriff*   861 Battle Road

Look, James   *reporter*   552 W. Newton Road

Look, Stanley   *county employee*   301 W. Oregon

Look, Helen (Mrs. Stanley)

Look, Ann   *student*

Love, Henry   *art teacher*   17 W. Ohio

Lund, Aaron O.   *clerk*   48 S. Meade

Lutz, Helen   *artist*   477 E. Main

Lyons, Eugene R.   *taxidermist*   277 E. Arizona

Lyons, Evelyn (Mrs. Eugene R.)

Lyons, Suzanne   *student*

M

MacClure, Lawrence   *banker*   580 N. Sheridan

MacComber, Rufus   *city employee*   465 W. Perimeter

MacComber, Mahalia (Mrs. Rufus)

MacDonald, Stewart   *hotel manager*   345 N. Sherman

Maher, Thomas O.   *detective*   104 N. Battle Road

Main, Roger   *accountant*   804 N. Sherman

Main, Virginia (Mrs. Roger)

Marks, Ellen   *registered nurse*   347 W. Arizona

Marks, Mary   *teacher*   120 W. Ohio

Marks, Patricia   *county employee*   12 S. Scott

Marks, Peter   *teacher*   305 N. Houston

Marks, Mary (Mrs. Peter)

Marshall, Joseph R.   *police officer*   234 E. Ohio

May, Earl   *county employee*   86 Beech

McGregor, James L.   *musician*   927 N. Stuart

McGregor, Vangie (Mrs. James L.)

McGuire, Edwin (Micky)   *trainman*   385 W. Wisconsin

McGuire, Harold   *retired*   85 River Road

McGuire, John   *insurance*   158 S. Stuart

McLaren, Joyce Ann   *publicist*   780 N. Grant

McLeod, Mary Margaret   *physician*   610 W. Oregon

Meade, Horace W.   *physician*   414 W. Ohio

Meade, June (Mrs. Horace)

Medford, John E.   *deputy sheriff*   35 W. Nevada

Medford, Stephanie (Mrs. John E.)

Medford, John Jr.   *student*

Meyers, Don   *court clerk*   150 E. Arizona

Miller, Kenneth L.   *school employee*   442 E. Wisconsin

Miller, L.L.   *editor*   216 N. Scott

Miller, Robert L.   *plumber*   807 S. Jackson

Miskell, William   *surveyor*   415 E. Maryland

Miskell, Sybil (Mrs. William)

Miskell, Raymond L.   *student*

Morris, Clyde   *package store manager*   560 S. Grant

Morrissey, William A.   *state employee*   27 Oak

Murphy, Wanda   *dressmaker*   980 N. Houston

N

Nelson, Fred W.   *city editor*   900 N. Sheridan

Newhouse, Harold H.   *postal worker*   682 N. Scott

Newhouse, Mildred (Mrs. Harold H.)

Nightingale, H.L., Rev.   *pastor*   715 N. Scott

Nixon, James   *firefighter*   217 S. Grant

Norton, Homer H.   *clerk*   271 Washington Road

Norton, Frances (Mrs. Homer H.)

O

Oberdorfer, Harry   *police officer*   604 W. Nevada

O'Byrne, John L.   *SBA ass't administrator*   187 Sycamore

O'Kelly, Sean   *police officer*   270 W. Vermont

Olds, Gerald   *hotel manager*   49 Beech

O'Neil, James   *detective sergeant*   75 Oak

Ormsby, Zelig   *retired*   347 W. Arizona

Ormsby, Harriet (Mrs. Zelig)

Orr, Marion   *city attorney*   811 E. Wisconsin

P

Palmer, Bernard E.   *retired*   350 River Road
Parks, Marshall   *SBA administrator*   408 N. Jackson
Peters, Don   *production manager*   79 W. Utah
Peters, Paul   *security guard*   87 Oak
Potter, Branson   *laborer*   506 S. Sherman
Powers, Hubert   *oil dealer*   108 E. California
Powers, Gladys (Mrs. Hubert)
Price, Flynn   *state police*   3 S. Meade
Price, June (Mrs. Flynn)

Q

Quill, Henry   *retired*   218 N. Lee
Quill, Martha (Mrs. Henry)

R

Reeves, Marshall   *dry cleaner*   487 N. Grant
Reimenschneider, Russell   *paramedic*   847 N. Battle
Rickles, Arturo   *salesman*   450 E. Ohio
Rickles, Thomasina (Mrs. Arturo)   *police officer*
Rickles, Arturo Jr.   *student*
Rigsby, Peter   *painter*   922 S. Territorial
Rivera, Carlos J.   *auditor*   87 S. Meade
Rivera, Marie (Mrs. Carlos)
Rivera, Diane   *student*
Rivera, Helen E.   *student*
Robbins, Benjamin   *retired*   336 S. Sherman
Robbins, Diana (Mrs. Benjamin)
Robinson, George T.   *designer*   321 S. Scott
Rogers, George A.   *city treasurer*   627 N. Jackson
Rogers, Hazel (Mrs. George A.)

S

Sawyer, Albert H. Jr.   *teacher*   640 E. Nevada
Sawyer, Martha (Mrs. Albert H. Jr.)
Scissors, Floyd R.   *restaurateur*   104½ N. Calhoun
Shanks, Hubert L.   *physician*   321 W. Newton
Shaw, Harlan   *computer specialist*   317 E. Oregon
Shaw, Roberta (Mrs. Harlan)   *teacher*
Short, Alice   *teacher*   604 Washington Road
Smith, Henry Clay   *teacher*   280 E. Wisconsin
Smith, Nancy (Mrs. H.C.)
Snell, Jacob (Jake)   *service station operator*   252 W. New York
Souza, Albert T.   *banker*   461 W. California
Souza, Donald   *civil engineer*   333 River Road
Souza, John   *retired*   458 S. Scott
Souza, Mary (Mrs. John)
Souza, Joseph   *plumber*   401 W. Arizona

Souza, Lewis   *dentist*   27 Beech
Spaulding, Ernest   *actuary*   273 W. Wisconsin
Spaulding, Evelyn (Mrs. Ernest)
Speizman, Harold E.   *public relations*   761 N. Lee
Spooner, Randolph M.   *insurance*   910 N. Sheridan
Spooner, Janet (Mrs. Randolph M.)
Spooner, Jane   *student*
Spooner, Joseph   *student*
Spooner, Randolph Jr.   *student*
Stahl, John   *county agent*   650 W. Florida
Stahl, Virginia (Mrs. John)   *teacher*
Stahl, Mark H.   *student*
Stephenson, William A.   *musician*   125 Indian River Place
Stephenson, Deborah (Mrs. William A.)
Stephenson, Mitchell   *student*
Stieber, Kenneth   *insurance*   822 E. Nevada
Strauss, Jacob O.   *firefighter*   280 S. Scott
Stroh, Walter   *railroad engineer*   250 N. Sherman
Sturdevant, Willis   *police officer*   201 E. Nevada
Sullivan, James J.   *editor*   35 Maple
Sullivan, Caroline (Mrs. James J.)
Swift, Franklin T.   *hotel clerk*   216 N. Scott

T

Talcott, John A.   *police officer*   210 W. State Road
Tate, Lawrence D.   *deputy sheriff*   409 S. Sheridan
Teacher, Walker E.   *salesman*   603 W. Utah
Timulty, John O.   *photographer*   410 W. Newton Road
Toefel, Mary Jane   *bank teller*   216 N. Scott
Tombs, Catherine   *court clerk*   216 N. Scott
Toy, Jack E.   *state police*   85 W. Utah
Trask, John   *court clerk*   212 S. Jackson
Trosko, Julia A.   *teacher*   347 W. Arizona
Tsui, Charles E.   *teacher*   212 N. Houston
Turnbull, Anna   *bookkeeper*   310 E. Virginia
Turner, Ralph   *chemist*   207 S. Calhoun
Twardzynski, Otto   *teacher*   104 E. Florida
Twardzynski, Maryann (Mrs. Otto)   *teacher*
Twardzynski, Lorie   *student*

V

Vanderpol, Ray E.   *rail superintendent*   805 N. Lee
Verway, Richard L.   *teacher*   111 W. Oregon
Vogel, Ralph E. Jr.   *foreman*   504 W. Vermont
Vogel, Helen (Mrs. Ralph E. Jr.)

W

Wagner, S.E.   *teacher*   510 W. Lexington
Waldron, Donald E. (Duke)   *service station manager*   115 E. Main
Wang, James   *teacher*   504 E. Utah
Wang, Helen (Mrs. James)
Wang, James Jr.   *student*
Warren, Richard   *stockbroker*   407 W. Virginia
Warren, Evie (Mrs. Richard)
Warren, Richard   *student*
Watson, Charles   *hotel clerk*   107 S. Meade
Watson, Myrtle   *cashier*   107 S. Meade
Wells, Roger   *steelworker*   105 E. Newton Road
West, Henry A.   *welder*   915 N. Meade
West, Thelma (Mrs. Henry A.)
West, Ellis   *student*
Wetherbee, Beatrice   *college employee*   216 N. Scott
White, Elmer   *public relations*   235 Maple
White, Betty (Mrs. Elmer)
White, Mark   *student*
Wiggins, John F.X.   *city employee*   75 W. Utah

Williams, Anne   *county clerk*   216 N. Scott
Williams, Deborah   *public relations*   450 S. Meade
Williams, Donna   *city clerk*   108 E. Oregon
Williams, Henry   *business agent*   710 E. Main
Williams, Samantha (Mrs. Henry)   *lawyer*
Williams, Nancy   *student*
Williams, James   *insurance agent*   70 W. Utah
Williams, Marcia (Mrs. James)   *accountant*
Willoughby, Roger   *mechanic*   234 River Road
Wilson, James L.   *state employee*   508 N. Scott
Wilson, Lamar   *county employee*   250 N. Sheridan
Wood, Helen   *college employee*   571 E. Maryland
Woods, Donald   *police sergeant*   S. Western Avenue
Worthington, Lorraine M.   *realtor*   450 E. Nevada

Y

Yaffee, Bette   *architect*   317 S. Scott

Carolton Business Directory

Acme Fire and Accident Insurance Co.   Airport Road
Applegate Books   604 W. New York
Barth Flowers   411. E. Vermont
Belk's   245 E. Main
Belle View Apartments   216 N. Scott
Bi-Low Supermarket   400 Washington Road
Bulldog Wine and Beer Store   103 E. Main
Carolton Construction Co.   245 Washington Road
Carolton, City of
  Carolton-Washington Adult Center   412 E. Main
  Civic Center   312 W. Newton Road
  Community Development Agency   128 N. Meade
    James L. Polk, director
  Community Mental Health Clinic   550 W. Maryland
  Fire Department
    Fire Chief   John F.X. Wiggins
    Fire Capt.   Jonathan Hope
    Fire Lieut.   Jacob Strauss
    Fire Marshal   Clayton Evans
    Central Station   381 E. Main
      Rescue Squad
    East Side Station   808 S. Territorial
    West Side Station   Airport Road
  Franklin Library   400 E. Vermont
  Jail   614 W. Vermont
  Municipal Building   210 E. Main
    Mayor Henry Clay Smith   Room 112
    City Clerk Donna Williams   Room 104
    City Treasurer George A.
      Rogers   Room 12

Carolton, City of (*cont.*)
  Municipal Building (*cont.*)
    Tax Collector Joseph E.
      Thompson   Room 318
    City Auditor John Lodge   Room 15
    Human Rights Commission   Room 328
    Planning Commission   Room 330
    Vocational Rehabilitation   Room 211
  Municipal Court   100 E. Virginia
    Judge Carol Brown
    Judge Arthur B. Hempstead Jr.
    Judge Charles E. Hughes
  Police   612 W. Vermont
    Accident Prevention   Room 211
    Detective Bureau   Room 215
    Uniform Division   Room 101
  Public Housing Authority   412 E. Main
  Receiving Hospital   700 W. Vermont
  Recreation Department   608 W. Florida
  Rescue Squad   381 E. Main
  Schools
    Central High   608 W. Florida
    District Offices   608 W. Florida
      Alfred Carew, superintendent
    Harvey O'Higgins Junior High 350 E. California
Carolton Country Club   158 River Road
Carolton Hardware Co.   12 N. Jackson
Carolton-Washington County Chamber of
  Commerce   304 W. Vermont
Cedar Village Apartments   550 E. Newton
Churches
  All Saints Episcopal   680 N. Jackson
  Congregational   301 W. Arizona
  First Baptist   604 W. Florida
  First Methodist   522 S. Meade
  Liberty Baptist   911 N. Grant
  St. Thomas Roman Catholic   480 W. Maryland
  Trinity A.M.E.   234 N. Stuart
City Rescue Mission   601 E. Main
College Standard Service   1182 S. Territorial
Colonial Village Apartments   510 W. Lexington
Commerce Club   427 W. Lexington
Copper Kettle Restaurant   450 W. Lexington
Curious Book Store   340 W. New York
Daily Student   357 E. Lexington
Delta Mall   Airport Road
Door Brothers Funeral Home   250 N. Scott
Duke's Shell Service   511 S. Territorial
Evergreen Cemetery   Airport Road
Farmers and Merchants Bank   250 E. Main
First National Bank   16 W. Main
First National Food Stores   Airport Road
Graham Associates, public relations 100 W. Main
Great Atlantic and Pacific Tea Co. 106 W. Vermont
Hawkins Antiques   515 W. New York
Higginbottom Sons Co., real estate 316 E. Main
Holiday Inn   350 E. Main
Hospitals
  Carolton General Hospital   250 S. Calhoun

Hospitals (*cont.*)
   Holy Cross Hospital   E. State Road
   Receiving Hospital   700 W. Vermont
   St. Luke's Hospital   850 N. Jackson
   St. Luke's Medical Center   852 N. Jackson

Hospitals (*cont.*)	
Holy Cross Hospital	E. State Road
Receiving Hospital	700 W. Vermont
St. Luke's Hospital	850 N. Jackson
St. Luke's Medical Center	852 N. Jackson
Hotel Lenox	450 W. Lexington
Hudson, J.L. Co.	Delta Mall
Jefferson Village Apartments	347 W. Arizona
Jenkins Funeral Home	217 N. Scott
Jollity Building	Airport Road
Kelly Construction Co.	Airport Road
Kroger	Delta Mall
Leamy, Goldstick and Gray, attorneys	211 S. Sherman
McKay Funeral Home	550 E. Virginia
McKim, Oglethorpe and Dodge, architects	100 E. Main
Medical Arts Building	317 E. Main
Meijer's Thrifty Acres	Airport Road
Mercy Ambulance Service	213 W. Main
Montgomery Ward	Delta Mall
Morning Record Publishing Co.	312 E. Main
O'Flynn's	104 River Road
O'Malley's Restaurant and Bar	104 N. Calhoun
Piggly Wiggly Food Stores	Western Avenue
Presbyterian Home	E. State Road
Quick Coin Laundry	210 W. Main
Reuther Building	106 River Road
Riley Brothers Funeral Chapel	426 W. Arizona
Sears, Roebuck and Co.	Delta Mall
Shook Chemical Corp.	950 N. Meade
Smith and Jones Funeral Chapel	Airport Road
Snell's Texaco	585 S. Grant
State Government	
State Police	Airport Road
Vocational Rehabilitation Services	211 City Hall
Territory and Western Railroad	T & W Depot
Tri-State Education Assn.	255 Washington Road
University City National Bank	604 W. Main
U.S. Government	
Federal Building	106 S. Lee
Internal Revenue Service	Federal Building
National Guard Armory Battery D., 36th Inf.	Airport Road
National Oceanic and Atmospheric Adm.	Airport
Postal Service	Federal Building
Harold E. Rogers, Postmaster	
Postal Inspectors	
Small Business Administration	Federal Building
Utilities	
General Telephone Co.	211 W. Main
Midstate Gas and Electric Co.	417 E. Main
Washington County	
County Clerk Anne Williams	
Coroner W.T. Door	
Sheriff Abel Look	
Carolton-Washington Adult Center	412 E. Main
Carolton-Washington County Airport	Airport Road
Extended Care Facility	512 Washington Road
Highway Department	
Lamar Wilson, superintendent	

Washington County (*cont.*)
Human Relations Commission   300 W. Main
Department of Public Health   516 Washington Road
Department of Public Safety   600 Washington Road
  House of Correction   612 Washington Road
  Sheriff   612 Washington Road
Welfare Department   300 W. Main
Women's Clinic   516 Washington Road
Washington County Courthouse   300 W. Main
  Circuit Court   Room 104
  Clerk of Court   Room 103
    Clerk of Court John Trask
  County Clerk   Room 115
  District Court   Room 204
  Family Court   Room 110
  Council on Aging   Room 120
  Human Relations   Room 208
  Jury Commission   Room 212
  Mental Health Department   Room 234
  Prosecutor   Room 308
    Harold S. Boylan
  Welfare Department   Room 310
Wirtz Building   128 N. Meade

Carolton Organizations and Associations

American Civil Liberties Union
American Federation of State, County and
  Municipal Employees   106 River Road
American Legion, John Hennessey Post No. 12   Airport Road
American Legion Auxiliary
Boy Scouts Of America, Troop 43
Carolton Association of Police   128 N. Meade
Carolton Community Relations Association   128 N. Meade
Carolton Day Care Council, Inc.   419 N. Battle Road
Carolton Labor Council   106 River Road
Carolton Professional Women's Club   501 E. Main
Carolton Senior Citizens Organization   100 N. Stuart
Carolton-Washington County Chamber
  of Commerce   304 W. Vermont
Citizens for the Arts
City Art Club   310 W. Newton Road
Daughters of the American Revolution
Forest Lawn Neighborhood Association
Friends of the Museum
National Association for the Advancement of
  Colored People
National Organization for Women
Northwest College Alumni Club
Parent Teachers Association
Service Clubs
  Challenge
  Civitan
  Rotary
Central State Professional Chapter, Society of
  Professional Journalists, Sigma Delta Chi

State AFL-CIO Council   106 River Road
Veterans of Foreign Wars Post 182   600 W. Newton Road
Veterans of Foreign Wars Ladies Auxiliary
Washington County Assn. for the Blind   128 N. Meade
Washington County Council on Aging
Washington County Democratic Women's
    Organization
Washington County Education Association
Washington County Foundation
Washington County Heritage Assn.
Washington County Historical Society
Washington County Human Relations
    Association
Washington County Mental Health Association   317 E. Main
Washington County Public Relations Club
Washington County Society of Professional
    Engineers

Northwest College Faculty and Staff

Arnold, Dalton   director, news bureau
Blaine, Harold E.   professor, history
Brown, Robert   professor, physics
Cook, Gerald A.   chairman, business
Dawson, Terry   news bureau
Donnelly, William T.   chairman, agriculture
Feldpausch, Julia   professor, physics
                          chairman, department of physics
Flores, Luisa   associate professor, Romance languages
Gibbs, Beverly   professor, business
                          assistant chairman, business
Harmon, Donald   professor, Romance languages
Hirsch, H.L.   professor, medicine
Holmes, Granville   professor, journalism
Huang, Charles O.   professor, physics
                          director, physics research lab
Lafferty, Charles E.   professor, economics
LaFrance, Genevieve   distinguished professor, entomology
Leavitt, Rollin R.   professor, family science
McKay, John R.   president
                          professor, economics
Morrissey, William A.   editor, news bureau
Nichols, Robert   professor and chairman, environmental design
Sawyer, Albert H. Jr.   professor, history
Shanks, Hubert L.   director, health service
Shaw, Roberta   assistant professor, natural science
Sherman, Amasa   registrar
Smith, Henry Clay   professor, psychology
Trosko, Julia A.   professor, agronomy
Tsui, Charles E.   research professor, agronomy
Verway, Richard L.   director, computer laboratory
Wagner, Sigrid E.   assistant professor, education
Wetherbee, Beatrice   assistant dean, student affairs
Wood, Helen   general manager, college press

Northwest College Students

Allen, Richard S.	freshman, journalism, Cleveland, Ohio 504 S. Meade
Fraser, Helene	senior, computer science, Atlanta, Ga. Hallowell Hall
Gould, Gregory	freshman, biology, San Francisco, Calif. Hallowell Hall
Henderson, William	freshman, Romance languages, Boston, Mass. 540 S. Meade
Lawrence, Joan	senior, journalism, Austin, Texas 240 Lawrence
Lawrence, Quimby	freshman, English, Dallas, Texas Hallowell Hall
Matthews, Harold	junior, speech, Dubuque, Iowa Hallowell Hall
Riley, John T.	senior, journalism, Carolton 27B University Village
Riley, Nancy	junior, business, Carolton 27B University Village
Roberts, Daniel B.	senior, computer science, Portland, Ore. 540 S. Meade
Simpson, Paul	senior, history, Memphis, Tenn. Hallowell Hall
Sims, Maryanne	senior, history, Lenox, Mass. 305 Lawrence

Northwest College Buildings

Administration Building	N. Campus Drive
Alumni Association	Administration Bldg.
Alumni Chapel	E. Campus Drive
Bloomfield Library	E. Campus Drive
Bookstore	Student Center
Center for Continuing Education (Conference Center)	Circle Drive
Chartwell Residence Hall	Old Brick Road
Cordell Hull Center for International Programs	Circle Drive
Dykstra House John R. McKay, president	N. Campus Drive
Forestry School	Circle Drive
Hallowell Residence Hall	E. Campus Drive
Information Services (public relations)	N. Campus Drive
LaFollette Auditorium	W. Campus Drive
Lawrence Residence Hall	S. Campus Drive
Mark Twain Hall	Washington Entrance
Married Student Housing	
Lexington Village	W. Campus Drive
University Village	E. Campus Drive
Medical College	S. Campus Drive
Memorial Hall (student center)	N. Campus Drive
Military Science	Western Avenue
Air Force Reserve Officers Training Corps	Room 110
Army Reserve Officers Training Corps	Room 210
Public Safety Department	Service Road
School of Agriculture	S. Campus Drive

318

School of Education   S. Campus Drive
School of Journalism   Greeley Road
School of Law   Marshall Drive
School of Veterinary Medicine   Research Road
Shaw Residence Hall   S. Campus Drive
State Arts Center   N. Campus Drive
Wells Graduate Residence Hall   Wells Road
Women's Studies Center   W. Circle Drive

Northwest College Organizations and Associations

Alpha Phi Sorority   210 E. Newton Road
Alpha Zeta Omega Fraternity   540 S. Meade
Angel Flight   military honorary
Arnold Air Society   military honorary
Daily Student   independent student daily newspaper
Delta Mu Delta   business honorary
Faculty Women's Organization   women faculty
Friends of the Library   106 Bloomfield
Maison Francais   575 W. Newton Road
Society of Professional Journalists,
    Sigma Delta Chi   journalism students

Reverse Directory

Airport Road, North

Acme Fire and Accident Insurance Co.
Delta Mall
    J.L. Hudson Co.
    Kroger
    Montgomery Ward
    Sears, Roebuck and Co.
Ferguson, Gerald S.
Jollity Building
Kelly Construction Co.
Meijer's Thrifty Acres
National Guard Armory
Smith and Jones Funeral Chapel
State Police
West Side Fire Station

Airport Road, South

American Legion Post No. 12
Carolton-Washington County Airport
Evergreen Cemetery
First National Food Stores
Weather Service, Airport

Arizona, East

150   Meyers, Don
180   Brown, D.

277   Lyons, Eugene R.
380   Daggett, Richard

Arizona, West

301   Congregational Church
347   Jefferson Village Apartments
    Marks, Ellen
    Booker, Louisa Mae
    Feldpausch, J.
    Ormsby, Zelig
    Trosko, Julia A.
350   Dwight, Robert
401   Souza, Joseph
408   Gold, Morris
426   Riley Brothers Funeral Chapel

Battle Road, North

104   Maher, Thomas O.
419   Carolton Day Care Council, Inc.
847   Reimenschneider, Russell
861   Look, Abel

Beech

18   Franklin, Ben
27   Souza, Lewis

319

Beech (*cont.*)

49	Olds, Gerald
84	Arnold, Dalton
86	May, Earl
215	Boise, Hardy C.
301	Brown, Robert
308	Bell, Alexander G.

Calhoun, North

104	O'Malley's Restaurant and Bar
104½	Scissors, Floyd R.
180	Gold, Harold S.
212	Latham, Eric

Calhoun, South

207	Turner, Ralph
227	Carter, Marilyn
250	Carolton General Hospital
308	Evans, Clayton

California, East

108	Powers, Hubert
307	Donnelly, W.T.
350	O'Higgins Junior High

California, West

210	Carew, Luther
461	Souza, Albert
570	Begg, John
708	Blaine, Harold E.

Florida, East

104	Twardzynski, Otto
212	Carter, Dawson
224	Hoffman, Rita
327	Huang, C.O.

Florida, West

462	Henderson, Maurice
505	Gibbs, Beverly
602	Barke, Willis
604	First Baptist Church
608	Central High School
	School District Headquarters
650	Stahl, John
710	Irving, William H.

Grant, North

216	Harris, Charles
411	Hawkins, Emma
487	Reeves, Marshall
780	McLaren, Joyce Ann
810	Dwight, Marion
911	Liberty Baptist Church
942	Dendramis, Sue Ellen

Grant, South

217	Nixon, James
512	Cordoba, Alexis
539	Cleveland, William R.
560	Morris, Clyde
583	Gilmore, Horace N.
585	Snell's Texaco

Houston, North

212	Tsui, Charles E.
305	Marks, Peter
604	Cook, Gerald A.
980	Murphy, Wanda

Houston, South

157	Ashford, John
308	Dawson, Ronald
327	Door, W.T.

Indian River Place

87	Bettencourt, Walter Jr.
120	Gibbs, John
125	Stephenson, W.A.

Jackson, North

12	Carolton Hardware
408	Parks, Marshall
627	Rogers, George A.
680	All Saints Episcopal Church
683	Evers, E.E.
714	Green, Virgil
850	St. Luke's Hospital
852	St. Luke's Medical Center

Jackson, South

247	Baker, Howard L.
304	Choate, Stephen P.
212	Trask, John
622	Floyde, Halbert O.
807	Miller, Robert L.

320

Lee, North

218 Quill, Henry C.
581 Fiore, Emil Jr.
761 Speizman, Harold E.
805 Vanderpol, R.E.

Lee, South

106 Federal Building
109 Cristo, S.
418 Funderburke, James L.
437 Gillette, Ralph

Lexington Road, East

357 Daily Student

Lexington Road, West

427 Commerce Club
450 Hotel Lenox
    Copper Kettle Restaurant
510 Colonial Village Apartments
        Coolidge, Calvin R.
        Flores, Luisa
        Wagner, S.E.
518 Harmon, Donald

Main, East

100 McKim, Oglethorpe and Dodge
103 Bulldog Wine and Beer Store
115 Waldron, D.E.
210 Municipal Building
245 Belk's
250 Farmers and Merchants Bank
312 Morning Record Publishing Co.
316 Higginbottom Sons Co.
317 Medical Arts Building
    Washington County Mental Health
      Association
350 Holiday Inn
381 Central Fire Station
    Rescue Squad
412 Carolton-Washington Adult Center
    Public Housing Authority
417 Midstate Gas and Electric Co.
477 Lutz, Helen
501 Carolton Professional Women's Club
601 City Rescue Mission
710 Williams, Henry

Main, West

16 First National Bank
100 Graham Associates

210 Quick Coin Laundry
211 General Telephone Co.
213 Mercy Ambulance Service
300 Washington County Courthouse
604 University City National Bank

Maple

27 Dickens, Henry
35 Sullivan, James J.
127 Ferreira, Richard Sr.
184 Gomez, Delores
202 Delaney, John R.
221 Leavitt, Rollin R.
235 White, Elmer

Maryland, East

415 Miskell, William
571 Wood, H.

Maryland, West

478 Flynn, George A.
480 St. Thomas Church
550 Community Mental Health Clinic
599 Kane, Wadsworth

Meade, North

128 Wirtz Building
        106 Community Development Agency
        112 Carolton Community Relations
              Association
        204 Carolton Association of Police
        311 Washington County Association
              for the Blind
141 Jones, Myron
915 West, H.A.
950 Shook Chemical Corp.

Meade, South

3 Price, Flynn
48 Lund, Aaron O.
87 Rivera, Carlos J.
107 Watson, Charles
408 Dean, E.S.
450 Williams, D.
522 First Methodist Church
540 Alpha Zeta Omega Fraternity

Nevada, East

201 Sturdevant, Willis
371 Hickock, Bruce B.

Nevada East (*cont.*)

450	Worthington, Lorraine M.
540	Hughes, Charles E.
590	Higginbottom, Ernest F.
640	Sawyer, Albert H. Jr.
822	Stieber, Kenneth

Nevada, West

35	Medford, John E.
304	Cooper, Herbert W.
386	Boomershine, J.E. DVM
604	Oberdorfer, Harry

Newton Road, East

105	Wells, Roger
210	Alpha Phi Sorority
550	Cedar Village Apartments

Newton Road, West

310	City Art Club
312	Civic Center
321	Shanks, H.L.
410	Timulty, John O.
550	Ivory, G.R.
552	Look, James
560	Krug, Herbert
575	Maison Francais
600	Veterans of Foreign Wars

New York, East

212	Courtwright, Fred III
340	LaFrance, Genevieve
409	Hope, Jonathan
510	Banks, Charles
520	Diaz, Mark L.

New York, West

252	Snell, Jacob
340	Curious Book Store
515	Hawkins Antiques
604	Applegate Books

Oak

27	Morrissey, W.A.
75	O'Neil, James
84	Baker, William
87	Peters, Paul
97	Jackson, Terry

Ohio, East

450	Rickles, Arturo
234	Marshall, Joseph R.
608	Clark, John

Ohio, West

17	Love, Henry
27	Leamy, Lillian
120	Marks, Mary
278	Barth, Julius E.
345	Lewis, Elwyn
414	Meade, Horace W.

Old Meetinghouse Road, South

Korth, Frank

Oregon, East

108	Williams, Donna
111	Johnson, Nancy
306	Handy, W.H. III
317	Shaw, Harlan

Oregon, West

111	Verway, Richard L.
258	Brewster, Alex
301	Look, Stanley
335	Gilmore, Horace A.
610	McLeod, M.M.

Perimeter Road, East

104	Blake, John

Perimeter Road, West

465	MacComber, Rufus
704	Hazelton, William M.

River Road

85	McGuire, Harold
97	Hardy, James
104	O'Flynn's
106	Reuther Building
	AFSCME, AFL-CIO
	State AFL-CIO Council
	Carolton Labor Council
158	Carolton Country Club
197	Lodge, John A.
215	Krug, Jessie W.
234	Willoughby, Roger

River Road (*cont.*)

333   Souza, Donald
350   Palmer, Bernard E.

Scott, North

216   Belle View Apartments
         Ellenberg, Kellie
         Miller, L.L.
         Swift, Franklin
         Toefel, M.J.
         Tombs, Catherine
         Wetherbee, B.
         Williams, A.
217   Jenkins Funeral Home
250   Door Brothers Funeral Home
508   Wilson, James L.
682   Newhouse, Harold H.
715   Nightingale, H.L.
782   Brackett, Marlene

Scott, South

 12   Marks, Patricia
280   Strauss, Jacob O.
317   Yaffee, Bette
321   Robinson, George T.
458   Souza, John

Sheridan, North

250   Wilson, Lamar
550   Lewis, John Q.
580   MacClure, Lawrence
657   Hempstead, A.B. Jr.
714   Applegate, Charles O.
900   Nelson, Fred W.
910   Spooner, Randolph M.

Sheridan, South

115   Jones, William F.
409   Tate, L.D.

Sherman, North

250   Stroh, Walter
345   MacDonald, Stewart
641   Anderson, H.C.
804   Main, Roger

Sherman, South

211   Leamy, Goldstick and Gray, attorneys
301   Hall, Henry
336   Robbins, Benjamin
506   Potter, Branson

State Road, East

Holy Cross Hospital
Presbyterian Home

State Road, West

210   Talcott, John

Stuart, North

100   Carolton Senior Citizens Organization
234   Trinity A.M.E. Church
850   Hirsch, H.L.
875   Davis, Theodore
927   McGregor, James L.

Stuart, South

158   McGuire, John

Sycamore

 15   Holmes, Granville
187   O'Byrne, John L.
211   Kirby, Helen
311   Bates, Alpha E.
350   Hickock, Walter
412   Crow, Emil

Territorial Road, South

511   Duke's Shell Service
808   East Side Fire Station
922   Rigsby, Peter
1182   College Standard Service

Utah, East

504   Wang, James
587   Boyland, Harold S.

Utah, West

 70   Williams, James
 75   Wiggins, John
 79   Peters, Don
 85   Toy, Jack E.
408   Elmer, John C.
603   Teacher, Walker E.

Vermont, East

400   Franklin Library
411   Barth Flowers
503   Buchanan, H.L.

Vermont, West

106	A & P
270	O'Kelly, Sean
304	Chamber of Commerce
504	Vogel, Ralph Jr.
612	Carolton Police Department
614	City Jail
700	Receiving Hospital

Virginia, East

100	Municipal Court
310	Turnbull, Anna
550	McKay Funeral Home

Virginia, West

407	Warren, Richard

Walnut

146	Carew, Alfred
210	Duttweiler, John R.

Washington Road

245	Carolton Construction Co.
255	Tri-State Education Assn.
260	Johnson, Harry O.
271	Norton, Homer
400	Bi-Low Supermarket

512	Washington County Extended Care
516	Washington County Health Department Women's Clinic
600	Washington County Department of Public Safety
604	Short, A.
612	Washington County House of Correction
618	Curtis, Raymond

Western Avenue, North

Piggly Wiggly Food Stores
Territory and Western Railroad Depot

Western Avenue, South

Chin, John
Kelly, James
Woods, Donald

Wisconsin, East

280	Smith, H.C.
434	Abrams, James
442	Miller, Kenneth L.
616	Howe, George A.
811	Orr, Marion

Wisconsin, West

240	Hillman, Walter
273	Spaulding, Ernest
385	McGuire, Edwin

Appendix

3 Maps

City of Carolton and Washington County

N

Territory and Western Railroad

Perimeter Road

Industrial Park

City of Carolton

West State Road

Main Street

East State Road

Airport Road

Lexington Road

Northwest College

Washington Road

U.S. 210

Newton Road

Western Avenue

Territorial Road

Old Meetinghouse Road

U.S. 210

County Airport

Lancaster Road

River Road

Battle Road

South Street

Boiling Springs Road

Indian River State Park

Indian River Place

Indian River

Boat Landing

City of Carolton and Northwest College Campus

N

Note: East-west streets are avenues unless otherwise identified. North-south streets are streets unless otherwise identified.

Appendix

4 Job Hunting

Mary T. Roe
43 Johnson Street
Athens, Ga. 30601

Home Address:
214 Blank St.
Augusta, Ga. 30905

(404) 543-1234

Personal:

    Age 22, born Feb. 27, 1967; height 5 feet 6 inches; weight,
125 pounds; health excellent; single.

Occupational Goal:

    Newspaper work. Prefer general assignment reporting or other
writing. Eventually would like to be editor of a daily
newspaper.

Education:

    Senior in journalism, The University of Georgia. Will be
graduated in June 1988.

    Major: news-editorial journalism. Courses in news writing,
reporting, news editing, photojournalism, newspaper management
and mass communication law.

    Minor: political science. Courses in American state government,
politics and elections and judicial systems.

    Grades: 3.4 on a 4.0 scale.

Honors and Awards:

    UGA Honors Program, member Phi Eta Sigma, Dean's List fall,
winter and spring terms 1986-87.

Extra-curricular:

    Intramural women's track; vice president Alpha Chi Omega
sorority; member Society of Professional Journalists, Sigma
Delta Chi; member School of Journalism Student Activities
Committee.

Work Experience:

    1986 - present -- Staff writer, The Red and Black, UGA daily
                     newspaper; contributor to UGA News;
                     stringer for Atlanta Journal and
                     Constitution.

    1986 --   Summer quarter internship with Macon
                     Telegraph and News, Macon, Ga., as general
                     assignment reporter.

Mary T. Roe

1985 --   Summer internship with Elberton Star,
                           Elberton, Ga., as general assignment
                           reporter; some experience in composition
                           and pasteup.

Other:

Fluent in Spanish; summer study program in Europe, 1981; have
private pilot's license; have camera and can handle routine news
assignments; own a car.

References:

George A. Hough 3rd, professor of journalism, Henry W. Grady
School of Journalism and Mass Communication, The University of
Georgia, Athens, Ga. 30602. (404) 542-5038

Ron Woodgeard, managing editor, Macon Telegraph and News,
Macon, Ga. 31213. (912) 744-4319

Glenn McCutchen, managing editor, The Atlanta Journal and
Constitution, P.O. Box 4689, Atlanta, Ga. 30302. (404) 526-5151

Check List for Resumes

1. A resume should be neat and attractive. An acceptable resume can be typed on an electric typewriter using a carbon ribbon. Resumes composed on a VDT can be printed out on a letter-quality printer and reproduced in quantity at a photocopy shop. Most photocopy shops will set and reproduce resumes at a reasonable cost.

2. Copy should follow news style. You are familiar with it, and so are the employers to whom you are writing.

3. Format is not as important as content. Resume should be neat, attractive and clear. It should be complete. The form suggested here is workable and neat. You may find another form more attractive — if so, use it. Just be sure you don't omit anything important.

4. List work experience in *reverse* chronological order. List all work experience, not just that which relates to your major.

5. List internships, part-time journalistic work and work for student publications or broadcasting as work experience.

6. Employers may not legally inquire about the personal data shown on the resume sample. However, it may be advantageous to point out some of these things. Good health, normal weight and height, the fact you are single may be in your favor. Include personal data if you feel comfortable about it. Omit it if you don't.

7. Include references on the resume. These should include:

   a. a faculty member who knows you well and can speak about your abilities without hesitation.

   b. a former employer or internship supervisor.

   c. someone who knows you personally: a family friend, high school teacher or counselor, your minister.

   The most important reference is a faculty member familiar with your academic record and your professional competence. Make it a point to develop this contact.

8. Include full names, titles, mailing addresses, zip codes and telephone numbers for references.

9. Check copy carefully. Check spelling, dates, names, titles and other data.

10. A one-page resume is good. But if you need more space to tell your story, use two pages. A neat, attractive, interesting two-page resume will be read just as carefully as a one-page resume.

11. Your cover letter should be brief. The resume should be complete.

243 Johnson St.
Athens, Ga. 30601

Feb. 4, 1988

Robert J. Cochnar
Editor
Independent—Mail
Anderson, S.C. 29622

Dear Mr. Cochnar:

Does the Independent—Mail have an opening on its staff for a June
journalism graduate with a lot of energy and some experience?

I'm looking for a newspaper job and would like to start work as
soon as possible after commencement on June 9.

I have worked several years for The Red and Black, the University
of Georgia student daily. Last summer I worked for The Macon
Telegraph and News as a general assignment reporter.

If there's a chance the Independent—Mail might have something for
me, I would like to come to Anderson to talk with you. I can get
away any weekday afternoon.

Sincerely,

Mary T. Roe

Enc: resume

alternate final paragraph:

I will be in South Carolina during the spring vacation, March 10
to 15, and if it is convenient, I would like to come in and see
you some afternoon that week.

334

Letters

Your letter should be neat, your message businesslike.

Editors are busy people. Don't waste their time. Get right to the point.

Your letter should:

1. Say immediately what you want.

2. Explain briefly why you consider yourself qualified for an internship or employment.

3. Say when you will be available for work.

4. Suggest that you are willing to make some effort to meet and talk with prospective employer.

5. Leave details to the resume.

All letters should be typed, of course. And they should be free of errors. Have someone else read your letter before you mail it.

Job Hunting/Internship Bibliography

Editor & Publisher

Weekly magazine, the bible of the newspaper industry. Classified section lists job openings.

Editor & Publisher International Year Book

Annually. Lists all U.S. daily newspapers and staff.

Gale Directory of Publications

Annually. Lists all daily and weekly newspapers, magazines and other periodicals published in the United States.

Georgia Newspaper Directory

Annually. Lists all members of the Georgia Press Association. [All but one or two states have press associations. Your state press association directory also lists all state and regional press associations and gives their addresses.]

Magazine Industry Marketplace

Annually. Lists major U.S. magazines.

Gebbie House Magazine Directory

Lists company publications.

Broadcasting/Cablecasting Yearbook

Annually. Indispensable source of information about radio, television and cable. Lists stations and news staffs.

Television & Cable Factbook

Annually. Everything you might want to know about television.

Standard Directory of Advertising Agencies

An alphabetical list of all advertising agencies in the United States with addresses, personnel and accounts.

Directory of Business and Organizational Communication

Annually by IABC. A directory of members of the International Association of Business Communicators. It provides a good list of businesses and organizations that employ writers and editors.

Public Relations Journal Register Issue

Annually by Public Relations Society of America. Lists PRSA members.

O'Dwyer's Directory of Public Relations Firms

Annually. A directory of U.S. public relations firms.

Student Guide to Mass Media Internships

A list of daily and weekly newspapers, radio stations and others that offer internships. Comprehensive and useful. Available from the Intern Research Group, School of Journalism, University of Colorado, Boulder, Colo. 80309.

College Placement Annual

Annually by College Placement Council. Describes corporate and government needs for graduates in many fields, including writing, editing and advertising.

Job Net

A national employment clearing house for minority journalists. Address: 1521 New Hampshire Ave. N.W., Washington, D.C. 20036.

Still Here

A newsletter published by the Job/Scholarship Referral Service for minority students. Address: School of Communications, Howard University, Washington, D.C. 20059.

(Acknowledgments continued from copyright page)

Pages 192–193: "Spending a Life in the Law," by James Vorenberg, from The New York Times, September 16, 1985. Copyright © 1985 by The New York Times Company. Reprinted by permission of The New York Times and the author.

Pages 194–195: "College Is Big Business," by Edward T. Foote, from The New York Times, November 13, 1984. Copyright © 1984 by The New York Times Company. Reprinted by permission of The New York Times and the author.

Pages 196–198: Excerpt from a speech by Ronald E. Rhody, given at the Virginia Public Relations Conference in Williamsburg, Virginia, on March 29, 1982. Copyright © 1982. Used by permission.

Pages 198–199: "Why Women Opt to Go It Alone," by John B. Parrish, from The New York Times, February 9, 1986. Copyright © 1986 by The New York Times Company. Reprinted by permission of The New York Times and the author.

Pages 200–202: Excerpts from a panel discussion about "The Future of American Newspapers," by Charles T. Brumback, Lloyd G. Schermer and Joel H. Walker at the Inland Daily Press Convention in Chicago, on October 22, 1985. Copyright © 1985. Used by permission.

Pages 202–203: Excerpt from "Where We Stand," a column by Albert Shanker, in The New York Times, November 10, 1985. Copyright © 1985. Used by permission.

Pages 204–205: Excerpt from speech given by Gilbert C. Fite at a Founders' Day Dinner in Athens, Georgia, on January 26, 1982, and reprinted in the Georgia Alumni Record, Spring, 1982. Copyright © 1982. Used by permission.

Page 262: Excerpt from "Our Country Relies on the Quality of Its Ideas," by John Chancellor, from The Chronicle of Higher Education, November 26, 1986. Copyright © 1986. Used by permission.

Pages 266–267: Excerpt from "The Three Blind Mice of Journalism," a speech given by Robert P. Clark at the ASNE Annual Convention in Washington, D.C., April 9, 1986. Copyright © 1986. Used by permission.

To the Student

We need your help. By answering a few questions below, you can have a hand in shaping the next edition of "Practice Exercises in News Writing." Please complete this questionnaire, tear it out and mail it to the following address:

Journalism Editor
College Division
Houghton Mifflin Co.
One Beacon St.
Boston, MA 02108

Thank you.

School name _____

Title of course(s) in which you used this book _____

_____

Is your school on a _____ quarter or _____ semester basis?

Instructor's name _____

Other books used in the course(s), if any _____

_____

1. What is your overall impression of the book? Did you find it

   _____ very useful _____ useful _____ not so useful. Comments, if any:

   _____

   _____

   _____

2. Did your teacher assign all sections and chapters of the book or only some? If any were omitted, please indicate which ones.

   _____

   _____

3. How did you find the reading level of the book?

   _____ highly readable _____ generally interesting _____ fair

4. Did anything about the book surprise you? That is, did you find new material that you hadn't expected in a text of this kind?

_____ yes _____ no. If yes, be specific:

_____

_____

5. Is there any material you would like to see added to the book?

_____ yes _____ no. If yes, be specific:

_____

_____

6. Did your instructor test you on the book? _____ yes _____ no

Describe the tests: _____ objective _____ short essay _____ other

7. Did your teacher's lectures _____ usually cover the same ground as the book _____ introduce entirely different material _____ something in between (describe) _____

_____